W9-CIE-667

Reprinted 1980 from the 1890 edition.
Cover design © 1980 Time-Life Books Inc.
Library of Congress CIP data following page 472.

"UNCLE DICK" WOOTTON

"UNCLE DICK" WOOTTON

"Uncle Dick" Wootton

THE PIONEER FRONTIERSMAN OF THE ROCKY

MOUNTAIN REGION

AN ACCOUNT OF THE ADVENTURES AND THRILLING

EXPERIENCES OF THE MOST NOTED AMERICAN

HUNTER, TRAPPER, GUIDE, SCOUT, AND

INDIAN FIGHTER NOW LIVING

BY

HOWARD LOUIS CONARD

WITH AN INTRODUCTION

BY

MAJ. JOSEPH KIRKLAND

CHICAGO

W. E. DIBBLE & CO

1890

ELECTROTYPED BY
G. M. D. LIBBY
CHICAGO

PREFACE.

In presenting to the public the story of " Uncle Dick" Wootton's life and adventures, I have been cautioned by the venerable frontiersman, not to embellish a single incident too highly, and to leave out of the work entirely the element of fiction.

" I have observed," said he, " in reading our frontier literature, that the tendency has been to exaggerate and overdraw everything, and the effect of this has been, to give the Eastern public a wrong idea of the conditions which existed in this country from twenty-five to fifty years ago, and of the character of the men who found their way into these savage wilds in search of wealth and adventure. Tell my story, so that those who care to read it, may draw from it correct conclusions as to the kind of lives the mountaineers have really lived, and avoid such coloring of truth as might lead them to think me boasting of my own prowess or exaggerating my own importance."

This admonition, which I could not do otherwise than respect, has restrained me from attempting to build upon a basis of truth, a superstructure of fact and fiction ingeniously combined, even had I thought a more attractive book could thereby have been given to the reader.

I am of the opinion, however, that no fiction which could have been devised, would have been more replete with thrilling incidents than the plain unvarnished story of one man's life and adventures, which is herewith given to the public.

Whether or not this impression of mine is a correct one, I leave to the reader to judge, trusting only that the story in its new form may prove not less attractive than when related by " Uncle Dick " himself in conversation with his friends.

In the absence of a formal dedication, which now-a-days is going out of fashion, I should say, perhaps, that " Uncle Dick," half dreaming of the olden time, suggested one day that the story should be dedicated " to the old hunters and trappers." Being reminded, however, that few if any of them were living, it occurred to him that to no one could he, with greater propriety pay such compliment than to his son, Hon. R. L. Wootton, Jr., in grateful recognition of his services in connection with the publication of this work.

HOWARD LOUIS CONARD.

HON. R. L. WOOTTON, JR.

TABLE OF CONTENTS.

LIST OF ILLUSTRATIONS.

INTRODUCTION.

Broad, grassy plains, shining in the sun; bordered by mountains rising, brown and huge, sheer into the sky until the snows on their summits become indistinguishable from the clouds above them. Vast herds of buffalo grazing undisturbed, spreading abroad so far and dense that as they move it seems as if the surface of the earth were changing its place. Mighty, lonely rivers wending their way slowly toward the Gulf of Mexico.

Occasionally, though very rarely—once in a hundred miles or so—a little clump of buffalo-hide "wigwams," "teepees" or "wickiups," with idle Indians, busy squaws, and dirty pappooses; and, somewhere near, a straggling band of thin, scrubby ponies—unless it happens that the painted braves have ridden them off on a wild chase after buffalo or a wilder errand to fight their brother savages on the horrid war-path.

How majestic is Nature in this aspect! Here in her own dominion of mountain, plain, forest, river, wild beast and savage biped, her reign has been unbroken for countless ages. Will it ever be disturbed? It seems impossible.

But what are those white specks approaching from under the sunrise? Slowly they advance, tracking the trackless plain, fording the unbridged streams, pushing bravely out into the unseen, unknowable perils, seeking the alluring hardship of adventure.

They are the wagons of the pioneers.

How puny and insignificant the outfit must seem to the invincible, implacable red men! So harmless and helpless that they might even spare it; except that in their insatiate thirst for blood they spare nothing, young or old, fair or foul, male or female, bold or gentle.

Spare or strike; it is all the same. It is their doom. Kill, scalp, torture, rob, enslave as they may, it is their doom; for with it comes the frontiersman; able to outwork, out-watch, outrun, outlast, outmanœuvre, outbrave and outfight them, on their own ground. When they have come to the very end of their efforts, he is at the very beginning of his; and when the long struggle is over, he is everywhere and they are nowhere.

Such is the vast panorama which Uncle Dick Wootton's simple, manly, artless, chatty narrative places before our eyes. Glad are we to have the story told once more; for this is nearly the last of the long list of authentic biographies of a time which is gone by never to return. Captain John Smith, before the landing of the Pilgrims; Daniel Boone and George Rogers Clark before and during the Revolution; Kit Carson in later days, and now old Uncle Dick; these are the famous adventurers; for these are the men who not only knew how to hunt and fight, but how to tell us about it.

Good bye to them! Hail and farewell, brave spirits! The advancing wave from the Atlantic has met the reflux from the Pacific, and the whole land is flooded with civilization; Uncle Dick and a few silent companions are left standing up like land-marks among the leveling waters.

Let every one who has had any of these wild sports, these bit-ter trials, these bloody fights and hair-breadth (scalp-breadth) escapes arise and put them in print; for they are vanishing like the smoke from their camp-fires. They must be perpet-uated; not by carved stone, for that passes away; but by the imperishable embalming of print.   "Words are the only things that endure forever."

Chapter seven, and the following portion of the memoirs, though not so full of exciting adventure as others, should be read with interest, for they give trustworthy information of the class of humanity whom the frontiersmen have ousted from their ancient dominion. Uncle Dick argues with force that much of the sympathy felt for those savages is misplaced. He says that before we appeared on the scene at all they were slaughtering each other more cruelly than we have ever slaughtered them; that carnage was their habit and cruelty their nature; that death was the only punishment they could understand, and the fear of it the only thing in the world that could keep them from inflicting it on us.

This view is gradually gaining ground among thoughtful observers. A late writer (Roosevelt, in "The Winning of the West") supports it to its fullest extent, illustrating native love of cruelty, for cruelty's sake, by citing the horror he himself has felt at witnessing the delight the children take in torturing little animals. Then, too, he combats the notion that an Indian can be said to "own" lands which he only uses as fighting grounds in internecine struggles, or only visits once or twice a year to hunt over. He "owns" them, at best, by right of conquest in his ceaseless wars with rival tribes; and when we take them from him we "own" them by the same right. The difference in our favor is this; we do not strive to exterminate our conquered foe; on the contrary, we give him all the land he can use (not all he can hunt over), and clothing and food besides.

At the same time, so tender-hearted are we—so different from the Indians—that to many readers the pleasantest narrative in this book will be the story of Uncle Dick's rescue of a suffering, perishing squaw, his returning her to her tribe, and his finding that whole tribe his firm friends forever after.

Uncle Dick's story seems to me fairly typical of the best border experiences. He starts out a poor, brave, and enterprising lad. He learns the trade of frontiersman—for a trade it surely is—and grows to love it. He knows the nature and habits of the bird of the air, the beast of the field and the savage of the wilds; he can understand their several tongues— even speak them to some extent. He is a trapper, and a hunter, and a fighter. He kills game for food, and Indians for defense. He gathers flocks and herds in great numbers, and money in plenty; always giving and spending as freely as he gains; but finally "rounding up" a store of the comforts of life and other good things. To-day his name is revered and respected, his son high in office, and himself personally beloved and honored. May his shadow never be less!

JOSEPH KIRKLAND.

CHICAGO, October, 1889.

SIMPSON'S REST.

CHAPTER I.

A FAMOUS MOUNTAINEER.

The man who has been fifty years in active life in any part of the world, must necessarily have had some interesting experiences, but the man who has lived for half a century along that border line of civilization, which we call in this country, "the frontier," has had fifty years of adventure.

It matters little what may have been the temper of the man who has been thus situated, his environments have been such, that thrilling incidents and wonderful experiences, could not have failed to be prominent features of his every day life. Even a quaker, loving above all other things peace and quietude, must have led an eventful life amidst such surroundings.

The western half of the American continent, which we looked upon in our boyhood days as the sundown land, and of which almost as little was known, by those who lived east of the Mississippi River fifty years ago, as is now known by the same class of reasonably intelligent people of "the Dark Continent," is to-day rapidly throwing off its old time wildness, in fact, has already thrown it off and donned the garb of Civilization.

The hunter and trapper have gone, and in their places we find the farmer and the cattle king; the

2

old time trader has given way to the modern merchant and the old style wares are no longer in demand; the occupation of the stage driver is gone, and transcontinental railways have taken the place of the primitive stage lines.

The freighters have gone into retirement along with the stage drivers, and railway freight trains are whirled by strong locomotives, over more space in a day than the ox-teams were able to cover in a fortnight.

The old camping grounds have been cut up into town and city lots, magnificent residences and massive business blocks have taken the places of tent and cabin, and the whole face of the country as well as the character of its population has undergone a most complete and remarkable change.

Not even the rocks and mountains have preserved their primitive character, and only here and there are to be found undisturbed, the old landmarks which were the handiwork of the early mountaineers.

The mountaineers themselves, those brave and hardy adventurers, the path finders of the Rocky Mountain region, who found their way into the country, in advance of the skirmish line thrown Westward in the march of civilization, with but few exceptions, have long since passed over the trail which ends at the silent camping ground of the dead.

They have been "gathered to their fathers," but not in the sense of being carried to the same burying ground.

Wherever the battle of life ended they found a burial place and in widely separated localities, those who faced the same dangers, braved the same perils and shared the same hardships, are sleeping to-day undisturbed by their isolation from old comrades and trusted friends.

Upon most of those who are still living, and their whole number may be counted upon the fingers of one hand, the weight of years rests heavily, and like the dismasted and dismantled man-of-war they are little more than a reminiscense of other days.

To meet and converse with one of these old time adventurers, who has borne up under the crush of years and who retains the full and unimpaired use of all his faculties, is to learn the secrets of the hills and hear the very rocks tell tales.

Passing westward over the main line of the Atchison, Topeka & Santa Fe Railroad, one follows, from the great bend of the Arkansas River to "the City of the Holy Faith," the line of the old Santa Fe trail.

Just before the line between Colorado and New Mexico is crossed, the attention of the tourist is always called to one of the most picturesque spots in all the Rocky Mountain region.

It is twelve miles from Trinidad, the metropolis of South Eastern Colorado, a town noted throughout the West for its extensive coal fields and superior manufacturing facilities.

When the west bound train reaches Trinidad, its motive power is always doubled, and pulled by two strong locomotives, it commences to climb a spur of the Rocky Mountain Range, or, perhaps, properly speaking, of the Cimaron Range, known as Raton Mountains.

Slowly the train winds its way upward, until it reaches an altitude of eight thousand feet or more, when it enters a long tunnel, cut through the "backbone" of the range, crosses the state line under ground, and drops down into New Mexico.

The Raton Mountains were named by the Spanish speaking natives of that vast territory acquired by the United States from Mexico in 1848. Like all Spanish names, it is supposed to have had, at the time it was given, a significant and appropriate meaning, but traditions differ as to its origin.

The word " raton," means in English, squirrel or mouse, and some say that the mountains take their name from the grotesque but strikingly squirrel like shape of one of the principal peaks, while others maintain that it was the large number of squirrels, which could always be found in the pine forests, and along the wooded ravines and cañons, which suggested to the Mexicans the propriety of calling these rugged hills the Raton or squirrel mountains.

Less than two miles from the crest of the range, and more than seven thousand feet above the level of the sea, is a charming little valley, not much larger than a good-sized New England garden, through which runs Raton creek, a mountain stream, fed by springs which send their waters rippling down from sun-kissed banks of snow, and fringed on either side by willow, aspen and cottonwood trees.

Rugged peaks surround the little valley, or rather lift themselves up on all sides of it, leaving openings at either end of the level space, through which the creek finds its way in and out of it.

The hills are broken, rock-bound and ragged. Some are brown and bare; others are covered with a thick growth of shrub oak, piñon and mesquite, while there are still others crowned with groves of always verdant pine.

Between the hills are narrow valleys and wooded cañons, which have the appearance of miniature parks, where the shadows chase each other all day long and on moonlight nights, through enchanted play grounds.

Nor are the surroundings of the place lacking in points of geographical and historical prominence.

"Fisher's Peak," which takes its name from having been the place where Captain Fisher and a party of soldiers got lost in 1846, when on their

way through to Santa Fe, towers above the surrounding hills, a few miles south-east of the valley,
while " Raton Peak " rises abruptly a little farther
away to the north.

" Simpson's Rest," another lofty, rock-ribbed
elevation, which is noted as having been the scene of
a thrilling adventure and now the burial place of the
pioneer whose name it bears, can be plainly seen
a dozen miles away, while the "Spanish Peaks,"
"Pike's Peak" and the " Snowy Range," distant
from sixty to one hundred and fifty miles, seem
almost near enough to be reached by a few hours
walk.

Standing upon the mountain top, the monument
which marks the spot where rests the remains of
" Simpson, the poet mountaineer," is a conspicuous
object of interest. It is seldom that even the most
ardent lovers of the mountains, select as a location
for their homes while living, one of these rugged
peaks, and still more seldom do they exact from loving friends the promise that such shall be their place
of burial. The least inquisitive observer never fails,
therefore, to inquire what prompted this man to ask
for sepulture in a place so isolated and inaccessible.
Legend answers the query and informs the curious
that " once upon a time" Simpson found here a
friendly shelter from blood thirsty savages. In after
years he expressed the wish to be buried near the
scene of his adventure in the following poem :

GEORGE SIMPSON.

1. Lay me to rest on yon towering height,
    Where the silent cloud shadows glide,
Where solitude holds its slumberous reign
    Far away from the human tide.

2. I fain would sleep near the old pine tree
    That looks down on the valley below,
Like a soldier guarding a comrade's grave,
    Or a sentinel watching the foe.

3. 'Twas a refuge once, in the by-gone time,
    When a pitiful fate was near,
When my days were young and full of love
    For a life I held too dear.

4. Thro' all the long years that have passed away
    Since that night of storm and dread,
I've prayed that the boughs that sheltered me then
    Might wave over my dust when dead.

5. Delve deep my grave in the stern gray rock:
    In its rigid embrace let me rest:
With naught but my name on the stone at my head,
    And the symbol of faith on my breast.

6. One mourner perhaps, may remember where sleeps,
    In his rock-bound tomb the lone dead—
May breathe for the loved one to heaven a prayer,
    A tear to his memory shed.

Taken all in all, the attractive little valley, which is but imperfectly described above, and which seems in some way to have been hewn out of the mountain side, in the beauty of its natural scenery and the interest which attaches to its surroundings, is hardly surpassed by any spot which attracts the attention of the tourist in passing over the great ridge of upheaved rock and earth, which forms the continental divide and separates the Mississippi Valley from the Pacific Slope.

Not less interesting than are his surroundings in this mountain niche, is the man who has for more than a score of years made it his home.

In a quaint old adobe house, closely related, architecturally, to the old style plantation residences of Virginia and Kentucky, lives " Uncle Dick " Wootton, so well known throughout Kansas, Colorado and New Mexico, that scarcely a citizen of either State or territory could be found who would be willing to admit that he had not seen or heard of him.

Surrounded by what we ordinarily term the comforts of life and as many of the luxuries as an " old timer " usually cares for, " Uncle Dick," as every body calls him, is growing old ; in fact, has grown old, with but a single untoward circumstance to cloud the afternoon of his eventful life. This was three or four years of almost total blindness, from which he was only relieved by a skillful surgical operation a year or two since.

It was not until his blindness came on, that the old hunter laid aside, with the air of a man saying good-bye to the dearest friends he had on earth, the rifle and hunting knife which had for years been his constant companions. It was this, which more than anything else made him chafe under his affliction and regard it as the most severe which could have fallen upon him.

The restoration of his sight was not complete. While it enabled him to look again upon the beauties of nature by which he is surrounded and with which he is in such hearty sympathy, to recognize old friends and look into the faces of new ones, to read the newspapers and attend to his ordinary business affairs, it did not bring back to him that acuity of vision which in former years made his aim unerring, and a shot from his rifle always deadly when fired with that intent.

And so it happens that the celebrated old hunter, trapper, scout and Indian fighter is now content to point out to his visitors the localities in which game is likely to be found and entertain them with reminiscenses of his palmier days.

No longer young, he has hardly yet grown old, except in appearance, and this belies his years. With

" Hair just grizzled
As in a green old age,''

an erect carriage, and almost youthful spirits, with intellect unimpaired, a memory never at fault, and

vigorous bodily health, time never hangs heavy on
his hands or on the hands of those who have the
good fortune to be thrown in company with him.

Richens Lacy Wootton, that was the full name
given him by his father, was born in Mecklenberg
County, Virginia, on the sixth day of May, 1816.

His ancestors were among the early settlers of
Virginia, his great-great grand-father having come
over from Scotland, where the head of the family
wore a title, in 1726.

David C. Wootton, the father of "Richens," was a
Virginia planter who removed to Christian County,
Kentucky, on the southern border line of the state,
when the boy who afterwards became the contempo-
rary of Governor Bent, Colonel Ceran St. Vrain,
Lucien B. Maxwell, "Kit" Carson and other equally
famous frontiersmen was seven years old.

Here he grew up, or rather partly grew up, as he
was but seventeen years old and had just secured,
what in those days was considered a fair business
education, when he tired of the tobacco plantation
and joined an uncle who was at that time in Mississippi.

There he spent a little less than two years on a
cotton plantation, when he concluded one summer to
make a trip to Independence, Missouri.

That was in 1836. At that time all the vast
country lying between the western boundary line of

Missouri and New Mexico, was known as the Indian Territory.

Ambitious traders and daring adventurers were then just beginning to establish trading posts at various points in this wild and little known region peopled entirely by savages. A pathway had been opened up to that very ancient metropolis of New Mexico, the quaint old town of Santa Fe and Independence was its eastern terminus. This pathway was not called a road or a highway, but was known as the Santa Fe trail, and traversed eight hundred miles of plain and mountain.

Commerce had begun to travel westward over this afterwards famous trail, and the wagon trains had succeeded the primitive pack mule " outfits."

When young Wootton reached Independence he found there a wagon train belonging to Bent & St. Vrain, which had been loaded and was ready to start westward to Fort Bent, located on the Arkansas River, a short distance west of what is now the line between Kansas and Colorado.

It was there that Charles Bent, who was made the first governor of New Mexico when General Kearney took possession of that territory, in company with Colonel Ceran St. Vrain, had established the most noted trading post of the far west.

To attach himself to the west-bound wagon train which he found at Independence, and start on a trip

to the Rocky Mountains, where it was thought fortunes were to be had for the seeking, was exactly
suited to the adventurous disposition of the Kentucky
youth, who had started out to see the world, with
an ambition to return to his home laden with wealth,
when he tired of sight seeing.

There was little formality about the men with
whom he was associated after that, and if they had
a particularly strong predjudice against any one
formality, it was against that of calling a man by his
full christian name, when it could be abreviated, or a
nickname devised to answer the purpose.

So it happened that the name of Richens Wootton
was shortened to "Dick" Wootton, or rather to
"Dick Hootton," the surname even not being quite
satisfactory in its original form, and "Dick" he was
always called by the "old timers," while to all the
boys and girls who have grown up around him of
late years, he is "Uncle Dick."

With his trip to the mountains the adventures of
"Uncle Dick" began.

That was fifty-three years ago, and it is three years
more than half a century since he became a frontiersman.   He is a frontiersman still, if we have any
"frontier" left in this country, and barring the past
few years, not only every year, but almost every
month of every year has been a period of adventure.

Not all of his adventures were thrilling and blood curdling as a matter of course, but in all the years of his active life in the mountains, I doubt if a week ever passed in which something did not happen which would set the blood tingling in the veins of a healthy man unused to stirring incidents.

If the reader will take a look at the portrait which adorns the frontispiece of this book, and he or she happens to be a reasonably good judge of physiognomy, it will be easy to form a correct idea of the general appearance, character and truthfulness of the man whose reminiscenses have been written down by a summer idler in the mountains, as they were related by the gray haired adventurer, to a group of interested listeners.

Here and there the rough corners have been knocked off a peculiar form of expression ; now and then a sentence has been more fully rounded out, and occasionally it has been found necessary to temper a frontier phrase to the shorn lambs of polite society, but the substance of the narrative is given to the boys who delight in stories of adventures and the older boys who are always fond of reminiscenses, without change or embellishment.

And now that I have fairly introduced him to the reader, and said as much as need be said about his early life, " Uncle Dick" himself shall take the story off my hands and tell of his adventurous career, since he has but to unlock the storehouse of his memory, to call to mind, not only all the interesting experiences of his own eventful life, but the day and date of almost everything which has happened in the mountain region, within the past fifty years, which even for the passing moment attracted the attention of the public.

In this connection I should add, that while it has never occurred to the old mountaineer, that what he has given to the public in this volume, would constitute any important part of the history of the country with which he has been so long identified, the reader will observe that he has thrown much light upon incidents of historic interest, which have never received in any former publication, historical or otherwise, the attention to which they were entitled by reason of their importance.

"UNCLE DICK" AT HOME.

CHAPTER II.

"UNCLE DICK" TALKS.

"If you want to hear something about what an old hunter and trapper, who has been in this country more than fifty years, has gone through, I reckon I can come as near telling you some things that will make your hair raise up and knock your hat off, as anybody you will find, if you travel from one side of this broad land to the other.

You might as well understand right now however that I wasn't cut out for a smooth story teller, and can't put on any flourishes.

I shall just begin at the beginning and tell you in an off hand way, which will sound natural to those who know me—and I reckon you will find a good many such people in one place and another—what my experience has been in the mountain region. I shall not try to make it appear that the mountaineers were a lot of highly educated, polished gentlemen, nor shall I make them talk like a pack of savages, as they generally do in frontier stories, because that would be doing all of them a rank injustice.

When I left Independence, in the summer of 1836 I was a little under nineteen years of age, but I was pretty near full grown and had been away from home long enough to know how to take care of myself.

I could use a gun as well as anybody, knew how
to handle a team, and while I was never particularly
in love with hard work, I wasn't afraid of it and
when there was anything to be done I was always
ready to do my share.   That was all that was
required of me as a "wagon man," and I got along
first-rate from the start.

We had only seven teams, or rather seven wagons
in the train I started with.   We didn't call a pair of
mules a team in those days because it took ten or
twelve mules to draw each of the wagons when they
were loaded with merchandise and ready to cross the
plains.

We had to travel all the way through the Indian
country, and the "red skins" were so troublesome
that only large parties or wagon trains accompanied
by good sized bands of well armed men, stood a fair
chance of getting through safely.

Two or three days before we started, a wagon train
in which there were fifty-seven wagons, and which
was accompanied by perhaps a hundred and fifty
men, had started for Santa Fe and we were to overtake them before we reached the most dangerous part
of the country we had to travel through.

Our own train being light, we could travel with
greater speed than the Santa Fe train and we soon
overtook it and were given a place in the long line
of wagons.

I learned then, what I did not know before, that all the movements of a big wagon train had to be made with military precision.

When we went into camp at night all the wagons were pulled up close together so as to form a sort of circle. Then the mules were unhitched and driven to water, after which they were "picketed," that is, hitched by long ropes to stakes driven in the ground, outside of the line of wagons, so that they could graze during the night. So many men were detailed every night to stand guard, and they were stationed far enough away from the wagons so that they could see all the stock and prevent any of the mules or horses from being stolen.

The mules were pretty good guards themselves by the way. If they slept any at all they were very light sleepers, because whenever anything, whether it was a wild animal or an Indian, came near the camp, the mules would commence snorting in a way which would at once attract the attention of the guard to the object of suspicion.

While the guards were on the lookout for unwelcome visitors of any kind, the men who were not on duty wrapped themselves in their blankets and lay down on the ground inside the circle of wagons to sleep as soundly as though there was no such thing as danger to be thought of. They slept however with their rifles by their sides, and the crack of a sentinel's gun would bring them to their feet full armed in a moment's time.

I remember very well the first night I stood guard. I remember it on account of an occurrence which gave me a good deal of annoyance at the time and furnished every man connected with the train an opportunity to get off a joke at my expense.

We had gotten about one-third of the way across the Indian Territory, or what is now the State of Kansas, and although freighting was a new business to me, I had managed to get along without making any bad breaks and stood mighty well for a tender-foot.

One night we went into camp on the banks of what was then called " Little Cow Creek." It is now called " Chavez Creek," and, by the way, I must tell you how the name came to be changed.

A very wealthy Mexican by the name of Chavez was doing business then at Albuquerque, New Mexico, purchasing his goods mainly from St. Louis. Once a year he would make a trip to St. Louis to purchase his goods and make settlements, and on these trips he always carried a large amount of money with him.

He traveled by carriage, in the old Spanish style, with outriders and all that sort of thing, and of course attracted a great deal of attention. When he reached the Missouri he proceeded by boat to St. Louis, leaving his splendid carriage and horses to be looked at

by the " border ruffians " of western Missouri, while
they speculated as to the amount of his wealth and
laid plans to secure a portion of it for themselves.

Along about 1841 a plot to rob him was hatched
up by a party of these Missourians. There were
nine men in the plot and they all lived at Westport,
which is now a part of Kansas City. Some of them
were well known citizens of that place, and one I remember, a doctor, was one of the most prominent men
in Jackson County. They found out in some way when
Chavez was coming through on one of his trips and
went out to meet him in the Indian Territory, where
there was very little law and where they seem to
have thought they could commit any sort of crime
with impunity. They met Chavez at "Little Cow
Creek," where they killed him in cold blood, and
secured sixty thousand dollars in money as their
booty. If Chavez had not been a man of so much
prominence, they might have escaped punishment,
but as it was, the matter was taken up by the government and they were hunted down and all of them
either hanged or sent to the penitentiary. On account
of its having been the scene of the Chavez murder,
"Little Cow Creek" became known afterwards as
Chavez Creek, and it is still called by that name.

Well, as I was going to tell you, it was at this
place that I stood guard for the first time over a wagon
train. My instructions were to shoot anything that

I saw moving outside of the line of mules farthest out from the wagons.   Nothing had happened so far on our trip, to occasion any alarm or anxiety about our safety, and I didn't expect anything was going to happen that night.   Still I didn't feel at all inclined to go to sleep, and kept a sharp lookout. About one or two o'clock at night I heard a slight noise, and could see something moving about, sixty or seventy-five yards from where I was lying on the ground.   I wasn't a coward, if I was a boy, and my hair didn't stand on end, although it may have raised up a little.   Of course, the first thing I thought of was Indians, and the more I looked at the dark object creeping along toward the camp, the more it looked to me like a blood-thirsty savage.   I didn't get excited, although they tried to make me believe I was afterward, but thought the matter over and made up my mind that whatever the thing was, it had no business out there.   So I blazed away at it and down it dropped.   The shot roused everybody in camp, and they all came running out with their guns in their hands to see what was up.

I told them I had seen what I supposed was an Indian trying to slip into camp and I had killed him. Very cautiously several of the men crept down to where the supposed dead Indian was lying.   I stood at my post and listened for their report, and by and by I heard one of the men say " I'll be cussed if he haint killed Old Jack." "Old Jack" was one of our lead mules. He had gotten loose and strayed outside the lines, and the result was that he met his death. I felt sorry about it, but the mule had disobeyed orders you know, and I wasn't to blame for killing him.

The next adventure I had was at Pawnee Fork, just about where it flows into the Arkansas River. This was right in the heart of the Comanche country, and of all the mean Indians I ever had anything to do with, the Comanches were the meanest. Mind I am not saying that there are or ever were any good live Indians. They were all mean then, just the same as they are now, only some were meaner than others.

There was no false alarm about the incident at Pawnee Fork. The Comanches always fought on horseback, and they were good fighters too. It was on a bright moonlight night that they attacked us, although it was not often that they made a night attack. There must have been two hundred and fifty or three hundred of them, and the first thing we knew they swept down on us, yelling like scared wild cats. A few of them had the old fashioned " fusees," but the most of them had bows and arrows and spears. What we called a " fusee " was a fire lock musket with a bore half as big as that of a small cannon, from which either slugs or ball could be shot, although not with any great degree of accuracy. The Indians used sometimes to shoot a copper ball from these guns. Where they got the copper I never knew, but I suppose it came from Old Mexico. They used both flint and steel pointed arrows, and the spears which they carried were long poles with bayonet shaped steel points, as long as a butcher knife. Among all the "varmints" I have seen since that time, I don't think I have ever seen any that looked as ugly as each of those Comanches did that night.

We heard them before they reached us and were up in time to give them a warm reception. They didn't try to break into our corral, but their purpose seemed to be to stampede and drive off our stock first. They charged through the camp three or four times, trying to make the mules break loose, and the arrows fell pretty thick inside the corral as well as outside of it. We made it too hot for them though, and when they finally retreated, they left three good Indians, where they had fallen from their horses. You understand, when I say good Indians, that I mean dead ones. Some people may not agree with me on this point, but I think I know what I'm talking about. If I don't I ought to, because I've been among 'em long enough.

That was my first brush with the Indians and I got credit for conducting myself pretty well for a youngster.

A few days later we left the Santa Fe train, and
went up the Arkansas River to Fort Bent, Colonel
St. Vrain coming out from the fort with a party of
mounted men to meet us. On the way up I shot and
killed my first buffalo. By this time my reputation
as a frontiersman was pretty well established, and
after stopping at the fort a few weeks, I was placed
at the head of a party of thirteen men and sent north
on a trading expedition with the Sioux Indians.
These Indians were scattered over what is now the
northern part of Colorado, all of Nebraska, and pretty
much all of Wyoming.

We started out with ten wagons, loaded with beads,
and other trinkets, hunting knives, powder and bullets, blankets, and a few old guns. When we
reached the trading country, we would camp outside
an Indian village, and find out first whether they
were in a trading humor. If they were we would
send in a pack mule or two, loaded with our wares
and establish headquarters at the lodge of some
friendly Indian. The Indian at whose lodge we
stopped was then authorized to act as a guard to protect our goods from the thieves who were always
hanging about to get something without paying for it.

We dressed the guard up in a militia uniform,
which we carried for the purpose, made him wear a
stove-pipe hat with a red feather in it, put shoulder
straps on him and gave him a sword.

We called these fellows " Dog Indians," but that made no difference to them.   They would put on more style than militia brigadier generals, and always took good care of our goods.

I reckon you don't know what a lodge of the kind I speak of is.   Well, I will tell you.   It's an Indian tent, made of white buffalo skins ; that is, buffalo skins that have been dressed on both sides.   They take three poles, about twelve or fifteen feet long, and tie them together at the top.   Then they are spread apart at the bottom and set on the ground. The buffalo skins are stretched around these poles, with short poles put in between so as to make the tent perfectly round.   An opening is left at the top of the tent, through which the smoke from the fire inside passes out.   At the top there are also a couple of wings, which can always be so arranged as to break the wind, and keep the smoke from being blown back into the tent.   One of these tents is usually as large inside as a good sized room, and they're as comfortable as a house.   The fire is built in the centre of the tent, and at night a dozen Indians will sometimes lie down in one of them, sleeping in a circle with their feet to the fire.   Generally they sleep on buffalo robes and other undressed skins, but sometimes they have a kind of willow mattress, which makes about as nice a bed as a tired hunter ever stretched himself out on.   We don't see many of these lodges among the Indians any more. Buffalo hides have gotten too scarce, and nothing else seems to answer the purpose in putting them up. Their peltry was piled up inside the lodges, and when we had held a pow-wow with an Indian, and arranged to do business at his lodge, we unpacked our goods and trading commenced. It was all a matter of barter, and no money value was ever placed on anything. We used to get pretty good bargains in these trades with the Indians, although I suppose everybody understands that.

Their furs, buck-skins, robes and ponies were what we traded for. For a good butcher-knife they were generally willing to give us a buffalo robe, and for a pound of powder, the gun caps, and about sixty bullets to go with it, we could almost always get two robes.

Sometimes when they were disposed to drive hard bargains, we had to give them two common butcher-knives for an extra good buffalo robe, but even that you know left us a pretty fair profit. A good beaver skin cost us about thirty cents in trade, and it took three bullets and three charges of powder to get a nicely-tanned buckskin.

On this trip we moved about from one Indian village to another until we got away north of Fort Laramie, in Wyoming, where we spent a good part of the winter of 1836–37.

Finally we traded out and started back to Fort
Bent with as fine a lot of peltry as was ever gathered
up among the Indians.

The way furs and robes were selling then, I am
satisfied I had as much as twenty-five thousand dollars worth to turn over to my employers when I got
into the fort.

Just before we got there we were met by Colonel
St. Vrain and a party of men with the startling news
that Charles Bent and several other Americans had
been imprisoned by the Mexicans at Taos, a town
about one hundred and fifty miles distant from Fort
Bent and across the Mexican line.

I suppose Taos was about as large then as it is
now ; that is, there were as many people there but
not more than half a dozen of them were Americans.
Bent had gone over there on business connected with
a mercantile establishment which he was about to
start in this old Mexican town.   The Texas war was
going on then, however, and the Mexicans looked
upon every American with suspicion.

It occurred to them that the little party of Americans, who happened to be in the town, were spies
sent there by the Texans, and Bent and his friends
were at once arrested and lodged in jail.

When Colonel St. Vrain heard of it, he didn't wait
for any diplomatic correspondence to be carried on
between Washington and the City of Mexico to bring

about the release of his partner, but picked up all the men that could be spared from the fort, armed them with the best guns and pistols in his possession, and started for Taos to liberate the imprisoned Americans at all hazards.

I went along with the party, but before we reached Taos we met Mr. Bent, who had been set at liberty by the Mexicans, they fearing that a party would come to his rescue from the fort, and that their town might be burned if they undertook to detain him for any great length of time.

I spent the balance of that winter and the spring at the fort and had little to do but have as good a time as possible.

I remember a funny thing that happened there that winter, and I laugh yet when I think of it. We had some visitors at the fort who were from St. Louis and were friends of Bent and St. Vrain.

Among them was the most comical fellow I ever knew, whom we called " Belzy " Dodd. I don't know what his first name really was, but "Belzy" was what we called him.

His head was as bald as a billiard ball, and by the way, we had the first billiard table brought to Colorado, at the fort that winter.

Dodd wore a wig, and one day when there were a number of Indians hanging about, he concluded to have a bit of fun with them.

He walked around, eyeing the Indians savagely for some time, and finally, dashing in among them, he gave a series of war-whoops which discounted the Comanche yells, and pulling off his wig, he threw it down at the feet of the astonished and terror-stricken red men.

The Indians thought the fellow had jerked off his own scalp, and not one of them waited to see what would happen next. They left the fort running like scared jack rabbits, and after that none of them could be induced to come near Dodd.

They called him "the-white-man-who-scalps-himself," and I think he could have traveled across the plains alone with perfect safety.

STARTING OUT AS TRAPPER AND TRADER.

CHAPTER III.

HUNTING AND TRAPPING.

" The Pawnee Indians gave us a great deal of trouble that summer. They would come around the fort and pretend to be perfectly friendly, but whenever they caught a man away from camp alone, on a hunting expedition or anything of that sort, his life wasn't worth a cent if they could get near enough to him to kill him. Every few days somebody would be run into camp, and now and then a man would be killed. One morning I remember, two of the herdsmen were killed not more than fifty yards from the fort, and the stock which they were driving out to graze was all stolen.

We got even with them though, soon afterward, when we went out one day with a party of eight men, to meet a wagon train, coming through to the fort from the east.

At Pawnee Fork, the same place where we had the fight with the Comanches the year before, we struck a band of sixteen Pawnee Indians, watching the trail and seeking an opportunity to rob some small party which could be taken at a disadvantage.

There was a strip of country in that region, which the Indians always seemed to consider their best fighting ground, and it was a lucky wagon train that got through without being attacked.

Very strong parties even, were attacked in this
locality and sometimes they fared badly. In 1846,
in the neighborhood of Pawnee Rock, the Comanches,
under the lead of the noted chiefs " Little Wolf " and
" Sitting Wolf " attacked a considerable force of
United States troops, who were on their way through
to Mexico, and the soldiers got a good deal the worst
of the fight.

They all had American horses, that is, horses
brought from the States, and until they get used to
the Indians, these horses are as much afraid of them
as they would be of any wild animal.

When the Indians swooped down on them, whoop-
ing and yelling, as they always did, the horses which
the troops were riding, got frightened and became
entirely unmanageable.

They ran away in every direction and the Comanches followed and killed the unfortunate riders, who
were carried away from the main body of troops.

There have been more people killed along that portion of the old trail, than have lost their lives at the
hands of the Indians in any other spot in the west.

The band of Pawnees that we ran across were on
foot and we were on horseback, so that although they
outnumbered us two to one, the advantage was with
us.

While we could keep entirely out of reach of their
arrows, we could still approach near enough to them

to do very effective shooting with our rifles, and we killed thirteen out of the sixteen of them in the fight.

The other three escaped by throwing down their tomahawks, bows and arrows and running up to our wagon train, which was in sight at the time.

It wasn't customary to take any prisoners in those days of Indian warfare, but when an Indian came into camp in that way, we observed the same unwritten law that governed most of the Indian tribes under similar circumstances. I suppose you would call it observing the law of hospitality, but whatever name you give it, it was a custom of the Indians never to harm the man who came into their camp voluntarily, so long as he remained there, although when he went away, they might follow and kill him before he had gone half a mile.

Another custom of the Indians was to spare at least one of their conquered enemies when they were at war among themselves. Bloodthirsty and vindicative as they were, and as near as one band sometimes came to exterminating another, one or two of the defeated braves, were always left to carry the news of the slaughter to the friends of the slaughtered.

We observed the Indian rule in dealing with the three Pawnees who had made themselves our prisoners.

First we gave them as much as they could eat, when we went into camp for the night, and after breakfast in the morning, supplied them with food enough to last until they could reach a Pawnee village. Then we told them to go back to their friends and tell them what had happened, giving them fair warning that we intended to kill all the Pawnees, if they didn't behave better in the future.

When I got back to the fort after this trip, I determined to start out on a hunting and trapping expedition on my own account.

I had gotten a pretty good insight into the business by this time, and had learned that furs of all kinds brought good prices, while beaver skins in particular were in great demand. Beaver skins were worth at that time about seven dollars a pound, and as each skin would weigh on an average two pounds, or a little over, we could count on getting fifteen dollars a piece for them. I knew that there were plenty of beaver in nearly all the streams of the country, and I thought catching them at fifteen dollars a piece, ought to be a speedy way of getting rich.

I got up a party of seventeen men and we started out in June of 1837. We traveled together, for the reason that it was not safe for one man or even a small party of men to travel alone, but every man trapped for himself, with two exceptions.

We had two men in the party, one by the name of Briggs and another named Burris, who were in partnership. These men were brothers-in-law, they having married two Indian women belonging to the "snake" tribe, who were sisters.

These two squaws shared the hardships of the trip, traveling along with the party. They did the cooking for their husbands, mended their moccasins and clothes, and took care of themselves quite as well as any of the men. Both Briggs and Burris, with their squaw wives, afterwards went to California, and settled in the neighborhood of Sacramento, where they became very wealthy.

I don't suppose any of you ever saw just such a looking lot of fellows as our party of trappers were, when we started out. Every man wore a full buckskin suit and a pair of moccasins. In a belt, which he always wore, he carried a couple of pistols, two large knives and a tomahawk. What we called a tomahawk was a kind of hatchet which we used to chop our meat up with, and in fact to do all the chopping that we had to do. In addition to this, of course every man carried his rifle, and amunition enough to meet any emergency likely to arise. Our stock of provisions consisted of coffee, sugar and tobacco. We didn't try to carry any flour, and never tasted bread from the time we started out until we returned, unless we happened to strike some fort or

4

trading post. Outside of our coffee and sugar we lived altogether on wild game. You might think that this would grow a little monotonous, but it didn't, as there were so many kinds of game in the country then, that we could have a change of meat every day. The different varieties of meat that we used to have sometimes in one day, would make a famous hotel bill of fare now-a-days.

It was no uncommon thing for us to sit down to a meal, with a buffalo steak, a piece of roast bear, a "hunk" of venison, elk or antelope, and a wild turkey before us. There was an abundance of all kinds of small game, such as rabbit, squirrel, pheasant and partridge, and we got choice roasts out of the beaver, although this is a kind of meat that a great many people never have heard of. These meats were roasted over our camp fires, and I have never tasted meats, cooked any other way, which were quite as good as those we used to serve up in the trapper's camp.

It was only when we were in camp at night, or moving from one place to another, that all the trappers came together. We would locate the camp at a point where it could be reached, without difficulty, by all the trappers in the company, and then we started out in different directions, to trap the various streams within eight or ten miles of the camp. Each man carried eight traps, which was called a "set." He started out in the morning, set and baited his traps, and the next morning went the rounds to see what he had caught.

We trapped altogether for beaver, but every now and then a bear, or some other animal would come along and make the mistake of getting caught. When a bear got into a trap he would pull it loose and travel away with it, stopping now and then to pound the ugly thing on the ground and try in other ways to get it off. Poor old bruin would cry over his bad luck, making a noise almost like the wail of a child, but the strongly made trap would stick to him until we killed him and took it off.

Sometimes we would have to follow him a good distance to recover the trap, and a bear was never in good humor when we found him under such circumstances.

The man who has never had an opportunity of studying the habits of the beaver, has missed an acquaintance with the most interesting and intelligent animal in the world.

In building the dams which constitute their winter homes, they go about the work as systematically as so many men. In forming these dams they sometimes cut down large trees with their teeth, and they never fail to make a tree fall just where they want it. I never knew them to lodge a tree in falling it, and they show the same intelligence in everything they do.

With all their intelligence, however, they fell
easy victims to the trapper, who understood his
business.

Their principal food is the bark and buds of certain kinds of green twigs, and all the bait we used
was one of these twigs of trees, stuck down in the
ground, in such a position that the beaver would
have to pass over a trap, to get to it, when he left
his home and started out in search of a meal.   That
was the bait proper, but in order to persuade the
beaver that a particular twig would make a safe and
satisfactory lunch, we dipped it in the strong smell-
ing castoreum or beaver oil. This led them to
believe that other beavers had sampled the tempting
bit of wood, and they fell easily into the trap.

Sometimes we would find a queer old beaver living in a lodge by himself. These were always
males, and we called them " old bachelors."

When we had good luck, each trapper would come
in with four or five beaver skins every night, and
it was no light day's work to visit eight traps, take
care of the game and set the traps again.

We had Indian ponies on which we rode from place
to place, and on which we packed our provisions.
The beaver skins were dried and put up into hundred
pound packs, which also had to be carried by the
pack animals.

Each man started out with as many horses as he
thought he should need and if he got more peltry

than he could carry he could easily trade with the Indians for more ponies.

On this trip we trapped the Rio Grande del Norte, the Arkansas River, and pretty much all the streams of Colorado and Wyoming.

We wintered in Wyoming and was gone about nine months from the time we left Fort Bent. Fifteen of our seventeen trappers got back safely, which made it a pretty lucky trip for those times.

Two poor fellows were killed by the Indians, or at least we supposed they were. They left camp one morning as usual and that was the last we ever saw of them. We made a search for their remains, but could find no trace of them and reached the conclusion that they had been killed by the Indians and their bodies devoured by the wolves and coyotes.

We were fortunate on that trip so far as having any fights with the savages was concerned. Although we were often threatened by them, they only attacked us once. That time it looked very black for us, for a while, but we only had one man wounded and his injuries were not serious.

It was when we were coming up Grand River on our way home.

We had followed Green River down to its junction with the Grand, and in going up the latter stream had reached Piny creek, when we noticed a large band of the " Snake " Indians hovering about us.

They kept at a considerable distance, but we could see that they were following us and evidently sought an opportunity to take us at a disadvantage.

While we could not tell just how many of the Indians there were, I am certain there were four or five times as many as there were of us. They knew that we had a valuable lot of peltry, and this, along with our horses was a great temptation to the red robbers.

The fact that they delayed making an attack, puzzled us a good deal, as we did not understand the purpose of the delay, and thought it more than likely that they were aiming to drive us into an ambuscade.

While we could not help getting a little nervous, we knew there was but one thing to do and that was to be prepared to fight at any moment.

We kept on our guard day and night and it was this constant watchfullness, which saved our lives and gave us a very substantial victory over the savages.

Just at daybreak one morning they attacked us. They expected to take us by surprise, but in this they were disappointed. They not only found us on our guard, but we had the advantage of being in a thick cottonwood grove, so that we fought them under cover of the trees.

We allowed them to charge almost up to our camp before we fired, and when our guns cracked it seemed that not a trapper missed his mark.

We had no time to count the number of Indians which fell at our first fire, but we could see a considerable number of them being dragged away by those who retreated. They made another charge which resulted more disastrously to them than the first, and then they gave up the fight.

I think we must have killed about twenty of them and gave them such a whipping that they remembered us and had a great deal of respect for us after that.

The next time we went into their country, we had no trouble in making peace with them and we never had a fight with them afterward.

When we got back to Fort Bent we had a splendid lot of peltry and that summer I took a notion to go back to " the States," to dispose of my share of the beaver and buckskins, which we had gotten together.

Going back to " the States " in those days meant going back to Missouri, or some point east of that.

I went as far as Westport, now Kansas City, and remained there several weeks. After disposing of my peltry and paying the expenses of the trip, I had about four thousand dollars left as the net proceeds of my nine month's trapping.

I was pretty well satisfied with the venture and like the early gold hunters I fancied I had a fortune almost within my grasp. A year or two more in the "Rockies," I thought, could hardly fail to put me in possession of all the money I needed to live on comfortably in Kentucky, and I wrote to the "old folks" at home that I should rejoin them in the near future.

Not long since, one of my boys showed me a copy of an old letter that I wrote to my mother about that time, in which I told her that I hoped to come home rich, the next year. It brought the tears to my eyes, when I looked at it and reflected that I had failed to keep that promise. When the next year came around, although I had made a good deal of money, it had somehow or other gotten away from me and I decided to stay in the mountains a while longer. That's the way I kept putting off going home from time to time, until after awhile my parents died, the ties which bound me to the old homestead were broken, and I have never seen it since the day I left it, to go to Mississippi in 1834.

It was about the same way with all the old trappers. When they once got into the mountains, they seemed some way or other, to get chained to the country, and a great many of them became lost entirely to their early friends and associates, and even to their own families."

"UNCLE DICK" IN TRAPPER'S COSTUME,

CHAPTER IV.

FIVE THOUSAND MILES ON HORSEBACK.

"In the fall of 1838 I started out on one of the longest trapping expeditions ever made by American trappers.

It was in September that we left Fort Bent, and not until nearly two years later did we see it again.

There were nineteen men in the party when we started, and fourteen of them got back, five of our number having fallen by the way, the victims of the Monarch Indians of Oregon and the Pah-Utes, or as they are sometimes called the Piutes of Utah.

Before I tell you about this trip, I should explain to you how the land lay in this far western country in those days, because there were no such divisions into states and territories as we have now.

I have already told you that when I came to the country, all the territory lying between Missouri and the Mexican bounday line, was called the Indian territory.

A more nearly correct statement in regard to what was considered the Indian territory at that time, would have been, that it was the vast country bounded on the east by the Mississippi River, on the south and west by Mexico and the Rocky mountains, and on the north by the British Possessions, with the exception of the territory contained in Missouri, Arkansas and Louisiana. I believe that congress had declared that territory to be the Indian country in 1834, and it took in what has since been cut up into the states of Kansas, Nebraska, Iowa, Montana, North Dakota, South Dakota, part of Minnesota, a corner of Colorado, about half of Wyoming, and the present Indian territory.

In the early part of 1838 Iowa was made a territory, taking in a good part, if not all of the territory now in Minnesota and all of Dakota. All of the territory belonging to the United States, which was east of Mexico and the Rocky mountains, and west of the states of Missouri and Louisiana and the territories of Arkansas and Iowa, was, properly speaking, the Indian territory in 1838.

At the same time all of the country now included in Oregon, Washington and Idaho, was called Oregon, while all the country lying south of the parallel which marks the southern boundary of Oregon and Idaho, and west of a line which followed the Rocky mountain range south to the source of the Arkansas River, the Arkansas River east to the present eastern boundary of Colorado, the eastern boundary line of Colorado to Texas, and the eastern boundary line of Texas to the Gulf of Mexico, belonged to Mexico, or rather was claimed by the Mexican government, although Texas had at that time declared her Independence.

New Mexico and California were Mexican states, the former including in its territory nearly all of what is now Arizona, and a considerable portion of what is now Colorado.   Only that portion of Colorado lying north of the Arkansas River and east of the Rocky mountains, belonged to the United States prior to the purchase of our Mexican territory.

Utah originally took in all of the present state of Nevada, and when the mormons went there in 1847, they got outside of the territory of the United States.   In 1849, after the region which they claimed had been ceded to the United States, they undertook to set up an independent state, which they called "The state of Deseret"—the land of the honey bee. The government took a hand in the matter, however, and organized the territory, which took its name from the Ute or Utah Indians, who were natives of the country.

Whether Oregon belonged to the United States or Great Britain was at that time a question.   Both governments claimed it, and it was not until 1846 that the present boundary line of the British Possessions was agreed upon.

In speaking of what happened on the long trapping expedition I am about to tell you of, I shall use the names of the present geographical divisions of the country, although, as I have explained, these divisions have all been made long since that time.

We had six or seven Arapahoe and Shawnee
Indians with us on this trip. These Indians were
then on good terms with the whites, and as they
were good trappers, we found it to our advantage to
take them with us. Starting with the regulation
trappers' outfit, we proceeded up the Arkansas River
and followed it to its source in the Rocky mountains.
Then we went north, trapping nearly all the streams
of Northern Colorado. Passing over into Utah we
struck the Green River, and followed it up into
Wyoming.

After trapping all the smaller streams in that territory, we followed the Big Horn River into Montana, going north as far as the Yellowstone. Then
we turned westward and passed through Idaho, trapping for months along the Snake and Salmon Rivers
and their tributaries.

It was while we were trapping on the Green
River, that August Claymore, the oldest trapper
in the mountains, who was a member of our party
met with an adventure which we all supposed
would end his life, but which he lived to tell
of not many years ago, when he was the only man
in the country who still followed trapping as a
business. He fell in one day with a party of Snake
Indians, and some way or other they got into a quarrel, the result of which was that the Indians attacked
him with their war clubs, and beat him until they

CLAYMORE, THE LAST OF THE OLD TRAPPERS.

thought he was dead. Some of the trappers came upon them before they had taken the old fellow's scalp, but his skull had been crushed, the brain had been lacerated and a portion of it destroyed. We held a sort of trapper's consultation and decided that we would have to bury Claymore before we broke camp. Strangely enough, however, he got well, and used to tell about his living to wear out the suit of clothes that one of the trappers donated for a burial suit.

We reached the Columbia River not long after Claymore's adventure, and followed that magnificent stream up through Washington territory.

Having by this time become pretty well loaded down with peltry we determined to go to Vancouver and try to dispose of a portion of it. There we succeeded in relieving our pack animals of a part of their burden, and concluding that we had gotten far enough away from home, we turned to the south, and passing through Western Washington and Oregon we entered California, and struck the Pacific coast at San Luis Obispo.

Then we went down through Southern California, spent some time along the Colorado River, and late in the summer started up through Arizona, following the Gila River some distance and then again going north into Utah.

We were disappointed in Southern California and Arizona. We found plenty of beaver in nearly all the streams, but they were not of the fine fur bearing species.   There was about the same difference between the Northern and Southern beavers, that there is between the Alaskan and California seals.

The furs which we took along the Colorado and Gila Rivers, were of little account, and the time we spent there was practically wasted, but we got to see some new country.   When we got back to Fort Bent we estimated that we had traveled over five thousand miles.

We didn't know until we got back just how long we had been gone.   Like the man who went around the world in eighty days, as the French novelist tells the story, we lost our reckoning.

When we got out in the mountains we found that nobody in the party had an almanac.   A Frenchman by the name of Charlefou agreed to act as timekeeper and recorder of days, his calendar being a square stick upon which he cut a notch every day.

After we had been out some time and had entirely lost the run of dates, so that we couldn't have told to save our lives, what day of the month it was, without taking a look at Charlefou's stick and figuring up, the Frenchman met with an accident and his calendar was lost.

Then we agreed not to make any inquiry about the time until we got home, just to see how far off we would be in our reckoning.

Coming through California, a country with which none of us were acquainted, and where the seasons were so different from anything we had been used to, led us to believe it was a month or two later in the year than it really was when we reached Fort Bent, and nearly all of us made wild guesses as to the date of our arrival.

"Old Charlefou," as we always called the Frenchman who lost our calendar, had the worst luck of anybody in the party, who got back alive, with the exception of Claymore.

While we were up in Eastern Washington, he was out several miles from camp one day when a band of Blackfeet Indians got after him. He was riding a fine Nez Perces horse and kept so far ahead of the Indians that he was out of reach of their arrows. It was a race for life, but he was gaining on his pursuers and had begun to feel sure of reaching the camp safely, when he saw only a few feet in front of him one of those deep fissures in the earth which are characteristic of the Great Plateau. He dare not stop, and if he had turned either to the right or left, the Indians would have gained so much on him that he could hardly have escaped being captured or killed.

He put spurs to his horse and undertook to do what it seemed was the only thing for him to do under the circumstances, and that was to make his horse leap across the chasm.

The horse made a noble effort to carry out his master's plan of escape, but the distance across the breach was too great and horse and rider went to the bottom together. Charlefou had both legs broken and the horse was instantly killed.

The Indians came up and looked down into the gorge but as neither man nor horse showed any signs of life, and there was no way of getting down to where they were, without going to a good deal of trouble, they were left without being molested.

We started out to hunt Charlefou when he did not return to camp as usual, but did not find him for nearly a day after he had met with the accident.

He knew that we would make an effort to learn what had become of him, but feared that any signal which he might give, to notify us of his whereabouts would bring back the murderous Blackfeet. Finally, however, he made up his mind that he must take the chance of being discovered by the Indians, if he was to be found by his friends. He fired a few shots from his rifle, of which we fortunately heard the report, and after a great deal of hard work we succeeded in rescuing him from his perilous position.

There were no surgeons within five hundred miles of us that we knew of, so we had to set the broken bones ourselves. Then we made a litter out of poles, which we placed on two pack animals, and in this way we carried him from place to place for nearly two months.

This adventure made a great change in the French-man's feeling toward the Indians. Before that he had been inclined to think that the red-skins should be shown rather more consideration than we usually gave them.

Not a great while before, he had been standing guard one night, when he saw something perched in a tree, a short distance from him, which changed its position every now and then and appeared to be keeping a close watch on the camp. Without knowing what it was he fired a shot at it, and a dead Indian tumbled out of the branches. The old fellow really seemed to feel a little sorry about having killed the Indian at that time, but after the almost fatal chase of the Blackfeet, the naturally kind hearted old Frenchman became about as vindictive as he had before been charitable.

They used to say several years later, that this bitterness cropped out when he was sitting as a juror in a murder case at Taos, New Mexico. An Indian was charged with having killed a white man, and was given a trial by jury. Charlefou was on the jury, and soon after the trial commenced he went to sleep. It didn't last long and they had to wake him up when the jury got ready to retire to one corner of the room in which the trial was held, to agree upon a verdict. Charlefou had slept all the time and hadn't heard either evidence, argument, or the charge of the Court,

5

if there was any, but when they asked him what he thought should be done with the accused, he replied very promptly, " hang him, of course ; if he ain't guilty now he will be."

It was the Blackfeet tribe, or rather the Monarch Indians, who were found in the same section of country and were of pretty much the same character who killed three of my companions on this trip.

We were encamped on what we called Mussel Shell River, although I do not know that it is still called by the same name, and the "Monarch" village was not more than a mile distant. It was only a village of tents or lodges, you know, as all these Indians were migratory, and never built any permanent villages or had any permanent locations. They were a thieving lot, and one night they stole three ponies belonging to one of the Shawnee Indians who was with us. The next day we went after the horses and found them picketed out with the ponies belonging to the " Monarchs." We expected to have a fight if we took them away, but we didn't propose to be robbed, in any event.

There was always just one way of gaining the respect of a tribe of Indians and that was to give them a thorough whipping. They always seemed to have a curiosity to find out what kind of fighting men a party was composed of, before they could be relied on to keep their promises and cease annoying the party in various ways. As it was certain that we should have to fight the "Monarchs" sooner or later, we thought we might as well fight for our ponies as anything else. We took the horses back to camp and had just turned them into our corral, when a dozen Indians who had followed us, dashed in and undertook to drive away some more horses. I don't know who fired the first shot, but I know the fighting commenced just about that time and was kept up three or four hours. It was about two or three o'clock in the afternoon, and all our men happened to be in camp when the firing commenced.

Everybody turned out and went into the fight on their own account. Nobody ever assumed command of our trapping parties when we got into a rumpus of this sort with the Indians. Each man understood that he had to fight and keep fighting as long as there were any hostile Indians in sight. There was no choice about the matter. There was no such thing as being taken prisoner and released on parole. We knew if we didn't kill the Indians, they would kill us, and all the understanding we had among ourselves was that each man should make every bullet count and that any such thing as a surrender was out of the question. I may say that we had a further understanding, that not all of us were to shoot at the first fire. It never mattered much how large a band of Indians was, they fell back when fired on. Their next move, however, was to make a charge, let fly a shower of arrows, and perhaps follow this up with an attempt to tomahawk their enemies if they found them with empty guns. As long as they knew that we had loaded rifles, they felt that somebody was going to get killed whenever they got in range of these guns, and they kept at a respectful distance.

The band of " Monarchs " who had invaded our camp, soon retreated to their village. We followed them and kept up a hot fire, picking them off as they ran. The war was carried into their village, and we soon had them scattering in every direction. We pulled down their lodges, and when we got through with our afternoon's work, not an Indian was to be seen in the neighborhood who would ever again go on the war-path, this side the " happy hunting grounds."

The first live Indian we saw after that, was a very old man named " Lone Wolf," who came to us the next day to say that his people wanted to make peace. I suppose this old fellow must have been eighty or ninety years old, and it was on account of his age that they thought it safe to send him to treat with us. He came hobbling along, and of course we allowed him to come into camp. He told us, through an interpreter, that his people had done wrong, and that they had been fools for stealing the horses from the " white men." It was some of the young men of the tribe, he said, who had brought on the trouble.

We had killed many of their people and they had been punished for their wrong doing. The " Monarchs" wished to make peace with the white men, that they might bury their dead, and set up the houses which had been torn down.

We told him we had always wanted to be friendly with them, and through him invited the chief of the tribe, "Sitting Buffalo," to come into our camp and talk the matter over. The patriarch of the tribe carried this word back to the chief, and a party of his warriors who were in hiding, and by and by they came in carrying a white rag fastened to a pole, as a flag of truce. I don't know how they caught on to this feature of civilized warfare, but that was the way they came into camp. We picked out three of our men to represent us in the long pow-wow which followed, while the rest of us stood around and watched for any manifestation of treachery or bad faith.

Finally the chief and his friends, and the three white men who represented the trappers sat down, according to the Indian custom, in a circle, and the old chief lit the pipe of peace. He took a pull at it and then it was passed around the circle, until it reached him again, each of the Indians and the white men too, taking a single puff as it went around. This concluded the ceremony and established a peace which lasted as long as we remained in their country. As I have already said we lost three men in this fight.

There were two other trappers who failed to answer to roll call at the end of this long trip. Both of them were French Canadians and both were killed by the Pah-Utes in Utah. The first one killed was Le Bonte, a noted character among the early trappers. He fell behind one day when we were traveling, and the Indians stole up quietly and killed him without attracting the attention of the rest of the party. Then the miserable cannibals cut off nearly all the flesh from his bones and carried it away to eat. We found the bones and buried them where we found them.

Le Duc, the other Frenchman killed by the Pah-Utes, met with a more horrible death even than poor old Le Bonte.

We were sitting around our camp fire one evening just at dusk, when without any previous warning, a shower of arrows fell around us. We sprang to our guns and caught sight of a little band of Indians running away from a thicket in which they had been concealed. We fired on them, but they were soon out of sight and did not return.

Le Duc was the only man who was struck by one of the arrows which dropped into our camp so unexpectedly, and he was only slightly wounded.

It was a poisoned arrow, however, which had hit the poor fellow, and he died after suffering terribly for twenty-four hours.

The Pah-Utes were a stoical lot of Indians who paid no more attention to the killing of one of their number than the least intelligent brutes. The Snake Indians used to make war on them frequently and sell their captives to the Mexicans for slaves. It was no uncommon thing to see a party of Mexicans in that country buying Indian slaves, in those days, and while we were trapping there I sent a lot of peltry back to Taos by a party of these same slave traders, some of whom I happened to know.

I went from Fort Bent across to Taos to get this peltry, in the fall of 1840, and when I was returning to the Fort, I did the Arapahoe Indians a good turn, which made them my warm friends ever afterward.

The Utes and the Arapahoes had been at war and the Arapahoes had been defeated. A great many of them had been killed, and some of the Arapahoe women and children had been carried away as prisoners. I had gotten into a place in the mountains where there was a good deal of snow and was picking my way along carefully, when I saw something floundering about in a big drift. I raised my gun to shoot, when I saw that it was an Indian woman.

I knew something of the Arapahoe language and she made me understand that she belonged to that tribe and had been taken captive by the Utes. She had

managed to escape and without moccasins, and with
scarcely any clothing, she had made her way through
the mountains until exhausted by hunger and fatigue
she had fallen in the snow where I found her. She
was badly frozen and would have perished in a short
time had I not picked her up. I put her on one of
my ponies and carried her along until we went into
camp for the night.

The camp fire and something to eat soon had the
effect of restoring her to her normal condition, and
after a day or two she left us and made her way to
one of the Arapahoe villages, where she told her
friends how she had been rescued and cared for by a
white man. They came out to meet me, and with a
great deal more warmth and enthusiasm than I had
ever thought them capable of manifesting, they
thanked me for what I had done. There was something substantial about their thanks too, for they
made me a present of two ponies before they left me,
and would not be satisfied until I accepted them.
They were always my friends after that, and I never
had any kind of trouble with them. I think every
member of the tribe who was old enough to know
anything, was told about the Indian woman's rescue,
because they all seemed to know me, and looked upon
me as an exceptionally good white man.

A VICTIM OF THE WOLVES.

CHAPTER V.

BUFFALO FARMING.

" Trapping had by this time become less profitable than it was formerly. The prices of peltry of all kinds had gone down, and from that time on I paid less attention to it. Now and then I made a short trip, but for the next two or three years I was engaged mainly in a new line of business.

It required a large amount of meat to supply Fort Bent, and I took a contract to furnish what was needed. Buffalo meat was what I was expected to supply, with deer or bear thrown in when a change of meat was wanted.

In this I combined business with pleasure, because the finest sport a man ever had was hunting buffalo.

There were millions of them on the plains at that time. I say millions at a venture, although the fact is it was impossible to make even an approximate estimate of the number we could sometimes see at one time. You might as well have tried to make an estimate of the number of ants in a big Colorado ant hill. As far as the eye could reach I have seen the plains black with them, and it would actually look as though the prairies themselves were on the move.

When the emigrants commenced traveling across Kansas a few years later, the buffalo used to get mixed up with their cattle, and sometimes the herds of cattle would get stampeded, and half of them would be lost.

I remember when I was freighting, I was in camp one night and my ox teams were grazing, under the care of a Mexican herder. About twelve o'clock at night, I rode out to see that everything was all right, and just about that time a big band of buffalo came along. One of my oxen took it into his head to join the buffalo and quit the freighting business. I undertook to drive him back, and the whole band started to run. The steer had either determined to desert me, or else gotten it into his head that he was a buffalo, because I never had a bigger chase than I had to get him back among the other cattle.

It never occurred to me then that I should live long enough to see all the buffalo killed off. I never expected to see the time when I could not go out and shoot a buffalo, butcher him, and have the meat ready for use, with about as little trouble as a ranchman has in getting a beef out of his herd of cattle.

They were hardly as wild in those days as range cattle are now, and I have killed thirty buffalo in a day, when I was supplying Fort Bent with meat. Now, the best informed sportsmen say that there are not two hundred buffalo in the United States, and these are in small bands, scattered about in the west, the largest band being in Yellowstone Park.

The Indians killed a great many of these animals, but as a rule they only killed what they needed for food. The "skin hunters" were the fellows who were mainly responsible for the extermination of the buffalo. As long as they were killed only for the purpose of supplying the people on the frontier and the Indians with food, we could not notice that their number was decreasing, but when an army of men came into the country, to kill them for the purpose of supplying the eastern market with robes, they didn't last long.

I used to enjoy seeing the Indians hunt buffalo; that is, when the Indians were friendly and were not hunting white men at the same time.

A large party of them would start out on horseback and when they had picked out a band of buffalo, they would form a circle around the game and gradually close in on it.

Then they started their horses on a run, bending their bows and adjusting their arrows as they neared the animals marked for the slaughter.

They did not shoot until they ran alongside the game, and then their arrows were quite as effective as the bullets of the white hunters. The little Indian boys, who followed the hunters, took part in the chase, and the buffalo calves were left for them to practice on.

When I went out after buffalo, I took a good saddle horse, the best I could find in the country, one or two men to do the butchering, and a lot of pack animals or a wagon to carry the meat. I never rode my saddle horse until I got ready for the chase, because it took a good horse, and a fresh one, to catch a buffalo when he started to run, and there was nothing sportsmanlike about killing, without giving him a chance to escape in a fair race.

About a month after I commenced hunting in the fall of 1840, I was waiting one day, after having killed about twenty buffalo, for the butchers to get through with their work, when I noticed a pair of twin buffalo calves, and it occurred to me that I might take them back to the fort alive and raise them.

They were easily captured but how they were to be fed was not so easily determined. When I got back to the fort, however, I tried an experiment which proved entirely successful. I persuaded a good natured and kindly disposed cow to adopt the kidnapped young buffalos, and they seemed to do quite as well as they would have done roaming over the plains with the herd to which they originally belonged.

Satisfied with that experiment, I then commenced buffalo farming, and although I am not the only man who has tried the experiment in the United States, I have never heard of anyone who made as much of a success of it as I did.

I succeeded in picking up about forty milch cows and located my farm where the city of Pueblo has since been built.

That was twenty years before the town was started, and I suppose few people now living there know that the city is located on the site of the only buffalo farm Colorado ever had.

I fitted up a corral there, and got together forty-four buffalo calves, which I turned in with the cows, after taking away from them their own calves. They were not inclined to look with much favor on the hump backed, ugly looking little animals, in the start, but by and by they began to think better of it, and in a short time they were getting along as well together as if they had belonged to the same family. When they were able to take care of themselves, the buffalo and the cattle were herded together, and one appeared to be about as much of a domestic animal as the other.

I kept them until they were three years old and then sold them to a man who took them to New York. There they were parceled out to showmen, and some of them I think were put into the Central Park Zoological Gardens. I delivered them to the purchaser at Kansas City, driving them across the plains along with a few cows, just as I would have driven a band of cattle. I had two or three pairs of them broke to work like oxen and they made first class teams.

The meanest enemy the buffalo ever had, aside from the " skin hunters," was the grey wolf. The wolves followed the buffalo and lived on them. Their killing of the calves has had a great deal to do with the disappearance of the finest game we have ever had in America.

Their slaughter was not confined to the buffalo calves either. I have seen a pack of hungry wolves single out a full grown bull, drag him down and tear him to pieces in about as little time as it takes me to tell of it. A single buffalo could not defend himself against them, because while some of the wolves charged him in front, others would fasten their sharp teeth in his hind parts, cut the " ham-strings " as we used to say, and the poor bull dropped down and was entirely at the mercy of his enemies.

The buffalo were intelligent enough to know that in union there was strength, in a fight with wolves. When a band of them lay down at night, it was usually in a circle, inside of which were the calves.

Then if they were attacked by wolves, standing side by side, with their heads down, they presented a solid fighting front, and could take care of themselves.

When hunting buffalo, I have sat many a time all night by a blazing fire, throwing the red-hot brands every now and then at a pack of wolves, to keep them from stealing the game which I had slaughtered.

One night I remember, when I was alone, there must have been hundreds of the vicious brutes in the pack that kept me company all night. They would come so close that I could see their eyes shining like balls of fire in the darkness, and all the time they kept up a snapping and snarling which would have set a man crazy who did not know what cowardly brutes they were.

I didn't care to waste much ammunition on them, but I killed three or four during the night and the dead wolves were at once torn to pieces and devoured by the balance of the dirty gang of cannibals. They sneaked away just before daylight came in the morning, but they had given me a mighty lively all-night serenade.

With as much game as there was in the country it would seem that we never ought to have suffered for anything to eat, but we did now and then get into a tight place. I remember about the time I have been speaking of, I went up one time to where the town of Greeley is now to trade with the Arapahoe Indians. While I was there a terrible snow-storm came on and lasted so long that the Indians ran out of food, because they could not get out to kill any game.

I got about as hungry that time as a man ever gets, and swam the South Platte River one morning when it was full of melting ice, to get a wild goose that I had shot on the opposite bank.

The Arapahoes, by the way, saved me from the Pawnee Indians that winter. I have told you how I

made them my friends by returning to them one of
their squaws, who had been carried away by the Utes.

The three chiefs, Roman-Nose, Buffalo-Billy, and
Big-Mouth had gotten their bands together, and had
a village of about six hundred lodges at the mouth
of Crow Creek.

That was only a year or two before Buffalo-Billy
and eighteen or twenty of his braves were killed, in
a drunken brawl on Cherry Creek, about a dozen
miles from the present city limits of Denver.

The quarrel which resulted in the killing was all
their own affair, as it was entirely among the Indians,
although the white man who traded them the fire-
water, was in a sense responsible for it.

I started out to tell you, however, that on one of
my trips from the fort to the Indian village, my horse
gave out, and I had to turn him loose. There was
a deep snow on the ground and I buried my saddle
where I thought I could find it when I came back,
and then started for the village on foot.

I had thirty miles to travel, but I shouldn't have
minded the walk particularly, had it not been in a
country where I was likely to run into a band of hostile Indians at any moment.

The Pawnees were the sneaking, murderous scoundrels that I was most afraid of, but I began to feel
reasonably safe, when I had gotten within a few
miles of the end of my journey, without seeing any
signs of the hostiles.

About the middle of the afternoon I was jogging along at a pretty good pace, because I wanted to reach the village before night, when I happened to cast my eye toward a low ridge, which was perhaps four or five hundred yards to one side of me, and saw moving objects which at once attracted my attention.

What I saw was something coming up over the crest of the hill, from the opposite side, and at first I thought it a band of antelope just coming in sight. I stopped and took a good look at them, and then the things began to look like Indians.

That's what they were too, and Pawnee Indians at that. They were on foot and saw me about the same time that I caught sight of them. There was but one thing for me to do, and that was to run for the Arapahoe village, six miles away. I knew that if I could reach it I should be as safe as I would be in Fort Bent, but the question was whether or not I could keep a safe distance ahead of the Pawnees in a foot race.

As soon as they discovered that I had caught sight of them, they commenced brandishing their toma-hawks, and with one of those yells which will always make a man's hair jump straight up, no matter how often he has heard it, they started after me.

I had no time to count them, but as I started to run, I reached the conclusion that there were about twenty Indians in the band. Two of the Pawnee

6

bucks shot ahead of the others at the beginning of
the race, and as I glanced over my shoulder from
time to time, I saw that they were gaining on me.
The others soon fell away behind, and I made up my
mind that I could escape, if I got rid of the two Indians nearest to me.   One of them was by this time
within two hundred yards of me and the other about
a hundred yards behind him.

Exhausted as I was by a run of two or three miles,
I was by no means certain that my aim would be
steady enough to kill him, if I turned and fired at
that distance from the foremost of my pursuers, and
if I missed, with an empty rifle and the two Indians
so close to me, the chances would be very much
against me.

Fortunately, just at that time, I had to run over a
little hill which hid me for a moment from the Indians as they were coming up on the other side.

At the foot of the hill I stopped, raised my gun to
my shoulder, and waited until the foremost Indian
reached the crest of the hill.   That brought him
within a hundred yards of me and when my gun
cracked he dropped.   I knew from the way he fell
that he was a dead savage and that there was no danger of his following me any further.

I ran on, loading my gun for the other Indian as
I ran, but when I looked back again, he had fallen
so far behind that he was out of reach of a bullet.

He waited until the balance of the band came up and then they all followed me until they caught sight of the Arapahoe village, for which I was headed.

Before I reached the village the Arapahoes saw me and knew from the way I ran that I was being pursued. About forty warriors mounted their horses and came galloping out to meet me.

I was so near exhausted by the long run, that I couldn't mount the horse which they offered me, to go with them in pursuit of the Pawnees, when I told them what was up, but they went back without me while I made my way into the village.

Being mounted on good horses they soon overtook the Pawnees, and when they came back that night they told me that but one of the band which had given me such a chase, had been left alive, and his life was only spared, in accordance with the Indian custom, that he might carry the news of the killing to his friends and inform them that his comrades had fallen at the hands of the Arapahoe braves.

They brought in seventeen scalps, and as one of the Pawnees escaped the slaughter, there must have been nineteen in the party.

I never saw a band of Indians so much elated over anything as the Arapahoes were over this killing of the Pawnees. They were pleased because they had saved the life of a white man to whom they thought themselves under great obligations, and still more

pleased over having taken the scalps of so many of
their inveterate enemies, the Pawnees.

I was in high favor among the Arapahoes at that
time, and if I had had a fancy for it, I think they
would have made me a "big chief" without hesita-
tion.

My shooting used to astonish them, and when a
difficult shot was to be made at game or any of the
wild animals which came near the village, they
would call on me to do the shooting.

I became very thoroughly acquainted with the
Arapahoes that winter, and learned more of their
habits and customs than I had ever known before,
although I had at that time been among them more
or less for several years.

When they came back from their fight with the
Pawnees, I noticed for the first time how each Indian
kept the record of those he had slain. In one place
on the handle of his tomahawk, he cut a notch for
each scalp he had taken. In another place he cut
a notch for each enemy found lying upon the
battle field after the fight was won, whom he had
been the first to approach and strike with his
tomahawk. It was looked upon by the Arapahoes,
Cheyennes and some other Indians, as an evidence
of great courage for a warrior to be the first to
strike an enemy who had fallen in battle, their idea
being that the prostrate enemy might be only

feigning death, and if wounded he would fight more desperately than under any other circumstances.

They called these notches on the tomahawk handles " coups," (koos,) and in addition to those which indicated the number of scalps taken and the number of killed or disabled enemies " struck," they had

A SNAKE RIVER VIEW.

another row of notches which indicated the number of horses captured, when they fought with mounted enemies.

The Indian who grew up to manhood without being able to exhibit any " coups" was looked upon by the tribe as a very worthless and good for nothing Indian, and he stood no show of securing any kind of preferment.

On the other hand the Indian who could show a
long string of " coups" was looked up to and loaded
with savage honors."

I had a little experience that same winter, in the
dangerous business of traveling back and forth between Fort Bent and Fort St. Vrain, carrying money
and other valuables which had to be transported from
one post to the other.

Fort St. Vrain had been built up by the owners of
Fort Bent, in the Arapahoe country, north of where
Denver is now, and a weekly express was established
in 1842, between the two posts. A portion of the
time I filled the position of expressman, and have
carried as much as sixty thousand dollars in silver
at a time from one point to the other. It was carried
on pack animals, and every dollar was delivered
safely to the parties to whom it was consigned. I
made several trips of this character, at one time and
another, not only between Forts Bent and St. Vrain,
but between Fort Bent and Taos, New Mexico, where
Bent and St. Vrain carried on a large business. I
was always fortunate enough to get through safely,
and never lost a dollar entrusted to my care."

A UTE INDIAN VILLAGE.

CHAPTER VI.

AMONG THE UTES AND APACHES.

" Trading with the Indians had its attractions, the chief of which was of course, the very handsome profits which we made out of the business, but it was always a perilous vocation.

When we started out to trade with a band of peaceable Indians, we never knew how many hostiles we should find roving about in the country we had to travel over. In the winter of 1843 I got together a lot of goods and took out a license to trade with the Utes. It was always necessary, before starting out on one of these expeditions, to take out a license which was issued by the Indian Agent having charge of the band or tribe with whom the trader wished to do business. We had to give bond in the sum of two thousand dollars, conditioned on observance of the law, in our conduct of the Indian traffic. That is, we bound ourselves not to sell or trade them intoxicating liquors of any kind, or anything which we knew it to be unlawful to put them in possession of. Although we generally found the Utes on Mexican territory, they occasionally came across the line and then we had to deal with them on the same terms as with other Indians we found within the United States.

We were not having any trouble with the Utes at that time, but the Apaches were at war with us, and while we were looking for Ute villages, we had to steer clear of every Apache camp. I had a big stock of vermilion and other cheap paints, beads, knives, amunition and guns which I carried on pack animals and had gotten so well acquainted with the country by that time, that I thought I could get through without taking a party of men along with me.

With only one man, and he a Delaware Indian, to accompany me, I started out to find a band of Utes, that I knew were moving about from place to place, and finally found them in the Canadian River country, in the Pan Handle of Texas. I came down through Trinidad, or rather through the pass in which Trinidad is now located — there wasn't any such place then—followed Raton creek up past the place where I am now living, climbed the Raton mountains, and went over into New Mexico. On the other side of the mountains I started down Sugarite creek, and not more than eight or nine miles from my present home, I came to an Indian village.

Supposing it to be a Ute village, we rode in, stopped under the shade of some cottonwood trees, and as it was getting along toward night, we began to make preparations to go into camp. There were perhaps thirty or forty lodges in the village, but it was sometime before we saw any Indians or anyone took notice of us. Then we only saw two or three old men, and so confident were we of being among friendly Indians, that we did not think to look at them closely, and it was not until we saw a group of squaws peering at us intently, that we began to think it necessary to make sure of our whereabouts.

All Indians look pretty much alike to one unaccustomed to meeting members of the different tribes, but there were always some distinguishing features or characteristics which enabled a frontiersman, even when he did not understand their language, to determine, without much difficulty, what tribe an Indian belonged to, no matter where he might turn up.

So when we began to look about us in the village, into which we had found our way, we were not long in reaching the conclusion that we were surrounded by the hostile Apaches, instead of the friendly Utes. You may be sure that there was nothing very pleasant about this discovery, but we had to make the best of the situation. It was evident that there was a reason for our not being disturbed, and the small number of men about the village, indicated that the band was out on a hunting expedition. We knew there was no danger of our being attacked by the few old men and squaws about the place, and thought if we could get a good distance away before the hunters returned, we should be safe.

We lost no time in mounting our horses, and riding as far as we could before night overtook us. Then we selected a camping place in a thickly wooded spot, and prepared to defend ourselves the best we could if the Apaches followed us. I had about fifty guns in my stock of goods, and plenty of amunition. I got out all of these guns, loaded each one carefully and put them all where they could be handled as rapidly as we could shoot, in case we were attacked; then my companion and I stood guard all night. We saw none of the Apaches, however, until the next morning, when a few of them came down to where we were, and wanted to come into camp. They did not show any disposition to be hostile, but we refused to allow them to come close to us, and after some parleying they went away, and as we traveled rapidly when we moved on again, we saw nothing more of them.

If we had happened to strike this village at a time when the fighting men of the band were at home, instead of being out after game, it is not at all likely that we should ever have gotten out of it alive. As it was, however, there happened to be nobody to interfere with us, or prevent our hurried departure, and when we happened to strike a favorable camping ground, and got our guns loaded, we could have defended ourselves to pretty good advantage, even if they had attacked us. I think one reason they did not follow us, was that they were very much afraid of the Utes, who were not far away, and whom they knew to be our friends for the time being.

I reached the Ute village a day or two later, and there I had the misfortune of finding the chief of the band, whose name I have forgotten, very sick. This was unfortunate for several reasons. In the first place, the Indians were all greatly distressed, and it was difficult to get them to trade. In the second place, as the old chief had been sick some time, and none of the Indians had been allowed to go out to kill game, they had very little to either eat themselves, or give to a stranger; and in the third place, there were some peculiar customs among the Utes in connection with the obsequies of a dead chieftain, which made it an exceedingly unpleasant time for a stranger to be in their immediate neighborhood.

What purpose it was designed to subserve I never knew; but the Utes considered it incumbent upon them, to kill the first stranger found in their village after the death of a chief. Possibly they thought the spirit of the dead chief might more readily gain admission to "the happy hunting grounds," if accompanied by the captive spirit of a stranger, or it may have been the design to furnish the prince of darkness with the stranger's spirit, and thereby persuade him to relax his grip upon the chief's immortal soul; but whatever the poetic idea of the thing, the unpleasant fact impressed itself upon me, that there might be a demand for the taking off of a stranger, at almost any moment, and that myself and my companion were in a position to be available should such an emergency arise. I felt sure that the poor old chief could not live a week, and I was exceedingly anxious to get through with my business and get away.   They came to me and insisted that I should give the sick Indian some of the white man's medicine, but this I refused to do, first because I knew it would not do him any good, and second, because if he died, they would just as likely as not think my medicine killed him, and then they would very promptly send me over the same road.

I determined to dispatch my business as quickly as possible, and decided to remain right in the village, and make use of every artifice I was master of to force the trading.   In order to do this it was necessary that I should live on such food as the Indians could supply me with.   They had but one kind of meat, and I ate that without asking any questions.   I knew it was no kind of game with which I was familiar, and I had a very strong suspicion that it was the flesh of a domestic animal, which is about the last thing a man usually thinks of butchering.   Before I had been long in the village I happened to see the Indians slaughter one of these animals, and then, as I suspected, found out that we had been eating dog meat, and very poor dogs they were at that.

It was three days before I could get the Utes in the notion of trading, and in the meantime the old chief was growing weaker all the time. Two or three times I was half inclined to move out, without doing any business, thinking that I ran too great a risk in remaining in the village. I finally got them worked up to the trading point, however, and when we once commenced bartering, it did not take long to get through.

I got a number of mules and ponies, and a fine lot of peltry, and you may be sure I lost no time in loading the furs and robes on my pack horses and starting for home. I learned afterward that the chief died two days after I left the village.

I carried my goods back to Pueblo, where a fort had been built by the trappers. It had become a sort of trading post by that time, and there I entered into a kind of partnership with a man by the name of Tharp, who was going back to Kansas City to dispose of a lot of peltry. I furnished him with ten or twelve mules and he was to take my buffalo robes, buckskins, and furs back east, sell them, and return me the money.

It was an unfortunate trip for me and still more unfortunate for poor Tharp. While he was crossing Kansas he fell into the hands of the Comanches.

He was killed, all the horses were captured and the
entire train-load of goods either carried off or destroyed. I lost a good deal of money through the
capture of that wagon train, but nobody was to blame,
and it couldn't have been helped. Soon after that I
made a trip up into Northern Colorado and traded with
old " Yellow Wolf's " band of Cheyennes, but didn't
get into any dangerous places or have any particularly interesting experiences.

I put in the next summer hunting and furnishing
supplies of game for the fort, and in the fall traded
again with the Utes, going over the line into New
Mexico.

The Indians were at war with the Mexicans about
that time, and that was a good time for an American
to trade with them. That was the time when they
always had plenty of mules and ponies. That they
ran a great many of them away from the ranches of
the Mexicans I had no doubt, but they were shrewd
horse thieves and had a way of effacing the brands,
so that I had no means of knowing what animals
rightfully belonged to them, and what ones were
stolen. Even if I had known, I could not have
refused to trade for anything that they wished to
dispose of, without giving them great offense, and
perhaps getting into serious trouble. They didn't
set a very high price on either their mules or the
ponies. The mules usually cost me ten or twelve
dollars a piece in trade, and the ponies a little less.

Sometimes when we had concluded a trade, they would say to me that I should come again after so many "moons," or "half moons," and they would have more ponies or furs, or robes. That meant that I should visit them again at the end of so many months or fortnights. It is well known that all Indians reckon time by "suns" and "moons," but not so well known, I think, that the Indians of the Rocky mountain region reckon also by snows. If you ask one of these Indians how old he is, he will tell you how many snows he has seen, and that means the number of years he has lived. His "snows" are years, his "suns" are days, and as I have already said, his "moons" and "half moons" are months and half months.

After telling me when I should come back, they would tell me where I should find them at that time, and they were always there on time, unless they went on the war-path, or something happened to make it impossible for them to keep their engagement. If I failed to find their village, the understanding was, that when I got in the neighborhood of the meeting place which had been agreed upon, I should kindle a fire and when they saw the smoke they would come out and find me.

I have been asked a good many times, how we managed, when we understood but a few words of the Indian language, to reach an understanding as to the basis of exchange, in bartering articles differing very materially in value. I will tell you how I traded with the Utes, which illustrates fairly how all Indian trading was conducted. They knew nothing about money, and when they occasionally got hold of a silver dollar they used it to make some kind of an ornament of. They knew, however, that a pony was worth more than a buckskin, and that a rifle was more valuable than a butcher-knife.

The trader always fixed the prices, and the first thing to do was to arrange the schedule, if such a term can be used in connection with anything so primitive in style as Indian trading. I got together a parcel of sticks, each representing one of the articles I had to dispose of. The Indian laid down a buffalo robe, for instance, and then I commenced laying down the sticks, representing different things, that he wanted to trade for. When I had put down sticks enough to represent, in my line of goods, what I thought was the value of the robe, I waited to see if the Indian was satisfied. As a rule he wasn't. I don't know whether or not the Indian has descended from the Jew, but I know he has some of the same instincts in trade. He would insist on having sticks representing other articles added to the pile, and sometimes it would take a good while to reach an agreement.

When the agreement was reached, however, it fixed the price on buffalo robes, and as fast as they were transferred to my side of the Lodge in which the trading was carried on, I dealt out the articles traded for. In the same manner the prices were fixed on all the other Indian commodities, and we got through with our business very rapidly. In this way I have traded to the amount of a thousand dollars or two in a half day, after we once got started.

That fall and winter I put in trading with the Indians and hunting about the fort, was a very prosperous one in a business way, and I scarcely had an adventure more thrilling than one which was a little out of the usual order, and very amusing. I was up at old Fort St. Vrain, something like forty miles north of Denver, and there was a party of fellows there, who had come out from St. Louis to see the wild west, and teach the "old timers" how to fight Indians. They were loud talkers, and almost every time they went out of the fort, would have a story of Indian killing to tell when they got back. Some of us had doubts about their ever having seen any real live fighting Indians, and one day we concluded to find out how they would act in case they had reason to think themselves in danger. We heard them talking about going out to gather wild cherries in a thicket some distance from the fort, and knowing that it was a good place for an Indian Ambuscade, I

7

took a companion along with me, and rode out in
advance of them to the thicket, where we secreted ourselves, after having picketed our horses where they
would not be seen. The Eastern Indian slayers
came along by and by, hitched their horses, laid
down their guns, and then went into the thicket after
the cherries. About the time they had gotten interested in their work, we commenced shooting off
our pistols and yelling like Comanche Indians; and
then you ought to have seen those Indian fighters
run. They never fired a shot, and didn't even stop
to pick up their guns, but made the best possible
time in getting to the fort. When they got in they
reported that they had been attacked by a large force
of Indians ; they had killed a good many of them
and had only sought safety in flight, when they
found that they could not contend against the over-
whelming numbers of the savages. To account for
the loss of their guns, they said they had to swim
the Platte River, and had been compelled to leave
their weapons behind them.

My companion and I rode in shortly after they
had finished the story of their thrilling adventure,
and in a day or two the facts leaked out. Then
those St. Louis braves wanted to go home, and they
embraced the earliest opportunity afforded them of
making a safe trip to the east.

UTE CHIEF AND MEDICINE MEN.

CHAPTER VII.

" I suppose I ought to tell you something about the Indian tribes of the far west, to give you a correct idea of where they were located when they were at home. That is, where you might expect to find them when they were not on the war-path, or away on some kind of stealing expedition. Of course I can't tell you just what territory each band claimed, but at one time and another I have seen and had something to do with all of them, and know in a general way where they lived and what kind of Indians they were.

To begin then at the western border line of Missouri, coming west we traveled through the territory claimed by the Sacs and Foxes, or if we kept further south, through the country claimed by the Cherokees, Choctaws, Creeks, Senecas, and other bands of what is now the Indian Territory proper.

The Pawnees and one or two other tribes which spoke the same language, were in the country at the mouth of the Platte, on the Missouri River, although they wandered pretty much all over Kansas.

The Comanches were scattered all over central and western Kansas and along the upper Arkansas River. North of them were the Cheyennes and Arapahoes, and then came the Sioux, who roamed over Nebraska,

Northern Colorado, and Wyoming, and were considered at home anywhere along the upper Platte River. There were more of the Sioux in the country when I first came west than there were of any other Indians. I think I must have known as many as thirty different bands of them, and possibly more.

In the country northwest and west of the Sioux were the Blackfeet and Monarch Indians, who lived together, the Nez Perces, the Crows, and the Flatheads, spreading over Montana, Idaho, Oregon, and Washington Territory. The Blackfeet Indians could always be found along the upper Missouri River and in the Yellowstone Park.

In the Salt Lake region, and other portions of Utah, were the Utes and Pah Utes. There were Utes further south and east too, in New Mexico and Colorado, and they frequently got a long way east and north on their marauding excursions. The Snakes and Shoshones, who spoke the same language, had about the same customs and traditions, and belonged to the same family, were scattered over a great deal of the country between the Rocky mountains and the Sierra Nevadas, and could be found almost any place in that region.

The Apaches belonged in lower New Mexico and Arizona, and the Navajos in Northern New Mexico.

When you went west from Arizona of course you came to the California tribes, of which there were so

many that it would take up a good deal of time and
space to enumerate them. The Yumas, the Pimas,
the Maricopas, and the Mojaves, were the Southern
tribes that I knew most about.

There were some Delaware and Shawnee Indians
and a band or two of the Kiowas in the same country as
the Cheyennes and Arapahoes, along the Upper
Platte and Upper Arkansas Rivers.

There were subdivisions of the tribes I have mentioned, and scores of different names for them, but I
have given you, I think, a pretty good general idea of
the names and locations of the different bands.
Now I am going to tell you what kind of terms they
were on with each other, and further along what kind
of Indians they were.

Some of those people who have never seen an Indian
more hostile than those with "Buffalo Bill's Wild
West Show," or more dangerous than the wooden
Indian in front of a cigar store, are always talking
about the extermination of the unfortunate natives
of this country, by the Whites. I want to tell
these soft-hearted, well-meaning, but not well informed people, that if there are fewer Indians in
America to-day, than there were when the Continent
was discovered, the white man is not to blame for it.
All the Indians who have ever been killed by white
settlers, traders, trappers, hunters and soldiers, between the Atlantic and Pacific Oceans, within the

past two hundred years, would not be a corporal's guard, in comparison with the army of red skins slaughtered in wars, quarrels, and brawls of various kinds, which they have had among themselves.

It is not true either as some people seem to think, that their treachery, cruelty and vindictiveness, have been the result of the treatment which they have received from the Whites. Long before a white man had found his way into this country, the tribes which had never seen a white man, and possibly never heard of one, had the same distinguishing characteristics, which they have had ever since the Whites came in contact with them. Before there were Whites to rob and plunder and steal from, they robbed and stole from each other. Before there were white men in the country to kill, they killed each other. Before there were white women and children to scalp and mutilate and torture, the Indians scalped and mutilated and tortured the women and children, and their enemies of their own race. They made slaves of each other, when there were no " pale faces " to be captured and sold or held for ransom, and before they commenced lying in ambush along the trails of the white man, to murder unwary travelers, the Indians of one tribe would set the same sort of death traps for the Indians of another tribe.

My opinion is,—and I think I have as thorough a knowledge of the Indian character as any man living, and have seen as much of them in their dealings

with each other,—that we only use the proper form
of expression in speaking of Indians, when we call
them savages.   They are about as wild by nature
as any other animal found roaming through forest
and jungle, hiding in caves, and climbing over rocks
and mountains.   They have never recognized any law
but the law of force, and the difference between a
" wild Indian" and a " civilized Indian," is about the
difference between the tiger at large, and the tiger
in a cage.   As we find them now, on their reserva-
tions, and under proper restraints, they are as harmless as the caged animal; but they were under no
such restraints when I first came west, and we had
to deal with them in a different way.

The Creek, Cherokee, Choctaw, Delaware, Shawnee, and other Indians that I used to have more or
less to do with, were the thoroughly tamed, or you
might call them perhaps, the domesticated animals.
They did very little fighting among themselves, and
we had no trouble in getting along with them.

The other tribes were, however, always fighting
with each other, and I have personal knowledge of
thousands of them having been killed in these wars.
The Arapahoes and the Cheyennes were closely related to each other, and were always allies.   Among
their inveterate enemies were the Kiowas, a tribe
which used to make its headquarters about where
Pueblo now is.   They kept up a war with the

Arapahoes and Cheyennes, until there was but a remnant of their tribe left, and then they joined the Comanche band, and I think have remained with them ever since.

The Arapahoes and Comanches, and the Arapahoes and Utes, were always at war. When they fought the Comanches on their own ground, that is in the mountain region, the Arapahoes were generally the victors, but on the Kansas prairies, where the Comanches were at home, the Arapahoes were badly worsted in several encounters.

There were bloody battles, within my recollection, between the allied Arapahoes and Cheyennes and the Utes, on Apishapa Creek, above Trinidad, on the Sugarite, in New Mexico, and at one or two other places. Both bands were good fighters, and neither seemed to gain much advantage in either of these battles.

The Utes and mountain Apaches were never on good terms. They quarreled on all occasions, and killed each other whenever opportunity offered.

The Comanches and Utes were always hostile to each other, and had a great many fights at one time and another. The Utes and Prairie Apaches—not the mountain Apaches—were allies once in fighting the Comanches and Kiowas. They met at Cimaron City, and left about as many dead Indians on the field as were ever left on a western battlefield.

The Sioux were continually fighting among themselves. As I have told you there were many different bands of these Indians, and while they spoke the same language, looked alike, and made common cause in fighting other tribes, they seemed to have some differences, which were always breeding trouble, and they hardly ever got together, without having a row of such proportions, that it might very properly be called a battle.

The Navajos did less fighting with their neighbors, perhaps, than most of the other Indians, but their thieving propensities would every now and then get them into trouble. They fought well when they did go to war, and had a sort of Spartan courage, which made them prefer death to capture. A Navajo Indian who allowed himself to be taken prisoner, was discarded by his tribe, if he chanced to return to it alive.

The Crows and the Cheyennes were the best warriors of all the Indian tribes of the West. The Comanches and Pawnees always sought to have the odds largely in their favor, and would sometimes hover for days around an enemy, waiting for an opportunity to kill without taking any chances of being killed. They were very skillful in preparing an ambush, as they could stretch themselves out on the plains and cover themselves with sand, or hide themselves so completely in the tall grass, that it was not an uncommon occurrence for them to fall upon unwary travelers, as suddenly and unexpectedly as though they had come up out of the ground.

Nothing better illustrates the Comanche character, than his queer notion about killing rattlesnakes. The only time they kill the rattlesnake, is when they find him in that sluggish condition, in which he fails to rattle, when approached. Judging the snake instinct by his own, the Comanche says, when the snake fails to warn the Indian of his presence, " he is on the warpath ;" that is, he is lying in ambush for an enemy and wants to bite him. There was never any such thing as honor among the Comanches, and it was on account of their stealing that they were in trouble so much of the time with other Indians.

The Arapahoes and Cheyennes were good hunters, had plenty of game in their country and were better Indians than any of the far west tribes, with the exception of the Delawares and Shawnees. When I say far west, I mean the mountain and prairie, Indians. We never had much serious trouble with them for a long time after I came west, I think about the only battle we had with them, being down on the Arkansas River, at the point where the old Santa Fe trail crossed it. We gave them a terrible whipping at that time and it was a good many years before they forgot it and went on the warpath again.

The Sioux would steal a few horses now and then, when they happened to take a fancy to those belonging to the mountaineers, or to some other tribe of Indians, but they were fairly honest and didn't give us serious trouble.   We could always get along well trading with them, although now and then they acted a little war-like in their intercourse with the white men.

The Apaches were always just what they are now; a dirty, thieving lot of cut-throats who would rather steal than live by any other means.   They lived on horses and mules stolen from the Mexicans, and other Indians, because they were too lazy to hunt game, although there were always plenty of deer in their country.

The Utes were more honest than the Apaches, but they were sometimes bad tempered, quarrelsome and vindictive, to a remarkable degree, even for Indians. You could never tell when they would take offense at some trivial thing and go on the warpath.   As a rule, however, they killed to satisfy revenge, rather than for the purpose of plunder.

The most degraded Indians I have ever seen, that is those who seemed to me to be lower down in the scale of humanity than any others, were the Pah-Utes, the Yumas and the Mojaves.   The Pah-Utes, as I have said in the account of my long trapping expedition to the northwest, were to some extent cannibals,

while the Mojaves aud Yumas went naked, were more
filthy in their habits than an average lot of hogs, and
lived on ants, lizzards, and anything else they could
get without exerting themselves.

This reminds me of an amusing thing which happened when I was trapping on the Colorado River.
There was a Yuma village near our camp, and one
night some of the trappers went into the village and
brought back with them, what they thought was some
kind of bread. Without noticing it very particularly,
they commenced eating, but it was not long before
they discovered, that if they were eating bread, it was
a different kind from any they had ever tasted before.

They made an examination of the stuff then, and
found that what they had supposed were biscuits,
were small cakes made of red ants, crushed together
and dried in the sun.

The Maricopas located on the Gila River, were a
good looking, industrious, and rather thrifty lot of
Indians, who were generally well behaved and so far
as I know, always friendly to the Whites. The
Pimas were also a peaceable and well disposed band.

The Navajos were always rather better than the
average run of Indians, although they never knew
what it meant to be honest. They were industrious
however, and while other bands were roaming about
over the country, they staid most of the time where
they belonged, made the blankets which we used to

like to get hold of, and which have since become famous all over the country, manufactured water-tight baskets to sell, and cultivated the soil to a considerable extent.   Outside of the Pueblo Indians, the Navajos are the only mountain Indians that I have ever seen doing anything of consequence in the way of planting and raising crops of any kind.

The Pueblo Indians were an entirely different kind of Indians from the roving tribes.   They have always been called Pueblo Indians, because they built permanent villages or pueblos.   They were all natives of the Mexican country and several of the Pueblos may be seen in New Mexico, where some thousands of this peculiar class of Indians still live.   The pueblo was a building or group of buildings, designed, when they were built, to subserve the purpose of domiciles and places of refuge at the same time.

As a general rule they were built of adobe or sun dried bricks.   These are the same kind of bricks by the way, that the Israelites were making for Pharoah, down in Egypt, when he cut off the supply of straw which has to be mixed with the adobe mortar, and raised such a row among them, that they went on a strike.

I have seen several ruins of pueblos, and you can still see them down along the Rio Puerco in the Arizona country, which are built of stone and are several stories high.   The first story is always without any entrance from the ground. The second story is narrower than the first and this makes a terrace, the floor of which constitutes the roof of the first story. This terrace is reached by ladders, and then the first story is entered through trap doors, while doors opening out on the terrace, are the entrances to the second stories. These tightly closed rooms on the ground floor, or rather on the first floor, because all the floors were ground floors, made a very safe retreat from an enemy, when the ladders leading to the entrance were drawn up and hidden away, in the days of bow and arrow warfare. Some of the pueblos still in existence, are very ancient, it being claimed that the Pueblo de Taos and the Acoma Pueblo, were built before the advent into the country of Coronado, the Spanish explorer, in 1540. They are queer buildings and the people we found in them and those found in them to-day, are queer Indians, very unlike any of the other tribes found on the American Continent. They have always done considerable farming, and have never so far as I have known anything about them, done any hunting of consequence. The only time they have ever shown any hostility to the Whites, was they were stirred up to do so, by the Mexicans in 1847. I shall have something to say about that, however, some other time."

THE WIFE OF A UTE CHIEF.

CHAPTER VIII.

INDIAN CUSTOMS AND SUPERSTITIONS.

" I have made mention of the fact that one of the customs of the Utes, in connection with the obsequies of a dead chieftain, gave me considerable uneasiness at one time when I was trading among them. This was their custom of killing the first stranger found in their camp after the chief's death. That, however, was not the only sacrifice necessary to give the spirit of the defunct brave a good start in the other world. It was a Ute custom to burn the bodies of their great men, and their horses, bows and arrows, and sometimes one or more of their ·wives were burned with them. Ute Indians, other than the chiefs and principal men were generally buried, but in a peculiar way. They did not dig graves for these common Indians, but would usually find a depression in some hillside, or a hole under the rocks, and in this they laid the body, and then covered it up with stones.

The Arapahoes, Cheyennes, Sioux, and some other Indians used to leave their dead in trees. The dead warrior was wrapped in his blankets, and then in a buffalo robe, with his weapons and ornaments, along with food and tobacco at his side. Then the body was fastened in the branches of some large cottonwood or other tree, and remained there until it

fell to the earth to be devoured by the wolves and
coyotes.

The Comanches left their dead in caves, and as a
sign of grief, in addition to the wailings and lamen-
tations common among all Indians, they cut off the
manes and tails of their horses.

All the Indians I have ever known, with the exception of the Pueblos, were polygamous, and there was
but one thing stood in the way of an Indian having
as many wives as he wanted, and that was a lack of
the wherewithal to buy them. Among nearly all the
tribes, marriage was a matter of barter and sale, and
in fact that was about all there was of the marriage.

Among the Navajos, for instance, an Indian who
has taken a fancy to a particular young squaw, goes
to her father and offers him so many ponies for the
girl. If the bargain is closed, the ponies are delivered, the Indian maiden is carried away to the lodge
of her purchaser, and that's all there is in the way of
a wedding, as a rule. Sometimes a marriage of this
kind is celebrated by a feast on horseflesh, and I
have heard, too, that they a have kind of marriage
ceremony at times, although I have never seen anything of the sort. In this ceremony, the prospective
bride and groom take seats on opposite sides of a
wicker basket, which is made so tight that it will
hold water. This basket is filled with some kind of
food, and when the bride and groom have eaten out

of it, dipping in at the same time, they are married. The Indian who marries the first of a family of daughters can have all the others, in preference to other suitors, if he can bargain satisfactorily with the father, and as a rule he prefers to marry sisters, for the reason that he thinks they will get along better together.

Among the Apaches, when a girl reaches a marriageable age, her parents advertise the fact by getting up a feast, at which they always have a great deal of singing and dancing.

After this is over they cut off the girl's eyebrows, and a month later pull out her eye-lashes. What the object of this is I don't know, unless it is to distinguish her from other squaws, who are not in the matrimonial market. Having thus made her *debut*, as I suppose it would be called in fashionable society, the Apache maiden is given a somewhat better opportunity of choosing her own husband than her Navajo sister. Her suitor comes at night and stakes his horse in front of her father's lodge. This may be called the Apache style of " popping the question." If the proposal is satisfactory to the young squaw, and her father feels assured that he will be properly compensated for the loss of this particular member of his family, she takes the horse, at some time within four days from the time it is left in front of her tent, feeds and waters it and then returns it to the owner's lodge.

This signifies her acceptance of the offer of marriage, and the details are arranged later, between her father and her lover, or rather the Indian whose slave she is to become, because the women of this tribe are very badly treated. When an Apache Indian has more than one wife, the one last married is mistress of the harem.

The Comanches, Utes, Arapahoes and Cheyennes, conducted their courtships and marriages on strictly business principles, and horses, robes or other Indian property always had to be given in exchange for a wife. For this reason the rich Indian always had more and better looking wives than the poor Indian, who had to put up with the old and ugly women of the tribe.

The wives of the Comanches were miserable drudges, and were not allowed to participate in any of the pleasures of the males. Even when they danced, they had to dance by themselves and out of sight of their brute masters.

The courtship of the Shoshones was a novel one. For some reason or other, the Indian maidens of this tribe always seemed to be more fleet-footed than the young braves. This gave them an advantage when they were being courted after the Shoshones fashion, and made the success of a suitor dependent upon the feeling which the squaw of his choice entertained toward him. She was given a reasonable start of him in a foot race, and then if he succeeded in catching her and throwing a lasso over her head the fact that she was to be tied to him for life was settled. If she thought well of her infatuated pursuer, of course she was easily caught, but if she was not inclined to favor his suit, she could generally distance him in the race.

The Pah-Ute lovers were of a more sentimental character, and their custom was to seat themselves on a log outside the village, and wait for the likely young squaws to take seats by their sides, when the courtship was considered ended, and married life began.

The Pueblo Indians had a kind of perpetual leap-year arrangement.

These Indians mated after the fashion of respectable white people. That is, one man had one wife at a time ; and it was the Indian girl who picked out her lover. She never had to wait for some timid young buck to "come a courting," but when she took a fancy to one, all she had to do was to inform her father that she wanted to marry him. The father then visited the parents of the Indian upon whom his daughter had bestowed her affections, and proposed a matrimonial alliance between the young people. The parents of the groom were expected, of course, to make suitable presents to the father of the bride, but there was much less of the barter and sale idea about the business, than there was about marriage among the roving tribes.

The divorce system in vogue among these Indians was one which I think would be popular among the crowned heads of Europe, and possibly among some classes of people in this country.

PUEBLO INDIANS AT HOME.

Whenever they tired of living together they could separate, and both were free to marry again. If they had any children, the grand parents were under obligation to take care of them. This was a very different arrangement from that in force among the Comanches, where divorced women had their ears and noses cut off and became perpetual outcasts.

These Indians, I mean the Comanches, differed from most other Indians in having a very vague idea of a Supreme being. They worshipped the sun and the earth, but so far as I could ever see, these objects did not represent any kind of deity. Their idea of the future state was, that it was "a happy hunting ground" where there would be plenty of buffalo and nobody but Comanches to kill them.

They believed in evil spirits of various grades and kinds, and always attributed a lack of rain or sunshine to the influence of some of these evil spirits. To propitiate the spirits and cause the rain to fall, or the sun to shine, their custom was to whip or flay alive one of their slaves or a captive whose life had been spared.

The Navajos always believed in the existence of a God, to whom they gave a name so long that no white man ever remembered it. They had, when I used to be among them, and I suppose they still have, hundreds of superstitions about the existence of spirits, good and bad, who had a great deal to do with Indian affairs. A few of these Indians believed that the soul of man passes, at death, into some one of the lower animals, but the idea most generally prevalent among them, was that when an Indian died his soul passed into the center of the earth, and then by some means or other, found its way into a place where there was nothing to mar the happiness of the

good Indian's spirit. Those Navajos who believed
in the transmigration of souls, as I suppose you
would call it, thought that every rattlesnake contained the spirit of a bad Indian, and that there were
spirits of bad men in the coyotes also; women they
thought, became fishes after death.

The Apaches were all strong believers in the transmigration doctrine, and they had more definite ideas
about the form which the spirit was to assume after
it passed out of the body of an Indian, or rather what
kind of body it would inhabit next, than the few
Navajos, who entertained similar notions. That the
spirit of a very mean Indian would find lodgment in
a rattlesnake, they all believed, but other spirits
would, it was thought, assume the form of the owl,
the eagle, or the bear, or that of some pure white
bird, the particular form to be assumed, being dependent upon the kind of life the Indian, whose soul
was to take up its abode in some other animal, had
lived. They had a superstitious reverence for all
the animals which it was thought might contain a
good spirit, and I never knew an Apache Indian to
kill a bear, an owl, an eagle, or any kind of a white
bird.

The Nez Perces and Flathead Indians had a queer
belief, which might be called a cross between the
Roman Catholic, and the Apache idea of the future
state. They thought that the spirits of all good

Indians found their way at once to the Indian Heaven, while bad spirits had to go through a sort of purgatory to atone for their sins. While going through this state, the spirits inhabited the bodies of animals which were hunted and persecuted, and all beavers were looked upon as Indians, who were doing penance for their bad deeds.

Montezuma, as everybody knows who has heard or read anything about the Pueblo Indians, was their principal deity, or properly speaking the representation of the supreme being. They prayed to him for rain, and in fact for almost all the favors that they had occasion to ask from the ruler of the universe. They had a sacred snake, to which they sometimes prayed also. I believe this snake was looked upon as the animal which Montezuma regarded with greatest favor,—on account, perhaps, of its wisdom— and the stories which they used to tell of its appearance in various places, rivaled some of the sea serpent stories which we hear now-a-days.

The "sun dance" of the Sioux, was one of the most peculiar outgrowths of Indian superstition.

The object of the dance was to gain the favor of the great spirit, and commencing always at sun down, it lasted three days.

I have seen the Mexican *Penitentes* torture themselves in various ways, but I have never known them to devise any kind of self torture, quite as sickening as that which accompanied the sun dance of the Sioux.

They made preparations for the dance by attaching strong rawhide ropes to good sized saplings, which were bent over until the tops came within eight or ten feet of the ground.

When the time came for the dance to commence, an Indian took his place under each of the ropes, dangling from the tops of the saplings, his body entirely naked above the waist.

With a keen edged knife, two deep gashes, a couple of inches apart, were cut in the back of the savage, and the rawhide rope was passed under the skin and flesh from one gash to the other. The rope was securely fastened, and the Indian *penitente*, sometimes lifted clear of the ground as the sapling swayed back and forth, kept up a sort of rhythmic motion, until the rawhide cut its way through the flesh and allowed him to drop to the ground.

Most of the Indians believed that sickness was due to the influence of evil spirits, and their medicine men usually cured, or pretended to cure, rather by incantations and charms, than by giving medicines, although, of course, they understood how to use a good many roots and herbs. When they went on the war path the medicine men always went along, more for the purpose of keeping off evil spirits, and propitiating the Indian deities, than to care for the wounded.

Their superstitions were carried to the extent of puffing the smoke in a certain direction, or toward a certain object, when they lighted their pipes, to bring rain or fair weather, or cause the wind to blow from a certain way, and when starting out on a trip, all their plans might be changed, by the appearance of a snake in the pathway, or the flight of a bird overhead.

I have never known any Indians, at least none of the roving tribes, who were not inveterate gamblers. This certainly is not a vice they have contracted from the Whites.   Of late years they have learned to use cards, but long before that, they had gambling devices of their own, and took to this vice as naturally as they took to the hunt.   I have seen them lay an arrow on the ground, and then one after another, bounce other arrows off their bow strings, bets being made as to which arrow would fall closest to the one on the ground.   Sometimes they would take three sticks and shift them from one hand to the other, after the style of three-card-monte, or change a bullet rapidly from one hand to the other in the same way, and all the time they were betting buffalo robes, or buckskins, or something else on some feature of the shuffle, although I confess I could never understand the games myself. On the result of a horse race,—and they were very fond of racing,—I have seen them stake great piles of robes and furs, and not infrequently a lot of mules or ponies in addition.   They were very shrewd too about

their racing, and I have seen them get the best of
white horsemen in many a match.   I remember not
many years ago, a band of Utes came over to Trinidad, and made a big winning off of some of the Americans, who haven't been in the country as long as I
have, but long enough to be called " old timers."
They always had a lot of horses with them, and they
knew just to a second how much faster one of these
horses could run than another.   They would use the
slower horses to test the speed of the horses brought
out against them, and finally, when they thought they
had a sure thing, would bring out the fast ones.   In
the Trinidad race the Americans had a blooded horse
which had been brought out from Kansas City, and
thought they were very sure of winning the race, but
the Indians had sized him up correctly and won, a
little Indian boy, who had to be tied on the horse, riding the winning pony.

Drunkenness was quite as much a besetting sin of
the Indian as gambling.   I never saw one who
wouldn't drink rum, and some of them had liquors
of their own before any were brought into the country
by the Whites.

The Navajos, as long ago as I can remember, had
a way of making whiskey out of corn, of which they
have always raised more or less, and they, as well as
other Indians of the Mexican territory manufactured
mescal.   This is a fiery and very intoxicating liquor
made out of the cactus.   Some tribes of Indians drank

much more than others, and I think there was more drunkenness among the Arapahoes, Cheyennes, Kiowas and Comanches, than among any other bands of western Indians.

You have heard, of course, that some of the savages poison their arrows before going to war, but I reckon you never knew how these arrows were poisoned. I have never known of many Indians who did this, but I have known some, and I know how it was done; and when I tell you about it, you will understand the deadly nature of the wound inflicted by one of these arrows.

They used to take the liver of a deer, buffalo, or some other animal, and inoculate it with the venom of the rattlesnake. There were thousands of these snakes in the country, in summer, and it was always easy to find one, and not at all difficult to stir him up to the fighting point. The liver which was to be poisoned, would be placed on a stick and held before him in such a way that he would strike it frequently. Then it would be laid aside where it would decompose, and in a short time become a mass of the most fatal poison. The points of the arrows would then be stuck into this deadly preparation and allowed to remain until they became thoroughly coated with it. The Pah-Utes, the Mescalero Apaches, and the Digger Indians, were the only savages among those of the far west, so far as I have known, who used these poisoned weapons of warfare.

The Navajos used to be charged by the Mexicans, and possibly by some of the mountain men, with poisoning their arrows before going to war, and they have figured in some of the story books, as a band of Indians to be dreaded on that account. I have never seen anything, however, to indicate that these Indians went into battle with any such advantage over their enemies. They were none too good to use a weapon of that kind, nor were any of the other Indians for that matter ; but the poisoned arrow was by no means a safe thing to handle. In adjusting it to the bow, or drawing it from the quiver, the Indian might inflict upon himself the death wound which it was designed to inflict upon an enemy. To be pricked or scratched by its envenomed point, was quite suffi· cient to bring about a fatal result, and the risk of using poisoned arrows was considered too great, by all the Indians I have ever known, with the exception of those above mentioned. Even these Indians did not use them to any great extent, and outside of the "wild west" novels, they have never figured prominently in Indian warfare."

THE MAD WOLF'S ATTACK.

CHAPTER IX.

PERILS OF THE PIONEERS.

" Now and then, when I get to thinking over the old times, and the dangers the mountain men were exposed to on every hand, I wonder that any of us have lived to tell of our adventures. Even when we thought ourselves on good terms with the Indians, something which we couldn't foresee or provide against might occur at any time, which would change our relations in a twinkling, and the peace was at an end.

One time I had started out to trade with the Utes, and had along with me, among others, a Shawnee Indian. We were twelve or fourteen miles below where Trinidad is now, on the Purgatoire River, when the Shawnee happened one day to meet a Ute Indian alone. Not long before that, one of the Shawnees had been wounded, or perhaps killed by a Ute, and when my Shawnee companion saw an opportunity for revenge, the Indian instinct in him was too strong to be resisted. Notwithstanding the fact that we were within a short distance of their village, the Shawnee shot and killed the Ute. As soon as I heard of it, I knew that we would have the whole band of Utes after us, and that nothing I could say to them would appease their anger.

I changed my plans very suddenly, and instead of trying to do any trading with the Utes, undertook to get out of their country as quickly as possible. As I had expected, they followed us, and overtook us in an open country, where there was no chance for us to secrete ourselves, or take any advantage in fighting them. I think we had eight men in our party, and with a big band of Utes against us it looked as though our time had come. We determined, however, to make a brave stand and be killed fighting if we had to be killed.

Our pack animals, of which we had quite a number, were gotten together and arranged in a circle, so that they might protect us to some extent from the fire of the Indians. We stationed ourselves inside this improvised fort and awaited the attack which the Indians were not long in making. Circling around us, they commenced shooting, and we returned the fire. There was not a man among us, not excepting the Indian, who was not able to make almost every one of his shots count, while but few of the arrows which the Utes discharged at us, reached us. They had some guns, but of a very inferior kind, and at that time they had not learned to use firearms to as good advantage as they can now. We suffered comparatively little while the fight was kept up, and were picking off so many of their horses, besides killing a few Indians, that they abandoned the contest, and gave us an unexpected opportunity to make our escape.

On another trip into this same country, when I was accompanied by " Bill " Williams — who was afterward a guide for General Fremont, and a noted scout — and a trapper by the name of Walters, we were one afternoon making our way along through a rocky and rather thickly wooded cañon, not knowing that there were any Indians near us, when I heard the crack of a rifle and saw Walters, who was a few feet ahead of me, throw up his hands.

He cried out that he was shot, and would have fallen from the mule which he was riding, had I not sprung to his assistance. He recovered himself in a few minutes, and realizing that we were ambushed and could only save ourselves by a rapid flight, he clung to his mule, and we started at full speed down the Cañon, with the bullets from a score of guns whistling about us.

When we emerged into an open space, where, if we were compelled to fight, we should not have an unseen enemy to contend with, we stopped long enough to ascertain the condition of our wounded companion. The shot had been fired at such close range that his clothes were almost powder burned, and my first impression was that the ball had passed entirely through his body. A closer examination developed the fact that the wound was less serious than that, but still bad enough. The ball had entered the left side just above the hip, but strangely

enough, its course had in some way been deflected,
so that it passed just under the skin, half way round
the body, and came out on the right side nearly opposite where it entered.

We dressed the wound as best we could, and made
our way back to Fort Bent, where Walters finally
recovered, although he was never much inclined to
venture into any portion of the Indian country, where
he did not know that he would be perfectly safe, after
that.

My own good fortune during all this time possibly
had the effect of making me somewhat more adventurous than I would otherwise have been. I had
had so many close calls, and, as the saying goes,
had escaped with a whole skin, that I began to think
I led a sort of charmed life. I had heard of the old
Scotch maxim to the effect that " the child that's
born to be hung will ne'er be drowned," and had
about made up my mind that whatever the future
had in store for me, I was not to be killed by the
Indians.

For that reason these hairs-breadth escapes did
not have the effect of frightening me out of the
country as it did a great many, or even inducing me
to follow some less hazardous vocation than that of
trapping, hunting, and trading with the Indians.

There was no adventure which promised good re-
sults in a business way, that I was not ready to

undertake, and I was rather disappointed than pleased, when I returned from one of these trips, without some thrilling experiences.

It's strange how we get used to all sorts of dangers, isn't it? I remember one incident of my life,—and it occurred about the time I have been speaking of too, which, while it hardly seemed more than commonplace at the time, to me, sends a cold chill over me when I think of it now.

A party of five of us were trapping in Northern Colorado near the present site of Fort Collins. There were a lot of what we called "half breeds" in that country, and they were as great a lot of cut-throat Indians as ever infested any part of the United States. I do not mean by half breeds that they had any admixture of white blood, but that the Arapahoes, Shawnees and Blackfeet had become mixed up, so that the Indians in this neighborhood were not pure bloods of either tribe. They were always at war among themselves, and ready at almost any time to make war on anybody else, where there was a chance of getting possession of a band of horses or mules, or securing any other kind of plunder. Several years later, when the half breed Blackfeet Indians undertook to leave the country and join the Blackfeet tribe further north, they were followed by the Arapahoes, who had against them a grievance of some kind, and the whole band, including women and children, were killed.

9

We had quite a number of ponies and mules along with us, and I suppose the Indians thought, as our party was a small one, they could easily take our animals and our scalps at the same time. A band of them attacked us about four o'clock one afternoon, and as we had nothing like a fighting force of men in our company, the only thing we could do was to find the most secure hiding place which was available. We crept in among some large rocks at the foot of a steep hill, where it was almost impossible for either their bullets or their arrows to reach us. They soon discovered our hiding place, and commenced trying to dislodge us. Arrows and bullets seemed to fall around us almost as thick as hail, and kept up a patter on the rocks that made us feel anything but comfortable. Whenever we caught sight of an Indian or a horse we would shoot, and with such good effect, that they suffered considerable loss.

In this way the balance of the afternoon wore away. Just before night they drew off, and for a time we heard nothing of them. We were not by any means certain that they had abandoned the fight, but we were beginning to feel a trifle easier, when just as the sun was going down, the crashing of rocks down the mountain side, advised us of a new mode of attack. Having discovered that we were not being harmed by the fusilade which they had kept up during the afternoon, they had climbed the mountain, and now sought to drive us out of our

place of concealment by rolling rocks down on us.
If you have ever seen a huge boulder started down
the side of a steep mountain, and noticed the fearful
velocity which it acquires before it reaches the foot
of the hill, you can understand with what terrible
force these rocks struck those behind which we were
sheltering ourselves from the savages. Some of
them would burst into fragments, which were scattered all about us, while others struck our rock fortifications like cannon balls, or battering rams,
bounded to one side or the other, and passed down
into the cañon below us.

It seemed to us, sometimes, that if we were not
crushed by the falling stones, our stronghold must
finally be broken to pieces, and then we should have
been left at the mercy of our bloodthirsty enemies.
The huge masses of rock by which we were surrounded, stood as firm, however, as the rock of ages,
although the bombardment, with now and then an
intermission, was kept up nearly all night. It was a
moonlight night, and we could see the Indians moving about from time to time, and lost no opportunity
of letting them know that we were still alive, had
plenty of amunition, and could shoot as well as ever.
The hostilities came to an end about daylight, when
the Indians seemed to reach the conclusion that they
had wasted amunition enough on us. They knew
that we had the most of our pack animals with us,
with provisions and amunition enough to enable us

to withstand a long seige. We had killed some of
their men and a good many horses, and they knew
we would kill more of them if the fight was kept up.
There may have been other considerations which
influenced them in giving up the battle, but at any rate,
as soon as it began to get light, we could see them
getting ready to leave. By and by they started off,
and we watched them until they were out of sight.
Then we crawled out of our fort and took an inven-
tory of damages. We found that none of our party
had been injured, although one man had been so
completely changed in appearance that we scarcely
knew him. That was Major Kilpatrick, who up to
that time had not had much experience in Indian
fighting. He was a brave fellow, but it happened
that he had been placed in a more trying position
than any of us, and must have been worse scared.
He was not with the rest of us when the fight commenced, but had sought the same kind of shelter in
the rocks. While the fight was going on he had no
means of knowing how many of us were alive, and
as his hiding place had been stormed in the same
manner as ours, he imagined he was to be made the
last victim of the slaughter. When he made his way
to where the rest of us were, his hair, which had
been black the day before, had turned as white as a
man's hair can get.

I expect there are a good many Colorado people living yet who will remember the Major, as he afterward

spent some years in the territory as an Indian agent, but not many of them I reckon ever heard the story of his lightning change from a young into an old man.

While I am telling you about the dangers we had to contend with, back in " the forties," in getting a foothold in this country, where it is so easy for anybody to get a foothold now, I am going to say something about another experience of mine just to show you that it was not from Indians alone that our lives were in danger.

Among all the wild animals with which we came in contact there were none that we dreaded so much as the mad wolf. There were thousands of these animals in the country, I mean thousands of wolves, and you know the wolf is peculiarly liable to attacks of hydrophobia at certain seasons of the year. Whenever a wolf runs mad, he attacks, or rather bites, whatever comes in his way, the same as a rabid dog, and I have had a good many animals bitten by them at one time and another.

One evening when I was in camp with several other trappers, I saw a big, gaunt-looking grey wolf trotting along, not very far from where we were. I had a couple of fine hunting dogs with me, who could hold their own well in a struggle with a wolf, and I started them after him, thinking I should see an interesting fight.

Before the dogs reached the wolf they stopped and seemed to hesitate about taking hold of him. Without noticing anything peculiar about the animal I went up pretty close to him to encourage the dogs. They attacked him then, but he broke loose and paying no attention to the dogs, came toward me. I had picked up a club two or three feet long, and as he came toward me I struck him with it, but the stick was rotten and the blow only stopped him for a moment. I saw then what was the matter with the wolf, and that I was in a dangerous place. I urged the dogs to come to my rescue, but some peculiar instinct seemed to warn them of the dangerous character of their adversary, and they stood back leaving me to make my own fight. The wolf had been crippled slightly in his first struggle with the dogs, and was not as active as he would have been if uninjured. I had my hunting knife with me, and just as he was about to make a spring at my throat I managed to drive it into his side, catching him at the same time by the back of the neck with the other hand and flinging him away from me. The knife-thrust killed him, and I escaped without being bitten or scratched, although it was just by the skin of my teeth. The adventure cost me two fine hunting dogs, as they both had to be killed, but it taught me to exercise greater care thereafter about coming in too close contact with wild animals in general and mad wolves in particular."

"JIM" BAKER.

CHAPTER X.

"Speaking of my adventure with the mad wolf, reminds me of some other adventures with the original inhabitants of the mountains and plains, who were only less savage than those other wild animals, the Indians, and who would now and then resent an invasion of their domain.

There was one native of the Rocky Mountain region, which the hunters and trappers always made a point of dealing with very cautiously and circumspectly, and that was the grizzly bear. The grizzly, cinnamon, and black bears were all natives of this region, but the "grizzly" was the "big chief" of the bear family. There used to be a great many of them in the mountains, but we rarely hear of one now. They have a strong aversion to civilization, and have gotten as far away from the settlements as they could get.

I have had a long and intimate acquaintance with the "grizzly," and what I tell you about him may correct some erroneous notions which are prevalent as to the kind of animal he is.

In the first place, let me tell you that he is not a professional man-killer, and never goes about " seeking whom he may devour," as some writers of bear stories would make us believe. That he has been guilty now and then of staining his "chops" with human gore is true, but it was usually under circumstances which would have made "justifiable homicide" a proper verdict, if the affair had been between man and man.   It was where he met an open enemy in fair fight, and got the best of it.

My experience has been that the bear will always sacrifice his reputation for courage, to avoid a conflict with the hunter, provided the hunter makes no hostile demonstration, when they come in contact with each other.

An experience which I had one time, just about forty years ago, when hunting in the Cimaron Mountains, will illustrate to what extent the bear is a peace-loving animal.

Early one morning I left my two companions in camp, and started out to get some bear meat.   I had not gone more than a hundred yards when I struck the trail of a "grizzly," and after following it about a hundred yards further, through a thick growth of shrub oak, which was about as high as my head, I stepped into a little open space and found my bear. I found him in company with four other bears, all full grown.

I was looking for bear, but I hadn't been appointed a delegate to a convention of "grizzlies," and I felt at once as though I was an intruder.   If I had not attracted their attention, I should have retired without making my presence known, or interrupting their deliberations, but they had seen me as soon as I saw them.

I knew that to open hostilities would be suicidal, because, while I might have killed one or two of the bears, I should have been torn to pieces before the row was over if it had once commenced. It was unsafe to retreat, because a bear has no respect for a cowardly enemy, and so I concluded to stand still and give the "grizzlies" to understand that I didn't propose to commence a fuss.

They eyed me closely for about half a minute, and then commenced growling savagely, first taking a few steps toward me and then walking back to where they started from, as though they were daring me to make any hostile demonstration or even to "come half way."

I didn't much like being bullied in that way, but I didn't allow my temper to get the better of my judgment. I stood perfectly still for about five minutes, when the bears seemed to reach the conclusion that they had no quarrel with me, and bringing the proceedings of their convention to an abrupt close, they started off on a run in different directions.

I let them go without firing a shot. Their conduct had been much more genteel than I had expected it to be, and I wasn't going to break the peace under the circumstances.

I think they were even more pleased at getting away from me than I was at getting rid of them. One of them at least must have been panic stricken, because he galloped away toward our camp, and when he reached it, was so much excited that he ran through the camp fire, scattering the sparks all over one of my companions, who happened to be roasting a piece of venison at the time.

There is one thing which a "grizzly" resents very promptly and emphatically, and that is being shot at or threatened with a gun. He understands as well as anybody, that the gun is a death-dealing weapon, and the snapping of the cap, or the click of the hammer, enrages him almost if not quite as much as being wounded. Under such circumstances he fights viciously and ferociously, without any further provocation.

One of the most desperate encounters I ever had personal knowledge of, between the trappers and a " grizzly," was one in which " Dick " Owens, who afterward became somewhat noted as a guide and scout, and John Burris, who, when I last saw him, was a California ranchman, were the participants.

They were out hunting one day and came on to an enormous " grizzly" very unexpectedly. Both the hunters shot at him and both missed. Before the smoke of their rifles cleared away, the bear charged on them, and they made for a small bushy cedar tree, hardly more than a shrub, which was the only tree in sight. Owens was ahead and got into the tree, but Burris had hardly gotten off the ground, when the bear caught him by one foot and dragged him back. He was a man of rare presence of mind, however, and as soon as the bear caught hold of him, he dropped to the ground, and notwithstanding the fact that his body was being scratched and torn in a score of places, he lay perfectly still.

The enraged bear, thinking he had disposed of one of his enemies, left Burris and climbed into the bush after Owens, who had thrown away his gun and could do nothing but engage in a hand to hand fight with old bruin. He struck at the bear with his hunting knife, but the brute caught him by the hand, and then a terrific struggle commenced in the branches of the tree, ten or twelve feet from the ground. Burris, although he was badly wounded, had by this time gotten hold of and reloaded his gun, but it was some little time, an age it seemed to Owens, before he could get in a position to shoot at the bear, without taking great chances on killing his companion, who was having a wrestling match with the animal in the tree top.

Finally he managed to send a bullet through the bear's body, and the big brute dropped to the ground, almost tearing Owens' hand off before loosening its hold.

This shot was not fatal, but the bear left the two hunters and charged down through our camp, which was not far distant from the scene of the encounter. Several more shots were fired at him, and we finally killed him, but both Owens and Burris were left badly crippled, and never entirely recovered.

The hunter who took any unnecessary chances in dealing with a " grizzly," always regretted it. He always discovered that to trifle with the " monarch of the mountains" under any circumstances, was a mistake. Old "Jim" Baker, who next to " Kit" Carson was General Fremont's most noted scout, and who has been my companion on many a trapping expedition, used to tell me how he learned this lesson very early in his experience as a mountaineer, and he would always wind up by remarking, " I haint forgot that lesson yet." Baker came to the mountains about the same time I did, and soon became known as one of the most daring fellows among the mountain men. Two or three years after he came to the country, he and a companion ran across a couple of young " grizzlies" one morning, when they only happened to have with them the butcher knives sticking in their belts. It was not more than a hundred yards to the camp where their guns had been left, but, as Baker said afterwards, " I lowed we could get away with the varmints with our knives, and we sailed into the fight." Baker had a hard tus-

sle with the bear which he attacked, but finally managed to kill him. Just about the time this contest
ended, he noticed that his companion had abandoned
the fight, and the second bear charged him without
stopping to give him a breathing spell, or waiting for
time to be called. The struggle which followed between the exhausted hunter and his second antagonist was a desperate one, and poor Baker was more
dead than alive, when he again found himself a vic-
tor. He could barely drag himself away from the
two ferocious animals that he had slain in close com-
bat, and he never again allowed himself to be invei-
gled into a rough and tumble fight with a " grizzly."

The closest call I ever had myself when hunting
bear, was not many years ago, and right here in the
Raton mountains.

Bears were beginning to get scarce in the country
then, and I hadn't seen one for a long time. I had
boys growing up, and a good many men about me,
who were doing different kinds of work, and every
now and then some of them would come in and report
that they had seen a bear.

I always laughed at them and teased them more or
less about their reports, because I thought if there
had been any bear in the neighborhood, I should
have caught a glimpse of one sometime myself.

One morning I walked out with my gun on my
shoulder, thinking I might see something to shoot
at, and had not gone more than three or four hundred

yards from my house when I came on to an old bear
with two good-sized cubs.   I thought to myself,
" well, the boys were right, after all, and now I'll just
teach them that the proper thing to do when you see
a bear is to kill it."   I calculated to kill the old bear
and then capture the two cubs to raise as pets, just
to show the travelers through the country what a
live Rocky Mountain bear looked like.   As I didn't
often miss anything I shot at, I had every confidence
in my ability to kill the bear at the first shot.   For
once, however, my confidence in the old rifle, which
had served me so many good turns, was misplaced.
A long period of idleness seemed to have impaired its
usefulness.   It missed fire, and the snapping of the
cap made just noise enough to attract the attention
of the bear.   I had gotten so close, that when the
bear started for me, I could only get out of the way
by making for the nearest tree.   I reached the tree
with the bear in close pursuit, and commenced to
climb.   It was a small pine tree, and I had grown so
stout that I weighed about two hundred and forty
pounds, so you can understand that I couldn't climb
like a squirrel, even under favorable circumstances.
The dry pine limbs that I caught hold of broke under my weight, and when I got about four or five feet
from the ground, not high enough to be out of reach
of the bear by any means, there I stuck.   I couldn't
get up, and I needn't tell you that I didn't want to
come down.   I expected every minute that the bear

would take a mouthful of me, but I commenced hunting for a pistol that I had about me, and made up my mind to kill her if she bit a leg off. Just when I thought the biting and clawing was about to commence, something frightened one of the cubs which the old bear had left behind, when she started out to pay her compliments to me, and it set up that peculiar cry, which always makes one think of a child in distress. The old bear left me and ran to the cub, and then they made off together in the bushes. I didn't follow them, because I had seen enough to satisfy me that the bear had an ugly temper.

I really wanted those two cubs, but I didn't want them bad enough to try to get them that morning, at the risk of another encounter with the old lady bear. I let myself down out of the tree, picked up my gun, and walked home. When they asked me what I had found that morning in the way of game, I told them "nothing of consequence." I never said a word about my adventure with the bear, but some way or other the boys found out about it, and for a while I had a hard time to live with them. Every once in a while they would want to know if I had seen any bear lately, and what I thought about there being any in the country.

The thieving propensities of the bear used to get him into trouble with the trappers very frequently. They would come about our camp at night and some-

times carry off meat or sugar, which they found
within two feet of a sleeping trapper.   If the trapper
happened to wake up while the burglary was being
perpetrated, the safest thing for him to do was to lie
perfectly still and let the burglar have what he
wanted, because, like most other burglars, the bear
was ready to do some killing if it was necessary to
enable him to get away with what he was after.

It takes a good deal of nerve to enable a man to
keep quiet when lying in camp at night, with a great
ugly brute snuffing about within a few feet of him,
but I have done it many a time and never lost my
head but once or twice.

Once I was trapping on Indian Creek, a small
stream of Southern Colorado, when our camp was
visited one night by a " grizzly."   A companion
named Kincaid slept under the same blanket with
me that night, and about the middle of the night, he
awakened me out of a sound sleep by giving me a
nudge in the ribs.   He said something which I
thought meant Indians, and pointed toward the foot
of our " bunk."   Not two yards from our feet I saw
a black object which looked to me as tall as a telegraph pole.   It was a bear, sitting upon his haunches,
as they do sometimes, but I took it to be an Indian,
and the next thing I expected was to have a tomahawk hurled at my head.   We always slept with our
loaded guns at our side, in such a position that we
could grab them instantly, and in case of emergency

shoot without getting on our feet. Without ever thinking of the thing being a bear, I raised my gun and fired.

As it happened he fell backward over a little bank, and then started off through the brush in an opposite direction from our camp. I had, however, given him his death wound, and he only went a short distance before he fell over a log, and we found him there dead in the morning. If my gun had happened to miss fire, or if I had wounded instead of shooting the bear fatally, I should probably have had as ugly a fight as a man ever had with a mad bear, and I doubt very much whether I should be here now telling stories about my hunting adventures.

I killed another bear under similar circumstances one night, with my hunting knife. I was sleeping soundly when I felt the bear's cold nose rubbed against my face. My hunting knife was in my belt, and when I awakened and found the bear standing alongside of me, I drew the knife and plunged it into his side up to the hilt, springing away from him so quickly that I received but a slight scratch. The knife entered his heart and he fell dead on the spot where I had been sleeping a moment before.

To train our horses to carry game, and particularly bear, into camp, was a difficult thing to do. There is nothing on earth that a horse has a greater instinctive fear of than bear, and you can understand how he would feel about having one of

10

the dreaded animals thrown across his back and being compelled to carry it. Even the best broke riding
horse would cut more antics than the trick pony at a
circus, until he got rid of a load of bear meat, if he
had not been put through a previous course of train-
ing.

When we wanted to train a horse to carry this kind
of a load, the first thing we did was to strip off the
skin of a bear, and wrap the green skin about the
horse's head. Of course he didn't take kindly to this
performance, and made a good bit of fuss about it,
but by and by he would quiet down, and then he
would carry any kind of a load of game we put on
him.

I saw, one time when I was hunting in the mountains along Grand River, a bear which seemed to belong to a different species from those usually seen in
this country. I have never seen or heard of any
other animal in the mountains that looked like this
one, and I have always been at a loss to know what
family he belonged to.

I suppose it is hardly possible that a polar bear
should be found in this latitude, and yet the animal
that I speak of, had every appearance of a polar bear.
He was of a dirty white color; would have weighed
perhaps five or six hundred pounds, and was certainly
the queerest looking bear I have ever seen in these
parts. I shot at him and wounded him in the shoulder, but did not succeed in capturing him. It may

have been that he was a grizzly, who had turned pale from some cause or other, but if such a thing as finding a polar bear anywhere outside of the region of which he is a native is possible, I shall insist that I have seen one in Colorado, and he wasn't in a cage either.

The bear is the only animal I have found in the Rocky Mountain region, which is at all inclined to attack a man, if there is any way of avoiding a conflict.

The mountain lions, wolves, and other animals, which have the reputation of being more or less fierce and bloodthirsty, will only show fight when they are wounded, so that escape from the hunter is impossible, or when they are driven into a corner and compelled to defend themselves.

They made the early settlers a good deal of trouble by killing their stock, but they were cowardly brutes, and the hunters, trappers, and explorers had no fear of them.

Children were not so safe, and the settler never allowed his little ones to get far away from his cabin alone. I once shot a mountain lion when he was about to spring on a little child, which had wandered two or three hundred yards away from home.

The child was a five-year-old boy, who was playing, boy fashion, in a little stream of water, entirely unconscious of the danger he was in. I caught sight of the lion, slipping along, like a cat watching a bird, on the bank of the stream. He got within ten feet of the child, and was preparing to spring, when I sent a bullet through him, and he rolled down into the water, almost at the feet of the little prattler, who would have been torn to pieces a moment later, had not my shot prevented the lion from carrying out his intentions.

I never could understand why this animal should be called the mountain lion. If there is anything about him which entitles him to such distinction, I have failed to observe what it is. He doesn't look much more like the native of the African jungles, after whom he is named, than he does like a rhinoceros, nor is he like the " king of beasts " in any other way. He belongs to the panther family, and is neither more nor less dangerous than the common run of those overgrown cats.

So many big stories have been told, however, about the ferocity of the Rocky Mountain lion, that a great many people have been led to believe that he makes a business of eating people, and that to meet him in the mountains, is to meet an enemy hardly less to be dreaded than the fierce inhabitant of the tropical jungles. Old hunters and mountain men know that this is all nonsense, and if they have been responsible for putting any of these wild stories into circulation, they must have told the stories just to see some tenderfoot's hair stand on end."

GOV. CHARLES BENT.

CHAPTER XI.

THE TAOS MASSACRE.

"In the fall of 1846 and in the early part of the winter of 1847, I was in and out of the old town of Fernandez de Taos, very frequently, but was fortunate in not being there at one particular time.

That was when the Mexicans stirred up the rebellion, which culminated in what has always been known as "the Taos Massacre."

In August of the year 1846, General Kearney had gone into Santa Fe, with the body of troops which he had marched across the plains from Fort Leavenworth, and had taken possession of the capital of New Mexico, as well as other towns through which he had passed on his way to that point, without opposition.

The Mexicans had taken the oath of allegiance to the government of the United States, and New Mexico was looked upon as a conquered and subjugated province. General Kearney then proceeded on his way to California, leaving Colonel Stirling Price, with a few companies of troops at Santa Fe. Colonel A. W. Doniphan came through from Fort Leavenworth with another body of troops later, and also stopped at Santa Fe.

Aside from the small force of soldiers stationed at Santa Fe, and possibly small detachments at Albu-

querque, and one or two other places, I do not think
there were any troops left in New Mexico, when
Kearney pushed on to the Pacific Coast.

For a time both the Mexicans and Indians professed to be very friendly, and the Americans got
along well in New Mexico. By and by, however, it
was noticed that a considerable number of the Mexicans were for some reason becoming dissatisfied with
the condition of affairs, and Colonel Price, who was
in command at Santa Fe, found it necessary to keep
a close watch on their movements. It was not long
before he discovered that Tomas Ortiz and Diego
Archuleta, two prominent Mexicans, had set on foot
a plan to bring about a general uprising of the Mexicans and Pueblo Indians. They were to act in
concert, and at a certain time were to fall upon all
the Americans and other foreigners in the territory,
and either kill or drive them out of the country.
The Mexicans didn't seem to have much of an idea
of the size of the contract they were undertaking,
and the Indians, of course, were led on entirely by
the Mexicans, who promised them an easy victory
and plenty of plunder.

This scheme was discovered in time to be nipped
in the bud, and Archuleta and Ortiz left the country
to escape punishment.

There was nothing like a general uprising at that
time or even after that, but a Mexican named Pablo

Montoya and El Tomacito, an Indian, concluded some time afterward, to go ahead with the proposed rebellion on their own account. They gathered together a considerable force of natives, and marched to Taos, on the night of the 18th of January, 1847.

As I have already told you, Fernandez de Taos, or Taos, as we always called it, for short, was a Mexican town, having a population of five or six thousand people.

The Pueblo de Taos was an Indian village about two miles from the town. It consisted of one large Pueblo building, six or seven stories high, and a church, which stood some little distance away, both built of adobe.

I suppose there were something like a thousand Indians in the Pueblo. It was at this point that the Indians and Mexicans met, to commence their march to Taos, and the slaughter of the foreigners, of whom they proposed to rid the country.

There were not more than fifteen white persons, or perhaps, properly speaking, persons who had no admixture of Spanish or Indian blood in their veins, living in the town of Taos, and several of these happened to be absent from their homes on the memorable 19th of January, 1847.

Those who were at home, when they got up in the morning, found the town surrounded by as merciless a band of savages as ever went on the war path, and

they quickly caused it to be understood, that their
intention was to kill every white man woman and
child in the place.

Charles Bent, who had been appointed military
governor of New Mexico, by General Kearney, lived
at Taos, and had come up from Santa Fe, which was
of course his official headquarters, only a day or two
before. His residence was one of the first places attacked, and he was butchered in his own doorway.
James Blair, a young attorney from Missouri, who
was a brother of General Frank P. Blair, was visiting
Governor Bent at the time, and he was also killed
before the murderers left the house. Stephen Lee,
who was acting as sheriff of the county, Pablo
Armijo, prefect, and Cornelio Vigil, district attorney,
were killed at about the same time, by different
bands of the allied conspirators. The two men last
named were both Mexicans, but they were loyal to
the oaths which they had taken, to support the laws
and government of the United States, and for this
reason they were among the first victims of the massacre. Several other Americans were killed, whose
names I do not now remember, and the savages then
turned their attention to the women and children.
I do not think there was a white woman of foreign
birth living in the Mexican town at the time, nor is
it probable that there were any full blood American
children there. The half breed children were, however, marked for the slaughter, and as the Mexicans

and Indians all had dark complexions, the color of the hair and eyes was made the test of blood.

Spanish women who were married to Americans, had to disguise their children who had light hair and blue eyes, and some of those children still have a vivid recollection of having their faces and hair colored, to make them look as much as possible like the natives. Those who escaped in this way were the fortunate ones, and there were comparatively few of them. A majority of the half breeds were dispatched as summarily as Governor Bent and his friends had been. Among them, I recollect, was Narcisso Beaubien, a son of Judge Beaubien, who had lived among the Mexicans for years, and befriended both them and the Indians, in a thousand ways. Beaubien was a bright young fellow, who had just graduated from an eastern college, and proposed to make his home in the country, of which he was a native. His sympathies, however, were with the Americans, and he was not allowed to escape the fate of all those who were supposed to lean that way.

The bodies of some of those killed were horribly mutilated. All of the victims were scalped, and Governor Bent's head was cut off and carried about the town, to terrify women and children, and those Mexicans whom it was thought were not in full sympathy with the rebellion.

When they had made an end of the massacre at Taos, these bloody butchers proceeded to Arroyo

Honda, twelve miles from Taos, where there was another American settlement, and killed everybody they could find there.

Two men made their escape from that place, and one of them started for Santa Fe and the other for Pueblo, to carry the news of the slaughter to those places. The distance from Taos to Pueblo was about one hundred and sixty-five miles. Pueblo was not a town at that time, you understand. What we called "the Pueblo," stood on the site of the present town. It was an adobe fort, built by the trappers, which had become headquarters for a considerable number of the mountain men, and was something of a trading post. I was there at the time of the Taos massacre, and about five days later John Albert, who had managed some way or other to make his escape from Arroyo Honda, came into the Pueblo, bringing the news of the Mexican uprising and its bloody sequel. He had traveled the whole distance on foot, and was almost exhausted when he reached us.

When Albert had laid before us all the details of the tragedy, our little band of trappers held a council of war, to determine what we should do. The situation was as perplexing as it was distressing. The friendships of the mountain men were warm friendships. We had never seen the time when we were not ready to attempt the rescue of a friend whose life was in danger, and it was seldom indeed that the killing or wounding of one of our number had gone unavenged.

Among those who had been so brutally murdered at Taos and Arroyo Honda, were men who had been my warmest and best friends, ever since I came to the country, and I felt that I should, if possible, do something toward securing punishment of their murderers, and protecting the property which they had left, for the use of those who were entitled to it. What to do, however, was the question. We should not have hesitated much about attacking an ordinary band of roving Indians, but to undertake to put down what seemed to be a formidable rebellion, was of course out of our line. We did not know what might be going on at Santa Fe, or how long it would be, before we could expect any help from the government forces, and without such assistance, the small party of volunteers that we should have been able to muster, could have accomplished nothing.

We parleyed over the matter awhile, and reached the conclusion that there were soldiers enough at Santa Fe to put down the rebellion, and having agreed upon this point we reached the further conclusion, that it was our duty to render them all the assistance possible.

This determined our action, and five of us mounted our horses and started across the country toward Taos. It took us several days to make the trip, and we approached the place very carefully. We made our way into the high mountains east of Taos, and from there we could look down on the town, and see pretty well what was going on, without being discovered ourselves. As we could discover no sign of the arrival of the soldiers, we knew that it was not safe for us to venture further.

In the meantime, Thomas Tobin, the messenger who had left Arroyo Honda, with the news of the massacre at that place and at Taos, had reached Santa Fe, and Colonel Price had lost no time in marching against the rebels. He met the first force of Mexicans and Indians at La Cañada, some distance out on the Taos road from Santa Fe, and soon had them on the run. He then sent Captain Burgwin, with two companies of troops, on toward Taos. Colonel Ceran St. Vrain, Governor Bent's partner, accompanied Captain Burgwin, with about sixty volunteers, picked up in Santa Fe. At Embudo they had another skirmish with the insurgents, and did not reach Taos until the third of February.

We were watching for them, and saw them when they marched into the town. The hostiles had all gathered at the Pueblo de Taos, and fortified themselves in and about the old church. The soldiers marched to the Pueblo and fired a few shots, but as night was coming on, they returned to Fernandez de Taos, and went into camp for the night.

The Americans were by no means certain that the entire force of the enemy had gathered at the Pueblo, but half suspected that a force was secreted in the town of Taos. Before going into camp, they made a careful reconnoisance, inspecting every building in the town, to find out who was inside. Where the doors were closed, they were broken down, and a thorough search made of the buildings, but where they stood open, it was taken as a guarantee of a friendly feeling on the part of the occupants, and their residences were not disturbed.

While the soldiers were in camp that night, I made my way down to where they were, along with my four companions, and joining the Santa Fe volunteers, was ready for the storming of the Pueblo, and the fight which was to commence in the morning. It commenced early, and the battle which followed was a bloody one, considering the number of men engaged in it.

It lasted until sundown, and I think we were resisted as stoutly as were the American soldiers upon any battle field of the Mexican war.

We soon drove our enemies out of the pueblo building proper, but their position in La Iglesia de Taos —the old church—was a strong one, and we found it difficult to dislodge them. We had three small howitzers and one six-pound cannon, but the walls of the church were so thick, that the shells from the howitzers would not go through them, and the solid shot from the cannon only made a round hole. As we were short of amunition, we could not afford to waste any, and for that reason volunteers were called for to breach the walls with axes. This was a hazardous business, as the work had to be done while a hot fire was being kept up from the inside of the building.

Thirty-five of us, however, volunteered to make the attempt, and we gained the cover of the walls with a loss of only three or four men. It took us but a short time to accomplish what we had started out to do, and when a few shells were thrown through the holes we had made, and exploded in the building, they created a fearful havoc. We lighted the fuses, and threw some of these shells into the church with our hands, in order that they might be sure to explode at the proper time and place.

This made it altogether too hot for the besieged party, and bursting open the doors and windows they undertook to make their escape to the mountains. James Q. Quinn, of Illinois, a cousin of Stephen A. Douglas, planted the American flag on the old church, but as the Mexicans were retreating, they stopped long enough to shoot it down.

The last stand made by the insurgents was at the old church. When they were driven out of there, they fled in every direction. Of course we pursued them, and not much quarter was asked or given. There was considerable hand-to-hand fighting, Colonel

St. Vrain himself, I remember, engaging in a contest which in spite of the peril of the situation, was amusing. The colonel was riding along with myself and two or three others, who were about to join in a pursuit of one party of fugitives, when he observed an Indian whom he had seen a great many times, and knew very well, lying stretched out on the ground, apparently dead. Knowing that this Indian had taken a prominent part in the massacre, Colonel St. Vrain dismounted, and walked a few feet from where we were, to see whether the red skin was really dead or only shamming. That the latter, and not the former, was the proper diagnosis of the Indian's case, the colonel was soon very thoroughly convinced. He had scarcely reached the side of the apparently dead Indian, when the latter sprang up, and grappling with him, undertook to thrust into his body a long, steel-pointed arrow. Both the Indian and the colonel were large, powerful men, and as each managed to keep the other from using a weapon, a wrestling-match followed the Indian's attack, which, it seemed to me, lasted several minutes before outside help terminated it in the colonel's favor. I sprang to his assistance as soon as I saw the struggle commence, but the Indian managed to keep the colonel between him and me, and was so active in his movements, that I found it difficult to strike a lick which would be sure to hit the right head. I managed after little, however, to deal him a blow with my tomahawk, which had the effect of causing him to relax his hold upon the colonel, and when he stretched out on the ground again, there was no doubt about his being a dead Indian.

We lost thirty-five men out of the comparatively small number we had engaged in this battle, and among them was Captain Burgwin, who was as brave a soldier as I have ever seen on the frontier. We buried him at Taos in a grave by himself, while the other thirty-four men who were killed, were buried side by side in a long trench near where they fell.

We never knew exactly what the Mexican and Indian loss was, but it must have been in the neighborhood of two hundred.

This battle ended the Taos rebellion, as it is generally called, although the conspirators had their plans laid to bring about a general uprising of Mexicans and Indians in New Mexico, and they evidently thought with this combination of forces, they would be able to drive the Americans out of the territory, and keep them out.

A detachment of soldiers remained at Taos after that, and the work of hunting down and punishing those who had stirred up, and been prominently connected with the insurrection, commenced.

Pablo Montoya and El Tomacito were both captured. El Tomacito, the Indian leader, was placed

under guard, and we proposed to give him, along
with the rest, a formal trial, but a dragoon by
the name of Fitzgerald saved us the trouble. Fitzgerald was allowed to go into the room where the
Indian was confined, along with others who wanted
to take a look at him. The soldier looked at the
savage a few minutes, and then quick as a flash, drew

PUEBLO DE TAOS.

a pistol and shot him in the head, killing him instantly. Fitzgerald then made his escape from the
building, and succeeded in getting away out of the
country. If he had been caught he would of course
have been punished. The Indian deserved to be
killed, and would have been hanged anyhow, but we
objected to the informal manner of his taking off.

11

Pablo Montoya was tried and hanged, and twelve others were disposed of in the same way.

They were all tried by drum-head court-martial, and there was no unnecessary delay about reaching the climax of the proceedings. The twelve that I have spoken of above, were hanged at the same time, and dangled from the same pole. I acted as marshal in making arrests under the military authority, and was kept very busy for some days. The only law we had was military law, but that was just what we wanted, and it was not long before order was restored and the rebellion experiment has never been tried there since.

The traders who had been absent from Taos when the massacre occurred, that is, those who lived there, found, upon their return, that their stores had been sacked and burned, and the most of their property destroyed, but they congratulated themselves upon having escaped with their lives, and after the fashion of the pioneers, set about building up other fortunes to take the place of those they had lost."

"KIT" CARSON.

CHAPTER XII.

A TRIP TO OLD MEXICO.

"Soon after the battle at Taos, I received a letter from Colonel A. W. Doniphan, who had left Santa Fe for old Mexico, with about four hundred troops, requesting me to join his command, to act as guide and scout on the expedition which he was about to undertake.

I had met Colonel Doniphan at Santa Fe, some time before this, and agreed to go with him into Mexico, should he desire me to do so, and when I received this letter I was under obligations to obey the summons promptly. I left Taos at once, on horseback, and after four days of as hard riding as a man ever did, I reached his command and was assigned to duty.

Doniphan had been reinforced by a detachment of troops forwarded from Santa Fe, and when I reached him, he had a force of about eight hundred men. With this force he was to march to Chihuahua to meet General Wool, who was marching toward the same point, from some place lower down on the Rio Grande. We had a rough country to travel through, and the position of guide was a responsible one. It was my duty to keep the commanding officer informed as to whether or not there were any enemies

in front of him, to pick out the easiest and most practicable route to travel over, to find water and select
camping grounds.

Finding a sufficient supply of water for eight hundred men and the large number of horses we had
with us, was not always an easy matter in as dry a
country as Chihuahua, but the men who followed
my guidance on that march, never had cause for
serious complaint.

Something which I can't explain, and which I
think must be an instinct, has always enabled me to
find water in any country where there was any water
to be found.

Every night when we went into camp I was able
to give Colonel Doniphan correct information as to
the character of the country over which we were to
pass next day, and in the morning I again went
ahead to learn the " lay of the land" beyond the
place which was to be our next camping ground.

I always had with me a detail of ten or fifteen
men, so that if we should have come upon any hostiles I should not have been entirely without support and assistance.

We had rather a limited supply of provisions to
start out with, and before we had gone very far, we
had to draw on the resources of the country. The
wild game which we found, particularly wild turkey,
helped out a little, but there wasn't enough of it,

and ammunition was too scarce to be wasted getting
it anyhow. There were large bands of wild cattle
roaming over the hills and *mesas*, however, and
whenever we wanted a supply of meat we " rounded"
up a lot of these cattle and butchered them.

When we first commenced killing the cattle, it
was thought advisable to lasso, instead of shooting
them, as some amunition would be saved thereby.
The experiment was tried by the soldiers with
varying degrees of success, and upon the whole was
by no means satisfactory.

Lassoing wild cattle was a new business to most
of them, and they had some very amusing experiences. That is, it was amusing to those who looked
on, although there was nothing funny about it for
the participants. They had practiced throwing the
lariat more or less, and did not, as a rule, have much
difficulty in catching a steer when they started after
him. It was right there, however, that the trouble
began. At first the soldier always thought he had
the steer, but before much time had elapsed he
usually learned that the steer had him. Being able
to lasso an animal of that kind is one thing, and
knowing how to land him on his back, instead of
being landed on your own back, and perhaps seriously hurt, is quite another.

The soldier cow boys made this discovery, and
soon abandoned the plan of catching the beef cattle,

for the more practical scheme of riding into a herd, and shooting as many as it was necessary to kill, to supply the demand for fresh meat.

Colonel Doniphan's march toward Chihuahua was unobstructed by the appearance of an enemy, until we reached the Rio Sacramento. The road to Chihuahua crossed the Sacramento River at the Rancho Sacramento, a fine old Mexican *hacienda*, which belonged to Angel Trias, the governor of Chihuahua.

This house and the adjoining corrals had been converted into a fortress, and was occupied by General Heredia, with a force of about four thousand Mexican soldiers.

A strong body of horsemen was sent out to meet Colonel Doniphan, but two or three volleys fired by our artillery sent them scurrying back to the rancho, where they soon got under cover of their fortifications.

Their position was one which gave them a great advantage, but after about three hours fighting, they were driven out of the fortress, and Colonel Doniphan and his troops entered the rancho, having gained their first victory on the soil of old Mexico.

Colonel Doniphan remained here some days before pushing on towards Chihuahua, the capital then, as it is now, of the state of the same name, which he captured a little later. Just before he started for Chihuahua, which was only eighteen miles distant,

he sent for me and wanted to know if I was willing
to undertake to carry some dispatches back to Santa
Fe.

I told him I should like to see the famous city of
Chihuahua, but if he wished me to return to Santa
Fe I would make the attempt. He asked me how
many men I wanted to accompany me, and I told him
I thought I could take care of myself, but wasn't
sure that I could take care of anybody else. For
that reason I thought I had best go alone. If I met
any enemies, fighting them would be out of the
question, and it would be easier for one man to get
through the country unobserved, than it would be for
a party of men to do the same thing. I was allowed
to have my own way about the matter, and made the
trip to Albuquerque, where some of the government
troops were stationed, in nine days.

I had to carry horse feed and a supply of provisions for myself, and that made it necessary for me
to have two horses.

My stock of provisions consisted of some "hard
tack" and dried meat, and I had to lay in enough of
it to last me until I reached Albuquerque, as there
was no prospect of my meeting any friends on the
way.

What I wanted was to get through without seeing
anybody, or rather without having anybody see me.
To do this I knew that I should not only have to

keep in the mountains as much as possible, but
travel by a different route from that over which I
had led Colonel Doniphan's regiment.   The hostiles,
—and all the natives were supposed to be more or
less hostile—had discovered, of course, after we
passed over the ground, what our line of march had
been, and they would very naturally be on the lookout for other parties; coming the same way, or mes-
sengers returning with news from the front.

Loading my traps and provisions on one of the
horses, and pocketing my dispatches, which, of
course, were in sealed packages, so that I don't know
to this day the nature of the information I carried, I
mounted the other horse and set out.

I think I managed to keep out of sight of everything in the shape of a human being, during the
entire trip.   Now and then when I looked down into
the valleys from the mountains, I would see either
Mexicans or Indians, but I never allowed them to
catch sight of me.   I never once kindled a fire, or
even lighted my pipe.   I refrained entirely from
shooting at game, or making any noise which would
attract attention.   Whenever I saw an open space
ahead of me, I spent a good deal of time looking
over the ground from some secure place, before I
ventured out from under cover.   I traveled much of
the time after dark, and had no such thing as a
night's sleep on the trip.   Now and then, at very

irregular intervals, when I reached what seemed to be a very safe place, I lay down and took a few hours rest, and I slept a little as I rode along.   I was almost worn out when I came within sight of Albuquerque, which was along towards sun down of the ninth day that I had been riding.

There I encountered a difficulty entirely unlooked for and unexpected. The Rio Grande had risen, and was flooding the country, so that when I reached it, it looked to me as wide as the Mississippi when it reaches high water mark. This stream is noted for its treacherous quicksands, and fording it at that point, is always more or less dangerous. I had to cross it someway, however, and I prepared to wade and swim until I reached the opposite bank, on which the troops were encamped.

I don't think I ever had a more trying experience than I had, in my exhausted condition, getting across that stream. Several times I sank in the quicksands, but floundered about, until some way or other, I don't know just how, I made my way out. Then the sentinel on the bank challenged me, for it was dark by this time, and wanted me to give the countersign. I was down under the bank so that he couldn't see me, and of course he wouldn't have known anything about who I was if he had seen me.

It was his business to demand the countersign, but I had no means of knowing what it was, and being cold, wet, hungry and exhausted, I didn't want to be kept waiting for any red tape proceedings.

The sentry's peremptory " halt" and his demand for the countersign, while I was still knee-deep in the ice-cold river water, put me out of humor, and I yelled back, "countersign be d—d. I am an American, with dispatches from Colonel Doniphan, and I want to get out of this water."

This appeal did not have the desired effect. He kept me where I was until the officer-of-the-day came out, and admitted me inside the lines in due form.

That night I ate the first square meal, and got the first night's rest I had had in almost a fortnight.

The next day I went on to Santa Fe, delivered my package, and ended my mission as a bearer of military dispatches.

I was anxious then to get on to Taos, which I had decided to make my headquarters, as I had established a business there, and it had begun to seem more like home to me than any other place. I learned at Santa Fe, that both the Ute and Apache Indians had gone on the war-path, in my absence, and that bands of the hostiles were somewhere between Santa Fe and Taos.

This was no very pleasant news, and I hesitated about trying to get home, but finally concluded to make the attempt. I knew the country so well that there was no necessity for my following the established trail in

order to avoid getting lost. I was careful to keep
away from it, when I got a few miles out of Santa
Fe, and it was to this precaution that I probably
owed my safe arrival in Taos, as a party which attempted to follow the trail across, the next day, fell
into the hands of the Apaches, and several persons
were killed. I did not see one of the hostile Indians
on the way, although I passed close to a large band
of Utes, when I crossed the Rio Grande, twelve miles
below Taos. I had to swim the river at that point,
and the Indians must have been in hiding very near
there at the time. Three companies of soldiers were
sent out against them only a day or two later, from
Taos, and at about the point where I crossed the river,
they were ambushed by the Indians and badly defeated, thirty-five or forty men being killed.

The officer who commanded this expedition had
requested me to go with him as guide, and had I not
been so much in need of rest, I would have done so.

I remained at Taos the greater part of the time for
several years after my trip to old Mexico, and was
there when General, then Colonel Fremont, made his
way into the town, after he and his little band of explorers had come so near freezing to death, in the
Uncompahgre mountains, in the winter of 1848.

Fremont, who was then on an exploring expedition,
was on his way to California, and had with him as
guide. "Old Bill" Williams, one of the best known

of the mountain men, who had been famous for years as a hunter and trapper.

Williams knew every pass in the mountains, and almost every foot of the Rocky Mountain country, and if General Fremont had taken his advice, he would never have run into the death-trap, which cost him the lives of three men, and in which he lost all his valuable papers, his instruments, and the animals which he and his men were riding.

They had followed the Arkansas River to its source, and General Fremont had picked out the route which he wanted to travel over in crossing the mountains. Williams told him that it was not practicable to cross the range by the route which he had selected, in the winter season, but the great "pathfinder" listened to an inexperienced member of the party, who volunteered to pilot him over.

Before they had fairly gotten started, they were caught in a terrific snow storm, in which all their horses and mules were frozen to death. Then they turned back, and undertook to make their way down the mountain, leaving all their accoutrements behind and carrying with them but a small stock of provisions.

The snow storm continued, and even old "Bill" Williams could not keep them from getting lost. They wandered about for several days before they finally found their way into Taos, in great distress, from hunger and fatigue.

Three of the eighteen men who composed the party that started into the mountains, had frozen to death on their way down, and the others were little better than dead men, when I happened to run across them, and brought them into town.

I took Fremont to the home of "Kit" Carson, who then lived at Taos, and the other members of the party were at once fed and cared for at other places.

After resting for some days, General Fremont de⁻ cided to again push on toward California, but not until three of the most noted mountain men in the country at that time, had consented to accompany him as guides. These were, "Kit" Carson, Lucien B. Maxwell, who afterward became owner of the famous Maxwell land grant, and "Dick" Owens.

Five members of his original party, concluded they had had enough of the exploring expedition, and declined to start out with the general, when he got ready to leave Taos, but he had no difficulty in finding others to take their places.

Before starting, he arranged with me to go into the mountains, when the spring opened, and bring down his instruments, papers, and such other things as he had left behind when caught in the fatal snow-storm.

After he had gone away, however, the five former
members of the party, who had remained behind,
laid claim to all the valuables which I had been
promised as compensation for making the trip, and I
came to the conclusion that they might go after the
stuff themselves.

They started out, and again took " Bill " Williams
as guide.   They found their way into the mountains
all right, found the saddles, instruments, and accoutrements of all kinds where they had left them, and
commenced the return trip, but they never reached
Taos.

Coming back, they passed a Ute village, and not
knowing that this particular band of Indians was on
the war-path, and had just been soundly whipped by
a party of soldiers, they went into camp within half
a mile of the savages.

At daybreak on the following morning the Indians
attacked them, and every member of the party was
killed.   Not even poor old " Bill " Williams, who
had been among the Utes for years, could speak their
language, and knew a great many of them personally, escaped.

That was the last trip made by the old mountaineer, who was known to everybody in the country
fifty years ago, and who figured more or less in nearly
all the old-time stories, written and told of the mountain men and their adventures.

He was a queer character. I never knew where he came from, or how long he had been in the country, although I have sat by the same camp-fire with him a hundred times. All I ever knew was that he had been a circuit preacher in early life in Missouri, and had been in the mountains longer than any of the other trappers. He had been so much among

THE LARIAT THROWERS.

the Indians, that he used to look and talk like an Indian, and had imbibed a great many of their superstitions and peculiar notions.

Among other things he had picked up from them, was a belief in the transmigration of souls. He had pondered over this matter and dreamed over it, until he had reached a conclusion as to the kind of animal he was to become, when he ceased to be a man.

One night when there were a dozen or more of us together in camp—that was when he was growing quite old—he told us, with as great an air of solemnity as though he had been preaching his own funeral, that when he ceased to be " Bill " Williams, he was to become a buck elk, and would make his home in the very neighborhood where we were then encamped.   He had pictured out, in his own mind, what kind of a looking elk he would be, and described to us certain peculiarities which he should have, which would enable us to distinguish him from other elks, and cautioned us not to shoot an elk of that description, should we ever run across one after his death.   Poor old fellow!   He was a warm-hearted, brave, and generous man, and in whatever state he continues his existence, I hope he is happy."

LUCIEN B. MAXWELL.

CHAPTER XIII.

A STAGE COACH MASSACRE.

" In 1847, the Utes fell out with the Mexicans, and from that time on, for several years, they were at war more or less of the time with everybody.

They robbed and murdered the Mexicans, killed a trapper or hunter every now and then, fought with the other Indian tribes and kept up a general commotion in Northern New Mexico and Southern Colorado.

I made peace with them at different times, and traded with them more or less, but they robbed me just the same as anybody else when they got a good chance, and some of their robberies were very extensive.

I had taken a contract to furnish beef for the troops stationed at Taos, and had to go a long distance away from there sometimes to get cattle. On every one of these trips I ran the risk of having my stock captured and driven off by the hostiles. I had cattle of my own in the Arkansas valley, and one time when my men were driving a hundred head of fine beef steers from the Arkansas over to Taos, the Utes met them at Clifton, now a station on the Santa Fe Railroad, in Northern New Mexico. The Indians wanted the cattle and they took them without asking anybody's permission, leaving me to pocket a loss of not less than five thousand dollars.

It was not long after that, that a horrible massacre in the same section of country, and not very far distant, attracted general attention, and compelled the military authorities to take some action which would look like an effort to suppress the savages.

The Santa Fe stage was on its way from Independence, Missouri, to Santa Fe, loaded as usual with passengers. Among the passengers was a Mr. White, a wealthy farmer of Jackson County, Missouri, who was accompanied by his wife, a small child, and colored nurse. They were on their way to Santa Fe to visit friends, as were also two prominent citizens and business men of Western Missouri by the name of McCoy.

I do not now remember the names of the other stage passengers, but including the stage driver and conductor, and the two men with the baggage wagon, which followed the stage, there were fifteen persons in the party.

When the stage reached Whetstone Springs, in Northeastern New Mexico, the head of the little stream called Whetstone River, it had to pass, for some distance, through a narrow defile, on either side of which were high, overhanging rocks.

The Utes, knowing it was about time for the stage to come along, hid themselves on these rocks, and

the first knowledge the travelers had of the ambuscade, was when they heard the crack of rifles, and
saw the mules behind which they were riding, fall
dead in the harness.

That of course brought the stage and baggage-
wagon to a stop, and the massacre of the entire party
was an easy matter.

Not one of them escaped from the merciless savages, and it was not until the failure of the stage to
arrive on time at the next station, occasioned alarm,
and a party was sent out to learn the cause of the
delay, that anybody knew what had happened.

Inquiry at the last station which had been passed
by the stage, furnished full information as to the
number of persons in the party when it left that
place, and at the scene of the massacre the bodies of
all of them, with the exception of Mrs. White, the
child, and its colored nurse, were found.

The horribly mutilated remains of the victims
were gathered up and buried in one grave, on a bluff
overlooking the place where their lives had been so
suddenly and unexpectedly cut short.

Then the news of the killing, and as much as
could be learned of the circumstances in connection with it, were sent to Taos, where several companies of troops were stationed, under command of
Colonel Greer.

As the bodies of Mrs. White, the child, and its nurse, were not found among the others, it was evident that these three persons had been carried away by the Indians, and Colonel Greer was appealed to, to undertake to rescue them and punish the red murderers at the same time.

It was more than two weeks after the massacre, which occurred early in January, before the news reached Taos, and two or three days later, before the soldiers got ready to go in pursuit of the Indians.

As was always the case when an expedition of this kind was planned, the services of the mountain men were in demand.

" Kit " Carson, Joaquin Leroux, " Tom " Tobin, and myself, along with several others who had been in the country a long time, and who had had a good deal of experience in Indian fighting, volunteered to go with Colonel Greer.

It was midwinter, the snow being a foot deep or more on the ground, and it was intensely cold. We knew that the trip would be a hard one, but that was not to be taken into consideration, when women and children were to be saved from the miserable fate which we knew always awaited them, when they had been carried away by these savages.

We started out with five companies of cavalry and went direct to Whetstone Springs, because we had no knowledge of the whereabouts of the Indians at that time, and could only gain that information by striking and following their trail.

That we should have expected to be able to follow a trail nearly three weeks old, will seem somewhat strange to persons who have never had any experience in that kind of business, but that was one of the things which a mountain man had to learn.

When we struck a trail, and had followed it for a little distance, we could always tell about how much time had elapsed since it was made.

Where we could discover the footprints, of course it was easy to tell what kind of track it was, and in which way the person or animal making it was traveling. We could tell the difference between the track of an Indian and that of a white hunter, because, although both always wore moccasins, the moccasins differed in shape. In the same way we could pretty generally distinguish the tracks made by Indians of one tribe, from those made by Indians of another tribe. Here and there, too, they would always drop an arrow,—because only a small proportion of them had guns,—and we could tell from the marks on these arrows what tribe the Indian belonged to who lost it. No two tribes made and marked their arrows exactly alike, and I used to hear the Indians say that each individual Indian could identify his own arrows, among those picked up on a battlefield.

In following a trail, where there were no well defined footprints, by looking ahead of us, we could
discover, now and then, a stone rolled out of place, a
bush or twig broken off, or the grass bent over, and
this indicated to us the direction taken by whatever
we were following.

The fact that considerable snow had fallen, after
the Utes left Whetstone Springs, made following
their trail unusually difficult. It happened, however, that there was no snow of consequence about
the springs, and this enabled us to see which way
the Indians had started out. It was evident that
they had gone down the cañon of the Canadian River,
or Red River it is sometimes called at this point,
and we followed them in that direction. Striking
the Canadian River proper, further down, we traced
them down the stream, until we had traveled nearly
four hundred miles.

I began to think then that we were getting close
to the red skins. There was nothing about the trail
to indicate this, and I suspect nobody but mountain
men or those who had had similar experiences,
would have reached that conclusion.

It was the flight of the ravens, which led me to
believe that we were nearing the hostiles, of whom
we were in pursuit. The direction of their flight indicated the location of a camp, where they could find
the carcasses of dead animals to feed on, and the

time of their flight in the afternoon, indicated the distance of the camp from us. When they passed over us, we calculated about how far they would fly before night fall, and my conclusions were that the Utes were not more than a days march distant from where we had gone into camp for the night.

We did not reach them the next day, but early on the morning following, we came in sight of two Indians driving up a band of horses. Then we knew that we must be very near their village, and soon located it in a grove of large cottonwood trees, on the banks of the river.

The Indians had not seen us, and we prepared to give them a surprise. We dismounted, and stripping off our overcoats, tied them behind our saddles and put everything in readiness for a fight.

The plan of attack which Colonel Greer had decided upon, was to charge into the village, giving the Indians no time to either mount their horses and escape, or obtain any vantage ground from which to fight.

The order to advance was given, and we started on a double quick toward the village.

When we had gotten within two hundred yards of it, and could see the startled aud surprised Indians dodging about among their lodges, one of the strangest ideas that ever entered the head of a commanding officer, who was about to engage an Indian

or any other enemy, suggested itself to Colonel
Greer.

What occurred to him was, that there should be a
parley before there was a fight, and he ordered a halt
for that purpose.

A storm of protests, coming not only from the little band of mountain men, who saw before them an
opportunity to practically annihilate the murderous
band of Utes, but from the subordinate officers of the
command, as well, greeted this remarkable order.
" Kit " Carson swore, and Joaquin Leroux, whose
French blood was up, railed at the Colonel in broken
English, and for a moment it looked as though the
battle would open with mutiny in our own ranks.

A delay of ten or fifteen minutes followed, and
while the soft hearted colonel was trying to convince
his subordinates that his course was a proper one, a
bullet struck him in the breast, but, as it happened,
a suspender buckle changed its course, and he was
not seriously wounded.

When the Indians opened fire on us, without waiting for any further orders, and disregarding the one
which had been issued, the troops dashed forward to
complete the charge, which had been so unexpectedly
checked.

That little delay had, however, been fatal to our
plan of capturing or annihilating the band of Indians,
and also to the prime object of our expedition, the rescue of Mrs. White.

It had given the Indians time to hide their women and children, to mount their horses and gallop down the cañon, or up the steep hill sides, into retreats to which we could not follow them, and worst of all, it had given them time to murder poor Mrs. White, when those who sought to rescue her, were within hailing distance.

When we rode into the village, which was almost deserted, we found her body still warm, and drew from her breast three arrows which had pierced her ʰeart.

Had the charge been made as originally contemplated, the savages would have had no time for this last act of fiendishness, and we should have saved the life of an estimable woman. Some of us would most likely have been killed to be sure, but we were there to fight and to take the chances on losing our lives.

What became of the child and its nurse we never knew. We could find no trace of them in the Indian village, nor did we discover anything to indicate that they had been killed while on the road to this point, or carried away by the Indians in their hasty flight.

While the mistake which we had made, or rather which our commanding officer had made, proved so serious a blunder, it did not enable all the Indians to escape. Some of them undertook to cross the Canadian River on the ice, and these were nearly all

killed.   Other small parties and stragglers met the
same fate, so that altogether, eighty or eighty-five
Indians were killed in the fight.

A pursuit of the scattered survivors of the band,
would have been unavailing, and after the fight was
over, we turned back, and returned by way of old
Fort Union to Taos.

Not long after I returned from this expedition, I
was called upon to act as guide to a company of
soldiers, sent out from Taos to rescue a party, of
which L. B. Maxwell was the most prominent
member.

Maxwell had left Taos two or three weeks earlier,
going up the Rio Grande, to gather up a band of
horses for government service.

He had succeeded in getting something like a
hundred horses, and was on his way back to Taos,
when he struck the trail of a large band of Utes.

To avoid this band, he turned down the Arkansas
River, and went one hundred and fifty miles out of
his way, intending to go over the mountains and
come into Taos from the east.   Whether the same
band of Utes that he had seen, turned back and followed him, or whether it was another band which
attacked him, is uncertain, but when he was within
two or three days ride of Taos, he had one of the
bloodiest battles with these Indians, that any of the
mountain men ever had.

There were twelve men in the party, including Maxwell himself, and they had with them two children, whom he was taking from one of the upper Rio Grande settlements to their friends in Taos.

While they were taking their breakfast in camp one morning, the Indians suddenly made their appearance, and in less time than it takes to tell it, had stampeded and driven off their horses. While a portion of the band was stealing the horses, thirty or forty mounted warriors rode up and fired on Maxwell and his party, killing one and mortally wounding another of his men. It happened that there was a small grove of trees not far from their camp, and hurriedly getting under cover of these trees, they determined to fight as long as there was a man of them left.

In that position they defended themselves against the whole band of red-skins, until the latter tired of the fight and withdrew. Then they found themselves in a sorry plight. All but two of them had been wounded, some very seriously.

They had no horses, and were a long way, not only from home, but from any white settlement. They could not stay where they were, however, and that night they set out under cover of the darkness to walk to Taos.

Traveling in this way by night, and hiding in day light, without food, and suffering at the same time from hunger and numerous festering wounds, they reached the point where we met them, about thirty miles east of Taos.

We had heard, through a friendly Arapahoe Indian, of their fight with the Utes, and knew that they were making their way toward home under great difficulties, but we had not expected to find them in so pitiable a condition as they were.

Some had lost nearly all their clothing in crawling through the thick growths of underbrush, all had been so much weakened by starvation, that they could scarcely stand on their feet, and their undressed wounds were in a fearful condition.

They had almost given up the struggle to reach home, when we found them, and several of those who were most seriously wounded were begging their more fortunate comrades, to leave them to die where they were, and take care of themselves.

I shall never forget how the tears ran down the cheeks of those poor fellows, when they caught sight of us, and realized that they were saved, just when they were about to give up all hope.

We dressed their wounds as well as we could, and carried them into Taos, where with careful nursing they all recovered in time.

The two children fell into the hands of the Utes, and were carried away. We got track of them, however, not long afterward, and the Indians made a proposition to return them for a certain consideration. This was their usual custom when they made a raid on the early settlers. Small children, if there were not too many of them, were usually taken prisoners. If the friends of the children could not be persuaded to ransom them, the little ones would sometimes grow up with the savages, and soon forgetting all about their early associations, they became as wild as the Indian children themselves.

The two children of whom I have spoken were promptly returned, however, when we counted out, and paid to the Ute chief by whom they were held, two hundred and fifty Mexican dollars."

CHAPTER XIV.

A CAMPAIGN AGAINST THE NAVAJOS.

"The Utes were not the only Indians to give us trouble at that time.

We had hardly gotten back from our campaign against them, when there was a demand for the services of the soldiers in another quarter.

MEXICAN WOOD CARRIERS.

The Navajos, as I have said, were the most industrious of all the Indian tribes. At the same time, I suppose I should have said that they were the greatest lot of thieves among the Indians. They had gotten an idea of stock raising, and as their flocks and herds did not grow fast enough to suit them, they added to the number of their horses, cattle, and sheep, by stealing what they wanted from the Mexicans. Like almost every other band of robbers, they committed other depredations and outrages in addition to stealing. They had not only taken a great many horses and sheep from the Mexicans, but had been guilty of some very atrocious murders, and had carried away several Mexican women and children as prisoners.

General Kearney had promised the Mexicans, in the name of the government of the United States, that they should be protected against the hostile Indians, and when an appeal for that protection came from those who were loyal, it had to be given the same attention that would have been given to the same request coming from Americans.

Colonel Newby was then at Santa Fe with a small force of soldiers, and he left there in March of 1848, with six companies, to whip the Navajos into better behavior, three of the companies, under command of Major Runnells, having been sent from Taos to join the expedition.

I joined that expedition as a guide, and put in about four months more in the service of the government.

We crossed the Rio Grande at San Felipe, and from there marched to Jemez. Then we proceeded in a southwesterly direction, striking the Rio Puerco, and crossing over into Arizona. It was while we were going down the Rio Puerco, which by the way means "dirty river," and it is well named, that I saw for the second time those famous old ruins of stone buildings, which I think are marked on the map as " Ruins Leroux."

Leroux was the Frenchman of whom I have spoken in connection with our campaign against the Utes. He accompanied us on this expedition, and I suppose must have gotten credit for having discovered these remarkable ruins, and had them named after him, although they had been seen by hundreds of white men long before that time.

I have never yet heard of any tradition, or read anything, which gave a very satisfactory explanation of the origin of these buildings. The Navajos, who have claimed and lived in the country, for I don't know how long, certainly know nothing about the people who built them or the purpose for which they were built. When asked about the ruins, the Indians say they have always been there, and seem to think they were built at the same time the world was made. One thing is certain, and that is they were built by people who thoroughly understood stone cutting and masonry. Both granite and sandstone were used in the construction, and some of the blocks of stone which have been placed in the walls would weigh, I should think, a dozen tons. The buildings are several stories high and very large, the style of architecture being similar to that of the adobe buildings put up by the Pueblo Indians, although in no other respect are they at all alike. A small party of us, ventured into the old ruins, and found rooms which had apparently been as well finished as those of the average modern residence.

I leave you to hunt up the history of these ruins, if they have any, or build up your own theory of their origin, if you can find nothing authentic about them in history, because, like the Indians, I can only tell you that they are there and how they look. Anyhow I didn't start out to talk about ruins, but about a war with the Navajos.

We didn't see any of the hostiles until we had gotten some distance away from the Rio Puerco. I was riding along one afternoon, a mile or two ahead of the soldiers, when all at once I caught sight of four Indians. They did not see me and I rode back a little distance, and waited until Colonel Newby came up. I told the Colonel what I had seen, and assured him that the four Indians belonged to a large band not far away. I pointed out to him the place where I thought we should find them, and advised him to halt his command and remain where he was until dark, when we could make a quick march, and take the Indians so much by surprise, that they would have no time to get away with their horses and other stock. If we captured their stock it would be easy to compel them to make restitution to the Mexicans who had been robbed, and this was one of the objects of the expedition.

13

It seemed to be a custom of some of the military officers we had in the country in those days, however, to employ guides, when they started out on an expedition, and pay no attention to their suggestions after they got started. When we were employed to find Indians we always found them, and then, knowing the character and habits of the savages as we did, we did not think it impertinent, now and then, to volunteer a little advice, as to the best method of affecting their capture or encompassing their defeat, and I can tell you that we always knew pretty near what we were talking about. Colonel Newby was one of those officers who didn't think that a mountain man's experience as an Indian fighter, was worth anything, and when I suggested that we should wait until night before marching against the Navajos, he very promptly squelched me as a military adviser, by ordering a forward movement at once. Before we had gone half a mile, we passed into an open space on high ground, and the four Indians I had seen, caught sight of us.

Away they galloped, and a few minutes later a slender column of smoke, shot up from a brush covered elevation, to warn the band, which we had not yet seen, of the approach of danger.

That was just what I had expected, and it was not long before a cloud of dust in the valley below, told us that the signal had been observed, and that our enemy was on the move. This was one of the things which always made it difficult to follow Indians in the mountains. I mean their system of signaling to each other. They knew the country so well that they had scores of what you might call signal stations. These stations were elevated points, from which a column of smoke in the day time, or a fire at night, could be seen over a large area of country. They had a way of sending the smoke up in puffs, and making their fires blaze up at intervals, which communicated any information they desired to communicate to each other, as satisfactortly as any code of signals ever devised.

It took us some time to get down to where the Navajos had been encamped, and when we got there, not an Indian or anything belonging to an Indian, which he cared to carry away, was in sight.

Of course we could see which way they had gone, but with jaded and worn out government horses, as I looked at the thing, we stood about as good a chance of overtaking them, as a bull pup would stand of catching a greyhound, in a race in which the greyhound had two or three hours the start.

Nevertheless Major Runnells was ordered to push forward with a detachment of troops, in pursuit of the Indians, and I was directed to go with him. Colonel Newby was to march to a point where I had informed him there was a spring, to go into camp for the night, and Major Runnells was ordered to return to that point, to rejoin the balance of the command, in case he did not overtake the Navajos before nightfall.

Well of course we didn't overtake them, but it was eleven o'clock at night when we got into camp. The camping ground was in a small valley which was surrounded by high bluffs. Before we reached there we heard firing, and I knew the Indians had gotten up on the bluffs and were shooting into the camp. We didn't much like the idea of riding in under fire, and so we moved along cautiously until we were within a short distance of camp, and then commenced shooting off our guns. At the same time we raised a yell and went in on a run, the Indians scattering as we approached, without firing at us.

They returned in a little while, however, and again commenced shooting into camp. No particular harm was being done, as we were well protected by over-hanging rocks, but the fire was annoying, and Colonel Newby, after a time, got exceedingly nervous, and ordered out a company or two of soldiers, and the fire was returned. The Indians fell back, and retreated in the direction in which the main band had gone, and the troops followed them.

Early the next morning a courier came in to inform us that they had fourteen Indians in their camp, a few miles distant. The Indians, it was said, wanted to hold a pow-wow, and were ready to make peace.

What seemed to me a very suspicious circumstance, however, was the fact reported by the messenger, that the Indians had come into camp with their guns, and still had possession of them.

We started for the front, but before we got there the rattle of musketry informed us that a battle, and not a peace pow-wow was going on.   Colonel Newby, who had ridden on ahead of us, had made a mistake which precipitated hostilities.   Instead of coming to an understanding with the Indians, and inducing them to lay down their arms voluntarily, at the same time that the soldiers laid down theirs, which was always a preliminary to a peace conference, he ordered his soldiers to disarm them.   This caused the Indians to believe that they were to be taken prisoners, or perhaps killed, and the fight commenced.

All but two of them got away.   One of these was killed and the other taken prisoner.   The other twelve retreated and we followed them, but as they had splendid horses, all but two soon left us a good ways in the rear.   I could see those two Indians, some distance behind the others.   One appeared to be badly wounded and the other was trying to aid him in making his escape.   Finally the wounded Indian was left alone and disappeared.   I knew about where he was and by and by caught sight of him. He had the appearance of being dead, but when I looked at him closely, I noticed that he had a bunch of arrows and his bow in his hand. Major Runnells had seen him also, and at the head of a party of six men, I being one of them, rode toward him. I called out to the major to be on his guard, but thinking the Indian dead, he paid no attention to my warning. We were riding single file, and as I was satisfied the Indian was alive, and would not be taken prisoner, I threw my foot out of the stirrup, so that I could instantly dismount, if he made a hostile movement. He lay perfectly quiet until we were within a few yards of him, and then, scarcely changing his position, I saw him bend his bow.

I threw myself off my horse on the opposite side from him, and the others followed my example. As I was the first man on the ground, the Indian very naturally expected me to be the first to shoot, and directed his arrow toward me. My horse got frightened, and as I had to hold on to him, before I could raise my gun to shoot, fourteen arrows whistled past my head, and I tell you some of them came awful close to it. Some of the other members of the party shot at the Indian but missed him, and it was not until I sent a bullet through his head that he dropped his bow and arrows.

I have often wondered how all those arrows happened to miss me, and I still credit it to my good luck, which in those days never failed me.

On the day after that, I think it was, I saw two Indians not far ahead of us, and Colonel Newby expressed a desire to have them come into camp for a conference. I told him if he would stop his command and allow me to go ahead, remaining where he was, until I should signal him to advance, I thought I could get to talk with them. He agreed to this and called a halt. I rode forward three or four hundred yards where the Indians could see me plainly, and dismounted. Then I held up my gun and other arms and dropped them on the ground.

This signified that I wanted a peace pow-wow, and the Indians understood it. They both had guns, which they laid aside, and advanced to meet me. We came together at a point about midway between those from which we had started, and sat down together.

I smoked the pipe of peace with them, and then explained to them that the representative of the Great Father at Washington, had come out to punish them for their stealing and other depredations, but that he was willing to make peace with them, if they would promise to behave better in the future.

They were very distrustful of Colonel Newby, but finally consented to talk with him. I signaled him then and he came up to where we were. A long pow-wow followed, of which the result was, that they promised to bring their band into camp, to turn over

to us three thousand sheep, in lieu of those which
had been stolen, and all Mexican captives.

Having completed this arrangement, we turned
back and camped at Cow Springs to wait for the Indians to come in.

We remained there twenty-seven days, and got so
short of supplies that each man's ration was two
ounces of pork and three ounces of flour per day.
It was in a barren country, where there was no game,
and as the only thing we found to add to our rations
was a few wild potatoes, we had mighty slim living.
Some of the Indians would come in every day or two to
report that they could not get together as many sheep
as the Great Father demanded of them, and ask for
more time and a modification of terms.   Finally, on
the twenty-seventh day, they all came in with something less than a hundred old rams, which they
turned over to us, and that was all the sheep we got.
They also brought in five Mexican children and the
treaty of peace was signed.

The next day we broke camp and started for Taos,
Major Runnells with a portion of the command going
ahead under my guidance.

We made our way to the San Juan River, and
then followed it up to where the Rio Chueco and the
San Juan come together.   There we crossed the
river, passed by the present sight of Fort Lowell,
and proceeded toward Abiquiu.

About half of the sheep which we had taken from the Indians, had been allotted to our party, and it was not long before they had been butchered, and not long after they were butchered before they had been eaten up. Then we were out of meat again, and in fact had very little of anything to eat. The day after we left the San Juan River, I rode ahead of the soldiers to see if I could not find some game. I killed a couple of deer, without much trouble, and was about to ride on after another one, when I heard a growl behind me, and looking around, saw a big "grizzly" about to take possession of my first deer.

It was no part of my business to kill deer for "grizzlies," and I wanted some bear meat anyhow, so I just laid the "grizzly" out alongside of the deer. The next morning I killed another bear, and this supply of meat had to last us a couple of days.

Major Runnells then directed me to go on to Abiquiu, and make arrangements to give the men a good feed there. Abiquiu is about forty miles from Taos, on the opposite side of the Rio Grande, near Ojo Caliente Springs. I knew if we reached so small a place, without making some preparations for securing provisions in advance, it would be impossible for us to get anything like the amount of supplies required to feed our men and horses.

I reached Abiquiu a day in advance of the troops, and soon found a man who agreed to have a supply

of bread ready by the time they came up. In addition to this I wanted meat for the men, and some kind
of grain for the horses.

MEXICAN BREAD MAKERS.

The only man in the
village who had any stock
or grain was a Mexican
padre, who had half a
dozen hogs and a big
granary full of corn.
This old fellow was an
unreconstructed native,
who cordially hated *Los
Americanos,* and when I
approached him on the
subject, refused to furnish
the desired supplies,
either for love or money. I did not press the
matter, because I knew very well that we should get
what we wanted when the troops came up, although I
should have preferred an amicable arrangement to
force of arms proceedings.

When Major Runnells came up next day, I
showed him my stock of bread, and then told him I
had corn and hogs, but it would require a detail of
soldiers to get possession of the meat and horse feed.
He gave me thirty men, and it didn't take us long
to convince the old *padre* that he had made a mistake in refusing to do business with me.

From Abiquiu we made the march to the Cienega, where we had to swim the Rio Grande. The men who couldn't swim, tied knots in their horses tails, and holding onto them, were taken across in that way.

We had expected to reach our destination before night fall, but crossing the river delayed us and we had to go into camp some miles out from Taos.

The soldiers had breakfasted at Abiquiu early in the morning, and when they got through with that meal, they had cleaned up about everything in the way of eatables in the town. Nothing was left to carry away, and the prospect was when we started out, that we should get nothing to eat until we reached Taos.

After marching all day without anything to eat, it was a hungry lot of men who began making preparations to go into camp for the night, with the prospect before them of another twelve hour fast, but before much grumbling had been done, I succeeded in providing a sumptuous repast compared with what we had been living on most of the time, since we started out on this campaign.

I saw a flock of goats coming down the mountain side, and suggested to Major Runnells that we appropriate to our use as many as were necessary to supply the soldiers with a meal.

He at once acted on the suggestion and about
eighty of the goats were killed to appease the hunger
of his half starved command.

In a little time an aged Mexican presented himself
before the Major, and after going through innumer-
able salaams and prostrations, informed us that he
was the owner of the goats, and that as they were
the only property he had, we had taken away his
only means of supporting his family.   The Major
informed him that he had only to present a claim in
proper form, and he would receive pay for his property.   This the old fellow did a day or two later,
and when he left the camp with the money to which
he was entitled in his pocket, he had no ill feeling
toward *Los Americanos.*

We reached Taos on the morning of the fourth of
July, where we learned that the treaty of Guadalupe
Hidalgo had been signed, and a peace concluded
with Mexico.   News traveled slowly in those days,
and although this treaty had been signed early in
February, we had not heard of it when our expedition started out in March.   We celebrated the event
that day in old fashioned style, and the soldiers
wound up their long campaign, by taking " a day
off " along with all the other Americans in the
country.

COL. CERAN ST. VRAIN.

CHAPTER XV.

DULL TIMES ON THE FRONTIER.

" We had dull times on the frontier for two or three years after the Mexican war, and we felt it particularly at Taos. The soldiers were all moved away from there with the exception of one or two companies. Money began to get scarce; that is, it was scarce in comparison with the amount which had been in circulation for several years prior to that time.

I don't suppose there ever was a place, outside of a bonanza mining camp, where a lot of frontiersmen got hold of more money, or spent it more recklessly, than at this old town of Fernandez de Taos, from 1840 to 1848.

I have seen men stand in the door of one of the old time resorts there, with their hands full of silver coin, and throw hundreds of dollars into the streets, just to see the Mexican urchins scramble after them.

About that time we heard of the gold discoveries in California, and quite a number of those who had gotten as far west as New Mexico, concluded to go on to the Pacific Coast. I was married then, and had settled down at Taos, or I expect I should have started out with the rest of the gold hunters, because

it promised to be just such a life of adventure as I
had learned to like.

As it was, however, I only had a mild attack of the
gold fever, and instead of going to California, I concluded to make a search for some of the famous old
Spanish mines we were always hearing so much
about, in New Mexico and Colorado.

Both the Mexicans and Indians used to talk about
marvelously rich mines in certain localities, but as a
rule they did not claim to know the real location of
such mines.

The same stories that were told to us forty years
ago, of lost mines, which were fabulously rich, have
been handed down to the present time, and every
once in a while we hear of a party of adventurous
miners, going in search of one of these mines.

They are always disappointed, just as we used to
be, and I reached the conclusion, long ago, that the
traditionary " rich diggins " of the Mexicans and
Pueblo Indians, would be considered very poor paying properties now a-days.

In the Sandia Mountains of New Mexico, for instance, I heard of a rich, abandoned mine, which the
natives called the " Devil's Palace," believing it to
be haunted. The stories that I heard of this mine
raised my expectations to the highest pitch. It
seemed to me that if what I heard was true, there

must be a vast amount of treasure hidden away in the dark recesses of the " Devil's Palace."

I was shown the entrance to the mine, but at the same time was cautioned by the Mexicans who acted as my guides, not to venture into it.

I had never had any fear of " spooks," however, and notwithstanding their protests, I went into the mine, with one or two companions, and explored it thoroughly.

What I found was a cave, or pocket, from which a considerable amount of lead ore had at some time been taken, and the bones of three or four miners, who had probably been crushed to death by falling rock. That was all there was in the " haunted palace," which the natives supposed contained more hidden wealth than King Solomon's mines.

At the time this lead ore was taken out, it brought a good price, and was probably looked upon as a " rich find," but at the time I was there, it would not have paid the cost of mining and transportation.

Hunting these old mines has always been about as unprofitable as " chasing a rainbow," and every time we entered the abandoned treasure houses, we were a good deal more likely to find a den of wild animals than gold or silver. I never saw enough of the precious metals to make my eyes sparkle, but in one of the mines of the Sandias, I caught sight of the fiery eye-balls, and heard enough of the growling of some kind of an ugly wild beast, to make my hair stand on end.

One of the old Spanish mines, from which, according to Indian tradition, a fabulous amount of gold had been taken, was said to be somewhere in the neighborhood of the Pueblo de Taos.

The Indians claimed they knew the exact location of this mine, and one of them finally agreed, for a consideration of three hundred dollars, to show some of us where it was. The night before the party to receive the much desired information, was to start out for the Eldorado, the Indian was murdered. We never knew who killed him. All we could ever learn was that he was found dead, and his secret, if he really knew anything about the gold mine, died with him. Our supposition was, that the Indians killed him to prevent him from telling the " white men " what he knew.

After that, those Indians who professed to know anything about the mine, refused to talk about it, and its location is still a secret. I fitted out one or two parties after that, to look for " old diggings " of this kind, but never made any discoveries which paid me for the outlay of time and money.

At one time when coming through the Sangre de Christo Pass, with a small party of prospectors, I came near running into an Apache ambuscade, where my career as a gold hunter would have been very suddenly cut short, had I not discovered the presence of the Indians in the nick of time.   I always made it a point, never to ride into any place which looked like a good hiding place for the savages, without taking a careful survey of the situation in advance.

That was what I did when we were about to enter a narrow defile in the Sangre de Christo, and a quick sharp eye, which has, no doubt, saved my scalp a good many times, enabled me to discover an Apache, lying flat on the rocks above us, so close to the road we should have taken in going through the pass, that we should have been powder-burned when they fired on us.

I could only see the one Indian,—although I knew there were more of them—and he had covered himself with dust and looked so much like a rock, that I think nine out of ten of the mountain men even, would have passed along without noticing him.

I didn't know how many Indians a shot would scare out, but I knew that the one I saw would be a dead one, and so I raised my gun and fired.   At the crack of my rifle he sprang up, but only to tumble over, as dead as Julius Caesar, a second later.

At the same instant the very rocks seemed to turn into Indians, and they jumped out of a score of places, where we could see no sign of them before. My party commenced firing on them then and the

14

Indians ran. They did not stop until they got out of reach of our guns, and we passed along in safety.

At another time we were prospecting along the Rio Grande del Norte, in the mountains bordering on San Luis Valley. One day we saw what looked to us like a band of Elk, down in the valley, on the opposite side of the river, from where we were. I suggested to a companion that we should ride down to where they were and kill a couple of them, as we were in need of meat.

We started, and had ridden, perhaps half the distance to where the elk were moving about, when they began to look rather queer to me. Just about this time we had to cross a deep ravine, and there we saw a band of Indian ponies, without their riders. We looked at the band of elk again, and made up our minds that there were Indians under the Elk skins, and that we had gotten altogether too close to them.

We turned back, and had barely gotten started towards our own camp, when just as we had surmised, the harmless looking elk turned out to be Ute Indians. They threw off their disguises, and running to their horses started in pursuit of us.

We had a pretty good start of them, and crossed the river before they reached it.

When we got up on the high ground, we were in a good position for fight, if that was what the

Indians wanted. We only had thirteen men, but the Utes knew, although they had a large band, that we would kill a considerable number of them while they were crossing the river. They stopped on the opposite bank, and watched us some time, but finally turned back and left us to make our way out of the country without molestation. We only waited until nightfall, however, to abandon prospecting in that section.

In the winter of 1849–50 I did the only trading I ever did with the Comanches. I got enough of it, too, and if I had kept on trading with Indians all my life, I should never have had anything to do with these treacherous scoundrels again, as the risk was entirely too great, even for a man who liked adventure as well as I did.

The Comanches never had even that small sense of honor which characterized the average Western Indian. They never made a pledge or promise of any kind for which they had any regard whatever. When they made peace it was always for a purpose. It was either to save their lives when whipped and cornered, or to obtain something which they stood in need of, and every such peace was made to be broken at the very first opportunity which presented itself.

It was at their request that we started out on the trip I am going to tell you about. Two or three of them came into Bent's Fort, and told us that they had a lot of buffalo robes and buck skins and wanted us to come out and trade with them. They agreed to make peace, and we were to meet them down on the Canadian River some time later.

I took twelve or fifteen men and two wagon loads of goods, and went down to the old adobe fort, the walls of which are still standing, on the Canadian River. Few people know, however, how it happened to be built. It was put up for the firm of Bent & St. Vrain, who at one time contemplated establishing a trading post there.

It was some time after we reached the fort that the Indians came in, and we were kept down there pretty much all winter, getting through with our trading.

The first thing of course was to make peace. This was arranged at a pow-wow at which we went through the usual ceremonies, and then made the Indians an unusually large number of presents. As I remember it now, we had to give them something like seven or eight hundred dollars worth of trinkets of various kinds, and some things which were not exactly trinkets, before they appeared to be satisfied that we would deal with them fairly and generously.

Among other things that they insisted on having, were some of our guns, and a considerable amount of amunition. Of course we expected to trade these things, but would very much have preferred to deliver the goods, just on the eve of our departure, because we did not feel by any means sure, that we were not furnishing them weapons with which to take our own lives.

The bulk of the presents which changed hands, came from us, the Comanches giving us in return a few ponies, of perhaps one-twentieth the value of the goods which they received from us.

We would not agree to go to their village, as we were in the habit of doing with other Indians, but stipulated that they should bring their peltry to the fort, and that the trading should be done there.

They went away after their robes and buckskins, and after awhile a big band of them came back. They were naturally so quarrelsome, ill-tempered and treacherous, that we anticipated trouble, if we allowed any considerable number of them to stay about where the trading was carried on. To make the busines as safe as possible, we shut ourselves up in the fort, laid out our goods, and then admitted two or three Indians at a time. When these had gotten through with their trading, others were admitted and disposed of in the same way.

Some of these goods we passed out through a hole in the wall, about as big as the ticket window in a railway station, and took in the robes and deer skins the same way. The Indians who had to remain outside were not pleased with being kept at a distance, and in order to impress upon us that fact, they would get off some distance and shoot at our general delivery window. Then we would have to suspend operations until the old chief and others who were responsible for the good behavior of their band, would get out and put a stop to the hostilities.

The tendency of such little episodes as this, was to make one feel nervous, and I assure you there was no one in the party who wanted to make a steady business of trading with the Comanches. We all liked excitement, but we didn't like it in quite that form.

From a business standpoint we got along well enough, because when we got through trading, and started home, we loaded twelve old-fashioned Pennsylvania wagons with robes and buckskins, which we had received in exchange for the goods we took out with us. We got away safely and reached home without having to do any fighting, although I have often wondered since, how we happened to have such good luck. There were very few frontiersmen who ever went among the Comanches for any purpose other than to fight, and all things considered, that was the most hazardous trading expedition I ever had anything to do with.

While I had been away from Taos a great deal of the time in 1848-49, I had built up quite a business in the merchandising line at that point, and after I got back from the Comanche country, I devoted myself mainly to this business, and to looking after my herd of cattle, which had grown to such proportions, that in those days I was something of a "cattle king."

A year later, I determined to take a trip back to St. Louis, to lay in a stock of merchandise. That was in 1851, and I had not seen the "Mound City," or been east of Independence, Missouri, since 1835. I had to go to Kansas City, either by wagon or on horseback, and from there I could go by river steamer to St. Louis.

I determined to go through on horseback, and set out with a small party, of which Colonel Greer, whose name I have mentioned in connection with a campaign against the Utes, was a member.

Going through from here to Kansas City now, on horseback, would be considered a pretty big ride, but I made the trip in a little over seven days, on a wager which I made with Colonel Greer, that I would beat him into St. Louis.

I did beat him very badly, because although he was an old army officer, and used to hard riding, his power of endurance was not so great as mine. He got laid up on the way, and I reached the end of our journey nearly two weeks ahead of him.

When I got through purchasing goods in St. Louis, it was a month or two before I could get them shipped, on account of low water in the Missouri River. I finally got started, however, and got up to Westport.

I had left my horses there, and had intended to stop several days to look after unloading my goods from the boat, and loading them on the freight wagons which were to carry them across the plains.

I changed my mind though, when I got there, and only stopped long enough to settle my bills and make contracts to have my goods forwarded after me to Taos.

My exit from Westport was very unexpectedly expedited, and I will tell you how it happened, just to show you that while I was a pretty good Indian fighter, and didn't run from anything we found in the mountains, I could be as big a coward as anybody sometimes.

The cholera broke out in the town, just about the time we arrived there, and as soon as I found out about it, I began to feel sick. There was no business important enough to keep me there long after that. After escaping all the dangers of fifteen years spent among the savages, I didn't want to be carried off by an epidemic disease, the first time I crossed the border line of civilization. So I just ordered out my horses and put about a hundred and fifty miles between me and Westport within the nexty forty hours. What I wanted was to get to the Rocky Mountains. I knew there wouldn't be any cholera there."

BRINGING CHIEF UNCOTASH TO TERMS.

CHAPTER XVI.

" Reports which reached us from California in 1852, induced me to make a trip to the Pacific coast.

I did not go as a gold-hunter, or at least not for the purpose of digging gold out of the ground, but planned a trading trip which I thought was certain to be profitable, provided I succeeded in getting through with it.

Thousands of people had flocked to California, and hundreds of thousands of dollars were being taken out of the mines. There was plenty of money in the country, or rather plenty of gold dust and nuggets, but there was a great scarcity of provisions of all kinds. Beef and mutton were particularly in demand, and cattle and sheep commanded prices which were almost fabulously high.

In New Mexico, where the Mexicans had large flocks, fine sheep could be bought, at about one-tenth of the price per head they were reported to be selling for in California, and it looked to me as though a handsome fortune might be realized as profit, on a large band of sheep driven through and disposed of at Sacramento or some other point on the coast.

Up to that time nothing of the kind had been attempted, but I thought the scheme a practicable one, and determined to try it.

I knew it meant sixteen hundred miles of travel over mountain ranges, across barren plains and still more barren deserts, and in addition to this I knew that there was scarcely a mile of the road which was not beset by savages, who were making it their principal business to rob and murder a white man or band of white men, whenever opportunity offered. I did not think the undertaking more hazardous, however, than others in which I had engaged, and I began making my arrangements to set out on the trip.

In the neighborhood of Watrous, New Mexico, I gathered together nine thousand head of sheep. They were driven through to Taos for me, where I supplied myself with everything that I thought would be necessary for the trip, got together the men who were to accompany me, said good bye to my family and started out.

I carried with me about one thousand dollars worth of supplies, which consisted mainly of flour, coffee, dried meat and amunition. My equipment was pretty much the same that it would have been if I had been going out on a long trapping expedition. All our supplies were loaded on pack mules. We took no horses with us, believing that mules would serve our purpose better.

I had with me when I started out, twenty-two men in all, fourteen of them being Mexican sheep herders, and the others Americans. I did not find it an easy matter to secure the kind of men I should have liked to have had accompany me on this trip. It was a different lot of men entirely from those I had usually had with me on hunting and trapping trips. On those trips my associates had almost always been men, who had demonstrated in many an Indian fight, that they did not lack either nerve or judgment, who never lost their heads in the presence of danger, feared nothing so much as being looked upon as cowards, knew what their guns were made for, and never failed to use them to the best advantage when there was occasion for it. The eight Americans who started for California with me were discharged soldiers and teamsters, whom I had found at Taos, and I knew nothing of their fighting qualities, and very little about their general trustworthiness. I had to pick up such men as I could find, however, and take the chances of their failing me at a critical moment, or perhaps planning murder and robbery on their own account.

I relied mainly upon the Americans to protect my property as well as our lives, and expected the Mexicans to look after and drive the sheep.

I armed each of the men, Americans and Mexicans alike, with a first-class rifle, a pistol, and knife, and

thus equipped we started on our long drive, on the
24th of June, 1852.

I had been over the greater part of the route I expected to take, before, and although there was no
such thing as a road or trail even, in some places, I
did not expect to have much difficulty in finding the
shortest and most available path to the Pacific Coast.

GREEN RIVER SCENERY.

Starting up the Rio Grande del Norte from Taos,
we followed it nearly to its source, and then turning
westward, crossed the divide. We had much difficulty in traveling the next two or three hundred
miles, and made slow progress, on account of high
water in the streams. Every river, creek, and it
seemed to me every arroyo was bank full of water,
the result of snow melting in the mountains. We

had to swim the sheep across all the larger streams, and then swim across ourselves. In crossing a few of them, such as Grand River, the Uncompahgre, Gunnison River, and Green River, we had to construct rafts on which to carry our provisions across.

It was just before we reached the Uncompahgre River, that we had our first trouble with the Indians. I knew that the Utes claimed all the territory through which we were passing, and intended to embrace the first opportunity to make peace, after the usual style, and obtain formal permission to go through their country. Instead, however, of coming to me, they made their presence known by attempting to steal my sheep, when we were in camp at night. My custom was to keep four men on guard all the time when in camp, each night being divided into four watches. We first kindled our camp fire, and then gathered the stock around us, so that the four men who stood guard did not have to patrol a very large area. The Indians crept up on us, and made an effort to stampede our pack animals as well as the sheep, but fortunately for us, they failed in the attempt, the guards discovering and frightening them away.

The next day they showed themselves, and demanded that we should compensate them for driving our stock through their country, before going any further. " Uncotash," the chief who acted as spokesman for the band, and made the demand, was very insolent in his manner of approaching me, but I paid no attention to this, and told him that when we reached the river, we would go into camp for the night, and that we should then have time to hold a pow-wow and make everything satisfactory to him.

I sent two or three of my men on ahead with him to the camping place, but before they reached it they began to get afraid of the Indians and made an excuse to leave them and come back where I was. This led the Indians to believe that it was not our intention to carry out the agreement I had made with them, and the first thing I knew, "Uncotash" and a hundred or more of his followers, came galloping back acting in a very warlike manner. At the same time that the old chief, with several other Indians, rode up beside me, I noticed that his band divided into small squads and each of these squads stopped beside one of my men.

I divined in a moment that their object was to kill or capture my entire party and then drive away the stock. We were separated so that we could not have fought them to any purpose, and as a matter of fact, I had made up my mind by this time, that I had very few fighting men in my company.

I tell you it was a critical situation, and just at that time, I think an old-fashioned Mexican dollar would have bought my entire outfit.

"Uncotash" was more insolent than he had been at first, and accused me of acting in bad faith. I had never been so badly scared in my life before, but I had sense enough not to let him know it.

I tried to pacify and explain to the old heathen, but he wouldn't listen, and kept railing at me until I got mad. I forgot for a moment all about the danger of the situation, and jumped off my horse, with the intention of making his body serve as a shield, or breast-work, while I convinced the Indians that I wouldn't be bullied if I was in their power. The chief jumped from his horse at the same time, and as it happened we both fell, coming down close together. I dropped my gun in falling, and knew well enough that I had no time to pick it up.

As I attempted to rise I locked arms with the chief, and being a much more powerful man than he, I held him down, at the same instant drawing my knife and threatening to kill him if he did not at once put a stop to the hostilities.

Our position was such that it would have been impossible for any of the Indians to come to his rescue in time to save his life, although of course there would have been no chance of saving my own. Life is very sweet to an Indian, and old "Uncotash," seeing there was but one way for him to preserve his, agreed to make peace. The Indians had commenced shooting my sheep, and I made him put a stop to this, and also call his band together, leaving my men to drive the sheep.

We then walked along together about two miles, down to the banks of the Uncompahgre, where I picked out a camping ground in a place that would afford us a fair show of successful resistance, in case we were attacked during the night. I arranged the camp as usual, and then we sat down for a peace pow-wow.

It didn't take us long to come to an understanding. I was so much pleased over my own deliverance from the danger which had threatened me only two or three hours earlier in the day that I was disposed to be liberal.

I gave them several hundred dollars worth of flour, amunition, and other things I had with me, that they happened to take a fancy to, as a consideration for their "love and affection," during the brief space of time that I expected to remain in what they were pleased to call their country.

As a guarantee of their good faith they left one of their number with me during the night as a hostage, the understanding being that his life was to be forfeited if any attack was made on us. I stood guard over him myself, because I wanted him to understand that there was no chance for him to escape in case hostilities were commenced, but they made us no trouble.

In the morning we crossed the river, and saw no more of that band of Utes, nor had we any further serious trouble with other bands.

Crossing the Grand River, a little later, was a dangerous business and it took me nearly two days to accomplish it. I have not told you yet about some of the help I had on this trip. I had eight trained goats and a shepherd dog, which were worth more to me than four times the number of men would have been. The goats led the flock and the dog brought up the stragglers. Two of the goats were picked out every day to act as leaders, and they could be guided as easily as a well-trained yoke of oxen. When we had a stream to cross, the two goats were driven into the water, just as you would drive a team of horses, and they always took the sheep across safely.

At Eagle Tail River I found a little band of Utes, who had large, fine horses, accustomed to crossing the river at all stages, and I called on them to assist me in getting my provisions, clothing, blankets, etc., across.

I made a bargain with them, stipulating that they were to take my men and the packs across for so much, and gave them the goods which they were to have.

They took everything over according to agreement, while I remained behind to see that nothing

15

was left.   All the men were on the opposite side of
the stream and I was left alone with the Indians.   I
told them I was ready to go, but they hesitated about
starting, and finally told me that I hadn't paid my
own fare, but had only compensated them for carrying over my men and goods, and would have to make
a new bargain if I wanted to get across myself.

I didn't think much of that way of doing business,
but they had the advantage of me, and I commenced
looking about among the few articles I still had with
me, for something with which to pay my passage
across the stream.   I laid out a cotton shirt, half a
plug of tobacco, five charges of powder, five bullets,
and five gun caps, and this paid my way across the
river on one of their big horses.

I anticipated a quarrel with another band of Utes
that I fell in with just before reaching Salt Creek,
in Southeastern Utah, and I expect I should have
had difficulty with them, had I not taken the precaution to hold one of them as a hostage for their good
behavior.

It was very evident to me that all the Indians
looked with longing eyes upon the large band of
sheep I was driving through the country.   We had
had fine pasture for them pretty much all the time,
and they had been driven slowly, so that they had
done as much grazing as if they had been running
at large.   As a result, they were in prime condition,

and every time an Indian looked at one of those fat sheep, I thought I could see his mouth begin to water.

The band which met us as we were driving toward Salt Creek, appeared to be very friendly when they first came to us. They rode along with us nearly the whole of one day, and insisted that we should go to their village to camp that night. I understood the purpose of this apparent hospitality. I knew well enough that their object was to get us into a place where they would have an opportunity of stampeding and stealing some of my sheep during the night, if they did not contemplate a more extensive raid, and I declined to go with them.

One of the Indians was rather an old man, who appeared to have a great deal of influence with the band. He spoke good Spanish, and as I understood that language well, I had no difficulty in carrying on a conversation with him.

Their village was a short distance from the trail which we were following and when we reached the point nearest to it, the Indians reined up their horses, and arbitrarily demanded that I should turn aside and go with them. Although I had not manifested any impatience I had been very much annoyed by them all day, and this was the straw that broke the camel's back.

I informed them in very forcible and possibly somewhat profane language that I would not go to their village and that I would camp where I pleased. Then I wound up by telling them that if they didn't like what I had said, and were not suited with what I proposed to do, I would fight them if that was what they wanted.

The Spanish speaking old Indian interpreted what I had said, and it created a commotion.

They had no arms with them, but without any further parleying, they started towards the village and I supposed that meant fight.

My interpreter was about to follow the other Indians, when I caught his horse by the bridle, and gave him to understand that I proposed to take him into camp with me, and that his life would depend upon the good behavior of his band during the night. His comrades noted the fact of his detention, and stopped long enough to learn the purpose for which he was held and the conditions upon which depended his safe return to them.

They gave neither my prisoner nor myself any intimation of what they proposed to do and I think he was left in a much more unpleasant frame of mind than I was. He knew his band was anxious to attack us, and felt very certain, as I intended he should, that the moment hostilities were commenced, he would be a dead Indian. He knew that his friends understood the situation and were fully aware of his peril, but he was by no means certain that regard for his safety, would outweigh their longing for white men's scalps, and the large amount of plunder in sight.

His anxiety deepened, as he looked from time to time toward the village, which could be plainly seen from where we went into camp. The Indians seemed to be gathering up their arms and sending the women and children to a place of safety.

I was watching these proceedings with no small uneasiness myself, but I could hardly help pitying the poor old savage, who sat in my camp, showing on his countenance the alternations of hope and fear, as he contemplated the situation. He sat down to supper along with the rest of us, but his appetite failed him, and he ate but a few mouthfuls, and that under compulsion.

Before it became quite dark I could see that the Indians had quieted down, but whether this meant that they had completed their preparations for a fight, or had decided not to attack us, I was uncertain.

I doubled the guard, and then after examining my rifle and pistols carefully, to see that they were all properly loaded and primed, in the presence of the old Indian, I ordered him to lie down, taking a seat a few feet away from him on a sack of flour, with my rifle across my knees.

Of course I didn't sleep, and if my prisoner slept any that night it was very little. Every few minutes he would raise up and look about, anxiously peering into the darkness to see if he could discover any signs of Indians about the camp.

The night passed away however, without anything happening to disturb or alarm us, and in the morning my old Indian ate his breakfast with a good deal better relish than he had eaten supper. Then I told him that as his people had behaved well during the night, and had shown that they were good Indians, I would not keep him any longer. I gave him the last cotton shirt I had, a little powder, some bullets and a few gun caps, and he left me feeling about as happy as any Indian I ever saw."

CHAPTER XVII.

" After getting across Green River, with a great deal of difficulty, but without any serious mishap, we turned to the north, and crossing the Wasatch Mountains at the head of Spanish Fork, followed it down into the great Salt Lake Valley.

There we saw the first evidence of civilization we had seen since leaving Taos, and struck the first well defined trail we had had to travel over.

This was five years after the Mormons had located in the valley, and Salt Lake City had become a place of some consequence.

I camped outside the city after a hard days' travel, and rode in alone to look after supplies for the balance of the trip, because the Ute Indians had drawn so heavily on my stock of provisions that I had very little left.

When I got into the town I met " Ben." Holladay, the famous old freighter and stage owner, for the first time. He was the man who started the noted " Pony Express," which got over the road almost as fast as a railway train, and also a stage line from Sacramento to Omaha. He was a partner in a large general store at Salt Lake City and happened to be there at the time. I purchased what I needed from him, and remained in the town three days, getting ready for the last half of my journey.

The day following my arrival in the flourishing " City of the Saints," as they called it then and still call it, I very unexpectedly met and formed the acquaintance of Brigham Young.

I was riding along at the head of my flock of sheep, when a stoutly built, florid faced, genteel looking man, whose hair was just turning gray, walked down to the street from one of the most pretentious residences in the place, and inquired whose sheep I had charge of.

I told him they belonged to me and that my name was " Dick Wootton."

He wanted to know then where I came from and where I was going.

I informed him that I lived in New Mexico, that I had been in the mountains a good many years, and was on my way to California.

He said then that he had heard of me, and after telling me who he was, he invited me into his house.

I hesitated a little about accepting the invitation, because I didn't know how many of the Mrs. Youngs I might be presented to, and I wasn't looking as handsome as I always liked to when going into the company of ladies.

I had on a buck skin suit when I left home, and I was still wearing that same suit.   It had changed wonderfully in appearance however, and it wasn't for the better either.   Swimming a dozen or more Rocky Mountain streams, had spoiled the fit of my buckskin garments, and had been particularly disastrous to my trousers.   Every time they got wet, the legs stretched out a few inches, and every time this happened, I had made it a point to cut them off at the bottom.   When I entered the Salt Lake valley and got into a hot, dry climate, I learned that I had made a mistake in cutting off those trousers.   They commenced to shrink, and when I got into Salt Lake, I should have been in just the fashion, if knee breeches had been the style.

It was a good enough suit for the plains and mountains, but I hardly liked to appear in it when paying my respects to the Chief of the Deseret Hierarchy.

Still I had a curiosity to see the inside of the Mormon apostle's residence, and as he insisted on my coming in, I got down off my mule and followed him into the house.

We sat down together and chatted for perhaps half an hour, while we drank a bottle of wine, which the hospitable " head of the church " brought out and set before me.   It was good wine too, and when I left him, I felt that I could commend his wine if I couldn't his religion.

I left him with a promise to call again in the evening, which I did, and received as courteous treatment as I have ever received before or since that time.

Two days later I left Salt Lake and started across the desert plains of Nevada. Several of the men who had traveled with me as far as Salt Lake, stopped at that point, and although I had employed others I only had eighteen men besides myself when I left there.

I heard of several parties of emigrants on their way through to California, having been massacred by the Indians, along the road we were to traverse, and was not sure that I should be able to defend myself successfully if attacked, but decided to take the risk. What was known as the "emigrant trail" had by that time become well established, and I followed it or rather kept close to it all the way through. It was necessary for me to leave the trail every few miles to find sufficient feed for my stock, and this made the trip longer than it would otherwise have been.

A few of my sheep were shot and killed by the "Digger" Indians as we were passing through their country, but aside from this we were not molested by Indians, after we left the Ute country, and the only serious trouble I had after leaving Salt Lake was with my own men. That was while we were crossing Nevada and some little time before we reached Humboldt Lake.

I had observed that several of my men were slack about doing the work which they had been hired to do. They were sullen and ill natured, and every now and then when we were in camp, I would hear them grumbling about something among themselves. I didn't know what their grievance was, or what they intended to do, but I became suspicious of them, and watched all their movements very closely.

One day I rode ahead some distance, and lay down to sleep, a little way off the trail, leaving orders with one of the men to wake me when they came up to where I was.

I was very much fatigued and soon fell into a sound sleep. When I awoke neither men nor sheep were in sight, and I discovered that they had passed by me.

They were several miles ahead, and it was some time before I overtook them. The man who should have called me, to move along with the train at the proper time, made some plausible excuse for not doing so, but I was satisfied that when they left me behind, they had done so with the expectation that some of the Indians who were near us all the time, would find me alone and kill me.

The next day I discovered that one of the mal-
contents, who was behind the sheep, was leaving
small bunches of them along the road.   I brought
up the sheep, and then riding up to one of the men
in whom I had most confidence, asked him what
scheme was on foot.

He told me that half a dozen of my employes who
had been behaving the worst, had entered into an
arrangement with an emigrant train, which had
been traveling alongside of us but had dropped behind, to steal enough sheep to pay their passage to
California.

That night when they got into camp, and had laid
aside all their arms, I unloaded the packs which belonged to these six fellows, and ordered them to pick
up their traps and march out of camp.   I enforced
the order by forming them into line, with the assistance of a trusty rifle and a pair of pistols, and
following them some distance.   I suppose they
joined the emigrant train that night, for I never saw
them after that, and had no further difficulty of consequence with the men who remained with me.

After leaving Humboldt Lake we crossed the desert
and struck Carson River.   We followed this to its
source, passed through Pleasant Valley and made
our way over the Sierra Nevada mountains.   We
got over the Sierra Nevadas, just in time to escape a
heavy snow fall, which came on as we were going

down the western slope. I followed the American River down into the Sacramento Valley, and went into camp twelve miles from the city, on the 9th day of October.

I had made the trip in one hundred and seven days, and had gotten through with eight thousand nine hundred of the nine thousand sheep I started with, having lost but very few outside of those I had butchered on the way.

After looking about for a day or two I arranged for winter quarters at Elk Grove, twelve miles out from Sacramento, on the Stockton road, where I remained until I had disposed of all my sheep, and the rest of my stock.

I found Sacramento a city with a resident population of perhaps six or seven thousand, and a floating population of ten or fifteen thousand more. It was the headquarters of the miners and was a fast town in those days.

Outside of the city there were very few settlers, and I did not think then that it would ever become the great farming and fruit raising country that it is to-day.

It took me all winter to get through with my business, and during that time I saw the City of Sacramento entirely wiped out by fire, and after it had been partially built up again, almost submerged in water.

The great fire, which had destroyed practically everything in the town, occurred on the night after the presidential election of 1852, when Pierce and Scott were candidates for president.

That was just after California had been admitted as a State, and it was the first time that her citizens had voted for a president of the United States.

It had been a great day in Sacramento, and at night the fire was started in a disreputable quarter of the town, and as the buildings were nearly all wooden ones, they were licked up like snow-flakes by a scorching sun.

Scarcely a building was left standing when the sun rose next morning, but before the embers had stopped smoking, hundreds of men were at work clearing away the debris and preparing to build anew.

I never saw just such a resurrection as followed that fire. Buildings seemed to go up almost as rapidly as they had been burned down, and within a few weeks the place again had all the appearance of a city. Then the flood came; the entire valley was covered with water, and people were driven into the second stories of their houses. That did a vast amount of damage, and altogether it was a bad year for Sacramento.

I had determined to return home by a different route from that which I had taken in going to California, not only because I thought I could save something in the distance, but because I should have an opportunity of seeing some new country.

After visiting San Francisco, which was then a straggling town, although there were a good many people there, I went by steamer down to Los Angeles.

There I purchased pack mules and mules to ride, and with three men besides myself, started overland for New Mexico.

At San Bernardino we fell in with a party of six Mexicans and two Americans, who were coming through to Taos, and we agreed to travel together.

The route that we were to take, was one over which a considerable number of people had been passing, but it had always been looked upon as a dangerous road, on account of the great difficulty in following any trail across the deserts, the intense heat, and the scarcity of water.

Had we traveled by the most direct route, we should have crossed Arizona and entered New Mexico, going only a little south of east from San Bernardino.

I was anxious, however, to avoid the Apache Indians, who, I had been informed, were then raiding Southwestern Arizona, and I determined to turn south and pass through Sonora.

We made good time to Fort Yuma, and then as I had intended, I turned south into Old Mexico. The party which had joined mine at San Bernardino, declined to follow my lead at this point, and I left them behind, but they followed along later.

We turned back into Arizona again, after a little time, and reached Tucson after a terrible experience in crossing the desert. I shall never forget that fearful ride over the burning sands, where not a drop of water could be found.

We had started on the perilous trip with well-filled canteens, but although we drank sparingly, this supply of water was exhausted long before we reached a place where the canteens could be re-filled.

For nearly two days we were without water, and my companions, and the animals we were riding, became almost crazed from thirst. I suffered less than the others, but nothing I had ever seen before, nothing I have ever seen since, delighted me as did the sight of a large spring which we reached, a few miles from Tucson.

People who live in a land of springs and streams, who have never known what it is to want water, can form no idea of the sufferings which travelers across these western deserts sometimes endured. As long as we had water we could struggle along, even if our supply of provisions ran out. We could find ugly-looking lizards and beetles, which, although they did not make very palatable food, would sustain life. There were roots and seeds which would satisfy to some extent the cravings of hunger; but there was nothing could take the place of water.

It was the failure to find water, in crossing these barren wastes, which in the early days of overland travel to the Pacific Coast, set the brain of the traveler reeling, and caused him to wander aimlessly over the broad seas of sand until death came to his relief.

Many of the early adventurers lost their lives in this way, and years after they had been forgotten, their bones were found whitening beneath the torrid sun, which, with its intense rays, had dried up the fountains of their lives.

The names of some of these deserts are significant and serve to remind one of the perilous journeys of old time adventurers. Having in mind, perhaps, the gold-hunters and emigrants, who perished when trying to make their way across it, somebody has given to one of these arid plains which lies in Southern California, the name of " Death Valley," and that is the name by which it is generally known on the Pacific Coast.

Another stretch of desert which lies in Southern New Mexico, the Mexicans have very appropriately named "Jornado del Muerte." That means, in English, the journey of death, and a journey of death it has been to scores of unfortunate travelers.

16

To get back where I left off telling you about my return trip from California, we camped at the spring which furnished us the only water we had found in traveling more than a hundred miles, and the next day rode into Tucson. There we found a company of Mexican soldiers, and secured some supplies, which lasted us until we got to a Mexican settlement further along on our way.

We traveled in a northeasterly direction until we struck the Rio Grande del Norte, just above the Jornado del Muerte, and from there we followed the river pretty much all the way to Taos.

On the 8th day of January, 1853, I reached home, having been thirty-three days on the road between Los Angeles California, and Taos New Mexico. It had been a little less than eleven months before that, that I had started, with my big flock of sheep, for California, and while I had been gone longer than I expected to be when I left home, financially and otherwise my trip had been entirely satisfactory. My trip westward had not been without some thrilling adventures, in which I narrowly escaped losing not only my property but my life. The return trip had, however, been characterized by no more stirring experience than our hard ride across the desert. We were never at any time harrassed or threatened by hostile Indians. Only twice on the way did we come in sight of the Apaches, the only Indians we had any occasion to fear at that time.

Once we met a few stragglers, with whom we held a friendly conference, and then proceeded on our way unmolested. At another time a large band came close to our camp one morning before we discovered them, but our pack animals were loaded and all we had to do was to mount our horses and set out. As the Indians were on foot, we soon left them far behind us, and escaped without firing a shot or hearing the whistle of an arrow.

The Yumas, Pimas and other Indians, through whose country we passed, treated us with the greatest consideration and kindness, the Pimas going to some trouble to direct us on our road.

The Maricopas, also, seemed to take a deep interest in our welfare, and were exceedingly friendly. They were a thrifty lot of Indians, and presented the best appearance of any Indians I have ever come in contact with. The Maricopa women struck me as the handsomest lot of Indian women I had ever seen. They were fine featured, well developed, and much fairer skinned than any of the other southern and western Indians, and the whole band seemed to be far above the average of the Indians in point of intelligence. I have never visited their country since, but I have heard of them from time to time, and my impression is that they have made considerable

progress in civilization, and that they are now engaged quite extensively in the cultivation of the
soil. If all the Indians had been as kindly disposed
toward the whites as were these Indians, we should
not have had much trouble in settling up the western
country. The Navajos and Apaches were the worst
enemies of the peaceably inclined southern tribes,
and it has been on account of the encroachments
and depredations of these roving robbers, that the
Pimas and Maricopas have not been more successful in farming and stock raising. They have not
always had the full protection that the government
should have given them, but they have fared better
of late years than they did before the Apaches were
gotten under control."

A PIONEER COURT SCENE.

CHAPTER XVIII.

OLD FASHIONED JUSTICE.

" I carried fourteen thousand dollars in gold, and more than twice as much more in drafts on St. Louis, back from California with me in a pair of saddle bags. Now-a-days the man who would carry that amount of money with him in going or coming through by rail, would be thought very foolish, and the chances of his being robbed would be about nine out of ten.

I don't know that people were any more honest in those days than they are now, but it is certain that there was a great deal less robbing and stealing going on. Of course there was less to steal, but what money there was in the country was not protected as it is now. We had no fire and burglar proof safes, or time locks, or anything of that kind. The man who got a few hundred dollars ahead, didn't carry it to a bank to deposit it, but laid it away in his house, and felt less concern about it, than most people do about a few dollars worth of silverware now-a-days.

I have seen men go to sleep in a room where they kept a trunk full of silver dollars, and if it wouldn't sound like bragging I might tell you that I had

done so a good many times myself, without ever
dreaming of being robbed. The man who has to
keep a thousand dollars in his house over night, in
these times, dreams about being murdered, and if
any considerable number of people know that he has
the money, the chances are that his dream comes
true.

I think the way we used to administer justice in
those days had a great deal to do with the remarkable security of property.

There was less security for human life than there
is now, perhaps, but every kind of property was certainly a great deal safer.

The fact is that stealing of any kind or character
was not a safe business in the early history of this
country. We had no jails filled with well fed and
well kept criminals, whose trials were postponed
from time to time, until all the witnesses against
them died or moved out of the country. There were
no delays in the trial of cases, and no scoundrel ever
escaped punishment on account of an error in the
indictment, or a technicality of the law. When a
man committed a crime against property, his punishment was certain, and the execution of justice
summary, if he remained in the country, or again
made his appearance in the neighborhood where the
crime had been committed.

What we looked upon as murder, although perhaps we didn't draw the line fine enough, was the killing of persons for the purpose of robbery, or of a man not prepared to defend himself, and such killings as these we punished promptly. There was a good deal of promiscuous shooting, and men were frequently killed in brawls and quarrels, but in such cases one party was usually as much to blame as the other, and we allowed them to take care of themselves, and settle their own difficulties in their own way.

We had just three grades of punishment for different classes of criminals. For minor offenses the punishment was thirty-nine lashes on the bare back of the offender.

For the most serious offenses the punishment was death. Where the offender was a man whose criminal transactions could not be so clearly proven as to warrant the infliction of either the whipping or death penalty, but who was known to be a bad man generally, we notified him to leave the country, and he always found that the only safe thing to do was to go.

I have told you that while engaged in other pursuits, I had been raising a herd of cattle. These cattle I kept at the mouth of the Huerfano River, where I had picked out a fine body of land and started a "stock ranch."

After my return from California, although my family remained at Taos until 1854, I spent a good portion of my time at the old fort on the Arkansas River, which we called the Pueblo, and from which the city which has since grown up in the same place, took its name.

Some miners were coming into the country at tnat time, and a great many emigrants were going through to California, Utah and Oregon. Many of the miners and emigrants passed by the Pueblo, and I remained there for the purpose of trading with them as they went along.

They generally had ox teams hitched to their wagons, and very frequently a party would come along with a lot of jaded and worn out cattle, which they were anxious to trade for oxen in good shape to travel.

I could always trade fresh oxen for these footsore and broken down animals, to good advantage, generally getting about three or four for one. I sent the lame cattle out to my ranch, and after pasturing them a few weeks in the Arkansas valley, I would have them in prime condition and ready to be traded for more disabled cattle. In this way I increased my herd very rapidly.

In 1853-4 we had a good deal of trouble with Indian and Mexican horse and cattle thieves, who would every now and then run off a few cattle or horses.

I had a neighbor on the Huerfano, who also had a large band of cattle. That was Joseph Doyle, who was for some years a man of considerable prominence in Colorado, and died while serving as a member of the territorial legislature.

Doyle and I noticed that our cattle were disappearing mysteriously, and there was complaint of the same thing from the bands of emigrants passing through the country.

It took some time to find out what became of the stock, but we learned after a while that our cattle were being stolen by an organized band of thieves, who ran them into New Mexico and disposed of them. The members of the band were all Mexicans and made their headquarters on the Fountaine River, not far from Pueblo.

We found it necessary to organize a little party of regulators to deal with this band of robbers, as well as to punish some Cheyenne and Arapahoe thieves, and they made me captain of the party.

We were not long in breaking up the gang. A close watch was kept on the stock, and whenever any of it was stolen, we took the trail and usually brought it back. Sometimes we brought back the robbers and sometimes we left them where we found them, but in either case they never stole any more of our stock.

Our court houses were like the primitive churches, and we could set up "a temple of justice" wherever it was most convenient. There used to be a cotton wood grove near where the union depot stands now in the city of Pueblo, which very frequently served that purpose.

We always had a jury and a judge, and counsel for the prosecution and defense, when we tried a man for the violation of frontier law. The judge, who would be selected for the occasion, would take his seat on a stump or log, or more frequently on the ground. The jury box was as primitive as the judge's bench, and the attorneys in the case didn't sit behind big desks, with a cart load of books piled up before them. Sometimes there were three members of a jury and sometimes a dozen or half dozen.

The witnesses were called and examined, and the lawyers never took up a whole day, questioning and cross-questioning a single witness, or arguing to convince the judge that a confession of guilt should not be admitted as evidence.

Our trials seldom lasted more than an hour or two, and the jury always brought in a verdict promptly. Sentence was then pronounced, and promptly executed, no time being given for an appeal from the decision of the court.

If whipping was the penalty to be inflicted, the rawhide was brought out, the culprit was tied to a tree or post, and some one of our number, who was thought to have a sufficient development of muscle, gave him the stipulated number of lashes.

If the judgment of the court was, that capital punishment should be inflicted, two men were selected to act as executioners. Two rifles, one of which was loaded, while the other contained only a blank charge, were handed to them, and the affair was soon ended. It is possible that judgment in these cases, may sometimes have been hasty, and now and then a mistake may have been made. I have never heard anybody claim, however, that the regularly constituted courts make no mistakes, and I doubt very much if we were in error any oftener than they are.

There was one bandit who commenced operations about this time, who eluded all efforts at capture, and terrorized the country for ten years or more. That was the notorious robber Espinosa. When I first knew Espinosa, he was living on the Conejos River, and up to the time of the Mexican war, he led a very reputable kind of a life.

The story runs, although I don't know how true it is, that in 1848, or perhaps a year later, he formed the acquaintance of a young American adventurer, who had with him a considerable amount of money. Espinosa and the American became intimate friends, and the latter became the guest of the Mexican at his home.

At the Espinosa homestead, the stranger met a beautiful, dark eyed, dark haired, but fair skinned *senorita*, sister to the man who afterward became the pirate of the mountains, with whom he fell deeply in love.

As a consequence of his infatuation, his intended visit of a few days, lengthened into a stay of several weeks, and in the meantime he had taken Espinosa into his confidence, to the extent of informing him what amount of money he had in his possession.

The cupidity of the Mexican then got the better of him, and he planned to rob his friend. With this object in view, he one night entered the room in which the American was sleeping, and had just placed his hands upon the buckskin sack which contained the coveted wealth, when the owner awoke, and with pistol in hand, sprang up to defend his property. A struggle ensued in the dark, in the course of which Espinosa was slightly wounded by a shot from the young American's pistol, and a moment later, to save his own life, he had struck his long, keen-edged Spanish knife, into the heart of the man who had entered his home as a guest.

The noise of the scuffle, and the report of the pistol shot, aroused the household, and just as the American sank bleeding and dying upon the floor, his Mexican sweetheart, followed by several other members of the family, stepped into the room with a light, and Espinosa's crime, in all its hideousness, was laid bare.

The unfortunate adventurer had not been more deeply enamored of the mountain maiden, than she had been of her handsome suitor. She had returned his love with all the warmth of her passionate nature, and when she saw him dead at her feet, her grief knew no bounds.

Falling upon her knees beside the body of her murdered lover, her tears rained down upon his face, while between her bursts of grief, she called down curses upon the head of his murderer.

Standing as he did, convicted of this fearful crime, in the presence of perhaps half a score of witnesses, Espinosa saw that he must henceforth be an outcast, and at the same moment, he appears to have made up his mind to become an outlaw as well.

In the confusion which followed the discovery of the murder, he slipped away unobserved, carrying with him the treasure which had incited him to robbery and murder, and mounting his fleetest horse, he made his way to the mountains which were afterward his home.

It was several years before he gathered around him a band of followers large enough to enable him to terrorize whole communities and defy the authorities, but for a long time he was noted as one of the most daring and desperate scoundrels that ever infested any country.

His headquarters were in the Sangre de Christo mountains, and from there he made periodical marauding expeditions into the surrounding country. There was nothing which comes within the province of a freebooter, which Espinosa did not consider a feature of his calling.   He would undertake the robbery of a stage coach, burglarize a Mexican *hacienda*, or drive away a herd of cattle or horses, just as the notion happened to strike him, and whenever murder was necessary to expedite or facilitate the carrying out of his plans, he committed murder.   He also committed many murders which were purely malicious, and for which there was not the shadow of an excuse.

He added to his other crimes, that of kidnapping, and many a handsome Mexican girl was carried away to his mountain haunts, to be held for ransom or kept for the purposes of debauchery.

It was not until 1864 or possibly a little later than that, that we finally got rid of Espinosa.   His raids had been so extensive and his crimes so numerous, that a large reward had been offered for his capture, either dead or alive, and I think the authorities preferred that he should be turned over to them dead.

He was captured by an old *compadre* of mine, who had been in the mountains many years and who is still living.

" Tom " Tobin, of whom I have spoken before, was the man who captured him, and to whom Colorado was indebted for ridding the country of " The Bandit King," as he has since been called by those who have written about him.

After keeping comparatively quiet for some time, Espinosa had come down from his hiding place, and raided the country about Cañon City. After paying his respects to the people there, he started towards the mountains, when Tobin, with four or five men who had been detailed to assist him, struck the trail of the robbers and followed them closely. I had gone over to the Sangre de Christo, to look after a wagon train which had been caught there in a snow storm, and stopped over night at a sort of public house on my road.

When I walked into the bar room, several men were sitting by the fire, and among them I recognized Espinosa and his nephew, who was a member of his band, hardly less notorious than the robber chief himself. They took a drink or two, and in a little while went out, quietly mounted their horses and rode away.

The next morning Tobin came along with his posse, and told me what his business was. I in-

formed him that the man he was looking for had
been there only a few hours earlier, and pointed out
the direction which he had taken when he rode away.

Tobin followed in the direction I had indicated, and
after a little time caught sight of a smoke, curling
up out of a grove of cottonwood trees. He left his
men behind and crept up, very cautiously, toward
the grove, until he could see Espinosa and his companion sitting by a camp fire.

Capturing the robbers alive, under the circumstances, was not to be thought of. Capturing them
dead was much easier and safer. Tobin laid his rifle
across a log, and waited until Espinosa stood up,
when the rifle cracked, and the robber fell dead. A
second shot killed the remaining bandit, and Tobin
had accomplished what he set out to do.

Before he could receive the reward to which he was
entitled, it was necessary that he should prove to the
satisfaction of the authorities, that he had killed his
man, and in order that this fact might not be ques-
tioned, he cut off the heads of the two brigands,
tumbled them into a gunny-sack and carried them
to Fort Massachusetts, located at the base of " Wet
Mountain," and afterward called Fort Garland.

The heads were identified as those of the two robbers, and in due course of time the reward which
had been earned at so great a risk of life was paid;

at least I understood at the time it was paid, although it has since been stated that such was not the case.

We managed to preserve pretty good order in the mountains, early in the fifties, and the lawlessness which disgraced the country at a later period, did not commence until immigration to Colorado set in.

Then the thieves and cut-throats and desperadoes flocked into the country, and we had single handed robbers, bands of robbers, vigilance committees, and lynchings by the score.

Some of these bands had to be hunted down by organized military companies, and a war of extermination was kept up until they were driven out of the country, killed or imprisoned. Comparatively few of them, by the way, had the good fortune to escape with a term in the territorial prison. Most of them were very summarily dealt with, and when their criminal careers ended, they ended suddenly and permanently. When the country had become to some extent settled up, the courts were organized, and the men who had been in the habit of taking the law into their own hands, have demonstrated that they are content to allow the law to take its course, as long as there is a reasonable certainty that justice will be administered promptly.

Now and then, when some particularly atrocious crime is committed, there is a revival of the old spirit, and a trial takes place in Judge Lynch's court,

17

followed by a prompt execution of the sentence pronounced. It is very seldom, however, that we hear
of a lynching, and taken all in all, the people of
Colorado are to-day quite as law abiding as the
people of older states. All they want is the assur-
ance that criminals will receive the punishment pre-
scribed by law, without unreasonable delay, and that
is something which the people of any community
have a right to demand at the hands of those whose
business it is to administer and execute the laws.

If their demands are not respected, if they receive
no consideration at the hands of the authorities, I
am inclined to think it is still an open question,
whether they have not the right to take the law in
their own hands, after the fashion of the "old-timers."

"OURAY" CHIEF OF THE UTES

CHAPTER XIX.

PENNED UP BY THE UTES.

"I divided my time between Taos and the Pueblo, during the closing months of 1853, and the early part of 1854. I had decided to try ranching, as we called it, stock raising it would be called now, on an extensive scale, and the first thing to be done was to build a fort, which would afford protection against the Indians.

As I have already said, I had started a ranch on the Arkansas River, near the mouth of the Huerfano, about twenty miles from the Pueblo.

I went down there with a number of workmen, and in a short time had completed a very substantial fortress. What I intended should be my dwelling house, built of logs, was protected by a high wall and stockade, and at two corners of the surrounding wall, diagonally across from each other, I put up strong bullet proof bastions. From one of these bastions, I could see two sides of my fort, and from the other the opposite two sides, so that in case of an attack I was prepared to receive an enemy coming from any direction.

My location was just above where the two rivers came together, and altogether the position was one which could be easily defended. I built a kind of primitive ferry boat, with which to get back and forth across the river, and then I had everything in readiness for the reception of my family.

It was not until July of 1854, however, that I thought it safe to attempt to bring my wife and children over the mountains, because the Indians were all the time on the war path. While I crossed over several times myself, it was only by hard riding—sometimes without stopping an hour for sleep during the trip—and aiming to keep clear of the established trail, rather than to follow it, that I managed to get through safely. I made one of these rides from the Pueblo to Taos, a distance of one hundred and sixty-five miles, in a little less than twenty-four hours. That time I caught sight of the Indians at several points along the way, and once they saw me. They fired several shots at me, and some of the bullets came so close that I could hear them whistle as they passed by.

I finally arranged to have my family sent to Fort Massachusetts, or Fort Garland as it was called afterward, and from there we had an escort of soldiers to accompany us to our new home on the Arkansas.

Our nearest neighbor was my old friend and partner, Doyle, of whom I have spoken before, and we lived only a hundred yards apart. Two miles up the river lived another old hunter and trapper, and eight miles further up, at the mouth of the St.

Charles River, were some traders, who had located there temporarily. Then the next nearest settlement was at the Pueblo, where there were a few people at the old fort.

I kept a few men with me at my place all the time, and after we had gotten fairly settled down we felt pretty safe.

Nothing happened to disturb us, or at least to cause us any particular uneasiness, until the early part of the winter, when the Utes swept down through the Arkansas Valley, leaving a trail of blood behind them, and frightening some of the settlers, who escaped with their lives, so badly, that they left the country, and never returned to it.

The outbreak was so sudden and unexpected that we were not entirely prepared for it. Of course we knew that the Utes might make a raid on us at any time, but we had gone along without receiving a visit from them, until we began to look upon their coming as a possibility rather than a probability.

My neighbor, Doyle, had gone up among the Arapahoes on a trading trip, in which I was interested with him, and I was to look after the safety of his family as well as my own during his absence. Just before Christmas, as I could see no sign of hostile Indians being in the country, I concluded to go with a party of friends on a hunting trip up the Arkansas.

There were five of us in the party, one of the number being a brother of James A. McDougal, the first Attorney-General of California, and afterwards United States Senator from that state. We found plenty of wild turkey and other small game, but no deer. McDougal was anxious to get larger game, and I had promised to kill a couple of deer for him before we returned. With this promise in mind, I rode out from the camp early one morning, when we had gotten as far up the river as Coal Creek, and soon caught sight of some elk track.

If I had seen nothing but the elk tracks, I should have been very much pleased with the discovery just at that time, but I saw something else, which at once made me decidedly uneasy. There were horse tracks among the elk tracks, and I could see that the game had been chased by hunters. The tracks were only a day old apparently, and I got down off my horse, and after examining them carefully, came to the conclusion that the hunters were Indians.

I went back to camp and told my companions that the Utes were in the country, and that I proposed to get out of it. They laughed at me, and intimated that I was easily frightened. I told them it might be that I was unnecessarily alarmed, but I was scared just bad enough to make me get back down the Arkansas as soon as possible, and if they didn't want to go with me I would go alone.

McDougal reminded me that I had promised him a couple of deer, and I told him I would go out and get them that day, if they would start home with me in the morning.

They agreed to this and I went out after the deer. I kept a sharp look out for Indians, and once, when I rode up on a little hill, where I could get a good view of the surrounding country, I caught sight of an Indian's head. I only saw it for a moment, but I knew just as well what it was, as if I had looked at it all day, and I knew that where there was one Indian there were more.

I turned toward the camp, and on my way back ran across two deer. They happened to be standing side by side and I killed them both at one shot. I loaded them on my horse, and carrying them to camp, told McDougal that my promise to him had been made good.

We remained in camp that night, but I didn't allow myself to sleep any. I thought it more than likely that the Indian whom I had seen had also seen me, and hardly expected we should get away without a fight, if we got away at all. Luckily, however, we were not attacked, and at three o'clock the next morning we started for home.

When we got to the Pueblo, an old Mexican came running out to meet us, and said that a big band of horses had crossed the river the night before, as they had discovered by seeing the tracks.

I told him that the Ute Indians had been riding those horses, and that they were evidently watching for a chance to attack the fort. He insisted that we should go into the fort and stop over night, but I refused to do so, telling him that I had my own family and that of a friend to protect, and should not stop until I reached my own place. I warned him however, that he and his people were in great danger, and that their safety lay in keeping the Indians out of the fort.

This was the evening before Christmas, and I cautioned the old Mexican particularly about allowing the Indians to come into the fort, knowing that the following day would be one of their feast days, and that they were likely to be caught off their guard on that account.

I went on down the river, stopping again where the traders were encamped at the mouth of the St. Charles, to warn them of the pending danger, and reached home late that evening.

The next day I kept close to my little fort, and spent a good deal of the time on the house top, looking for Indians. The traders above me on the Arkansas, whom I had warned of the danger, the night before, gathered up what they could carry with them, and started down the river to what they thought would be a more secure place. They wanted me to go with them, but I thought it better to stay where I was, and if necessary make a fight to protect my property. I could not induce the traders to stop with me, and I was left with only four men to do garrison duty.

About the middle of the afternoon I happened to be on the lookout, and saw a man on horseback, riding as fast as his horse could carry him, from the direction of the Pueblo. I was satisfied then that the trouble had commenced, and the information that he brought me was of a most startling character.

The Pueblo, he said, had been captured by the Indians, and every man, woman and child in it, had probably been killed. He had been riding towards the place when he saw the Indians enter the fort. He rode up on to one of the high hills overlooking the old rendezvous of the trappers, and witnessed the beginning of the conflict between the Utes and the Mexicans. He had not waited to see the finish, because he knew well enough what the result would be, and his statement that every man, woman and child in the place had been killed, was justified by his knowledge of the situation and the Indian custom under such circumstances.

As they had started in to raid the valley, I had no doubt they would soon reach my place, and I prepared to give them as warm a reception as possible.

I stationed two men in each of my bastions, and as we had plenty of arms and amunition, I did not feel that our lives, and what little property I had in the fort, were in great danger, but I fully expected that my large herd of cattle, which I could see grazing down along the river, would be driven away by the red skins.

The traders whom I have mentioned as moving down the river, sent a party of nine Cherokee Indian teamsters, back to their old camping ground, to bring away some goods which had been left behind, and early on the morning following the massacre at the Pueblo, they passed my house. I had seen nothing of the Utes in the meantime, and began to think it possible that they had turned back up the river from Pueblo. The teamsters had scarcely gotten out of sight, however, when I heard shooting in the direction they had taken, and a little later, saw the smoke rising from their wagons, which the Indians had captured and were burning.

None of the teamsters escaped to tell how they were attacked, or how many Indians they killed in the fight which followed. We found all the bodies and buried them later, and the position in which we found them, indicated that they had made a brave fight, but they had driven into an ambuscade, and had no show for making a successful resistance.

After killing the teamsters, the Indians came on down the river and passed the home of my neighbor two miles above me. This neighbor was Charles Auterby, a Frenchman, who had been in the country a long time, was a good Indian fighter, and had his place as well protected as mine. He had several men with him, all of whom were inside his fort, and ready to fight, with the exception of one. This one was outside the fort, digging a grave for poor old Charlefou, one of the early trappers, whom I have already mentioned once or twice. The man who was digging the grave, did not see the Indians, but heard them coming, too late for him to gain the fort. He dropped down in the nearly finished grave, and the Indians passed along without seeing him.

They did not stop to make an attack on Auterby's place, but divided into two parties, evidently with the intention of rounding up, and driving off a lot of our cattle.

There were about sixty Indians in the whole band, but only a small number in the party that came nearest to my place. I had been reinforced by this time, by something like a dozen men, who had come up the river, and they mounted their horses and dashed out of the fort toward the small band of Indians, although they were careful not to get far away.

The Indians ran, and this little sally led them to believe that we were prepared to fight outside the fort

as well as from the inside.   They withdrew to a considerable distance, gathered up what cattle they
could, without coming any nearer to us, and started
back in the same direction they had come.   They
did not succeed in getting one of my cattle, and I
escaped without any loss whatever.

One thing which perhaps hurried the Utes out of
the valley, was the fact that they were getting dangerously near the Arapahoes, with whom they were
at war.   As it was, the Arapahoes followed and overtook them at Coal Creek, where they had a hard
fight.

The Arapahoes gave the Utes a thorough whipping in that fight, but they were themselves the
greatest sufferers in the long run.   They destroyed
the Ute village, torn town their lodges, and carried
away their blankets, and such other things as they
cared for.

It turned out that the small pox had broken out
among the Utes, and the plunder which the Arapahoes carried away, being infected, many of them
caught the disease and died of it.   They rendered
the whites a great service, however, and one which
we fully appreciated at the time.

As soon as it was safe for us to do so, we went to
the Pueblo, to learn, if possible, whether any of the
people there had had the good fortune to escape with

their lives, or if we could do nothing else, to give the victims decent burial.

We found but one person alive in the fort; that was an old Mexican who had been badly wounded, and died a few days later.

We learned from him about all that was ever known about the fight. This was that the Indians came to the fort on Christmas morning, professed friendship, and asked to be allowed to come inside, for the purpose of holding a peace conference. All those who had taken refuge in the old fort, or Pueblo, were Mexicans, and I had expected the Indians would undertake to outwit them in this way. That was my reason for cautioning the old fellow—of whom I have spoken as having come out to meet us, as we were returning from our hunting trip,—not to allow the Indians to come inside the fort under any pretext.

Notwithstanding the warning, the Mexicans, thinking perhaps they might be able to do some trading with the Utes, allowed the whole band to come inside, and the result was, that a wholesale massacre followed.

Of the seventeen persons whom the Indians found in the fort, all were killed, with the exception of the wounded man whom we found there, and a woman and two children who were carried away as captives. The woman, a good looking young Mexican girl, was killed before the Indians left the valley. We could never learn what became of the children, but they probably met the same fate. Besides those killed at the Pueblo, and the nine teamsters killed near my home, there were some others who fell into the hands of the Indians, so that altogether, they probably murdered between thirty and forty people on this raid.

So far as myself and my family were concerned, however, we found when the hostiles had been driven out of the country, that we had only suffered to the extent of a good scare.

I took this as another evidence that I had been born lucky, and felt more secure than ever from that time on.

That was the only time I was ever threatened by hostile Indians while I lived on the Arkansas. The " Plains " Indians used to visit me frequently; that is, the Cheyennes and the Arapahoes did, but I was on good terms with them always, and their visits were at all times friendly ones. What trading I did during this time, was with these Indians. My relations with these two tribes, were always friendly, and even after the Cheyennes went on the war path some years later, I had no difficulty in making peace with them on my own account.

When they were plundering other wagon trains and killing scores of emigrants, my wagon trains were always safe from attack, so far as the Cheyennes were concerned, and I could trade with them at any time when they had anything to trade. I had to be liberal in making presents, but I thought their good will cheaply purchased, as long as it only cost me a few sacks of flour, sugar or coffee, when I met them with a train load of goods.

This trading with hostile Indians, had by the way, to be carried on in a sort of clandestine manner. In the first place, the Indians themselves did not want to show their friendship for any white man openly, or allow it to be understood that they had any favorites among them. In the second place, no license could be procured to trade with the hostiles, because those in charge of Indian affairs, sought to prevent them from procuring arms and amunition and other supplies, and were under the impression that if they could keep the traders away from them, the Indians could not get those things.

In view of the fact, however, that the authorities seemed at times to be powerless to afford us any protection from hostile Indians, I used to think I had a right to protect myself, even if I had to pursue a course which was not strictly in accordance with the rules laid down to govern us in our intercourse with the Indians.

A single visit which I made to one of the Cheyenne villages, resulted in our coming to an understanding, which prevented any trouble between us thereafter. The Indians kept a close watch on the trails all the time, and they generally knew about when I should be passing through their country. When they caught sight of my train, one or two of the Cheyennes, or perhaps a small party, would show themselves long enough to apprise me of their presence, and then I was expected to drop a few sacks of sugar, coffee, or something else, which would be a sufficient token of my good will and friendship, out of the wagons, so that the Indians could come along by and by and pick it up. In this way we got along without having any open dealings with each other, and at the same time kept up our friendly relations."

JOSEPH DOYLE.

CHAPTER XX.

COLORADO'S OLDEST FARMER.

"I remained on my ranch more than a year after the Pueblo massacre, and did fairly well in a business way, trading with the emigrants, and raising cattle, along with a little farming, but it seemed a very quiet life for me, after almost twenty years of constant changing about, and almost daily adventure.

There were two things about it I didn't like. One was, that it was too tame an existence, and the other was, that I wasn't getting rich as fast as I wanted to.

I had had some bad luck in the two years before I commenced "ranching." When I returned from California, I found that several thousand dollars in silver coin, which I had left at home, had been loaned to a friend, who squandered it all, and misplaced confidence on my own part, lost me nearly fifty thousand dollars more soon after that.

We didn't mind the loss of a fortune so much in those days as we do now, because they were more easily, or at least more quickly made. Still I had not entirely given up the idea of going back to my old home, by and by, with enough to live on, and I was anxious to make up what I had lost, as rapidly as possible.

After the Ute scare, neighbor Doyle thought it unsafe to keep his family in that country any longer,
and moved down to Fort Barclay, seven miles from
where Fort Union is now. My next nearest neighbor abandoned the country too, and I was left alone
in the valley.

This made it necessary for me to remain about
home most of the time, and interfered with my trading and hunting trips.

I made several trades with the Indians, which
served to break the monotony of living on a farm,
and did some trapping along the Arkansas, not because there was any profit in it, but because I wanted
something to do.

My hunting trips were short ones, and I killed just
about enough buffalo, deer and bear, to keep me supplied with meat. On one of these trips I killed the
queerest specimen of a deer, that anybody ever shot
at in the Rocky Mountains. It had a full grown
deer's body, perfectly formed, and large antlers, but
its legs were no longer than those of a six month's
old pig.

That was the only dwarf deer that I ever saw, and
if its skin had been properly " stuffed " and mounted
it might have attracted more attention than the skeleton of a mastodon, in the Smithsonian Institute or
some other museum.

The only company I had at my ranch home, outside of my own family, and a few employes, was now and then an old trapper, who would come out of his way to see me, or a company of emigrants who would stop long enough to trade for fresh cattle and put their wagons in repair.

Those who cross the plains to reach the mountain country, or go on over the mountains to find homes farther west, nowadays, sometimes imagine that they are undergoing great hardships, but their experiences are pleasant, compared with those of the early emigrants. On the long, tedious trip across the plains, they were menaced continually by Indians, suffered sometimes for food and water, were buffeted by wind and hail storms, and what was worse than all the rest, women and children, and sometimes men, fell sick, when they were hundreds of miles away from any place where medicines, or the attendance of a physician, could be procured. Those who died were buried on the plains, and to their friends this seemed almost like casting the remains of their loved ones overboard into the sea.

When these bands of emigrants reached my home, they used to tell me that it seemed to them like finding an oasis in the desert. It was the one spot which they found by the wayside, in traveling hundreds of miles, where they saw growing wheat and corn, and other "crops," which reminded them of the farms and homes they had left behind. They would almost always stop with me a day or two to rest, and trade, and at the same time to obtain such information as I could give them about the country they had to travel through before reaching the end of their journey.

I used to hear some sad stories of their sufferings on the way, and sometimes would be a witness of their misfortunes.

I remember one peculiarly unfortunate family, which started from Independence, Missouri, with a party of emigrants that reached my place in the summer of 1855. This family, which came originally from Western Pennsylvania, had stopped for a year or two in Missouri, and then, like hundreds of others, had concluded to seek the golden west.

When they left Independence, the family consisted of George Shaw, a young man perhaps thirty years of age, his wife, and two small children, a boy and girl, and Mrs. Shaw's mother, a lady about fifty years old.

Their troubles began when they reached the Indian country. First one of the children and then the other sickened and died. Then about two weeks before they reached my house, the Comanche Indians attacked the train, and in the fight which followed, young Shaw was fatally wounded and died two days later.

The heart broken wife never recovered from the shock caused by the loss of her husband and children, and when the train stopped at my house, she was lifted tenderly out of the wagon, in which she had been made as comfortable as possible, and carried into the house, that she might die, as she said, " surrounded by some of the evidences of civilization."

She only lasted a few hours, and the next day, which happened to be Sunday, an old Methodist minister, who was with the party, preached a funeral sermon and they buried her under a cottonwood tree on the bank of the Arkansas.

The grief of the poor old lady, who was thus left alone, having been bereft of son, daughter, and grand-children, was one of the most pitiable things I have ever seen, and the tears ran like rain down the rough, bearded cheeks of a score of men who witnessed it. There was no way for her to return to her friends in the East, and the only thing she could do was to journey along with the kind hearted emigrants, who promised to care for her to the best of their ability in the future.

This incident was unusually pathetic, but there were many similar occurences, which came under my notice at that time, and I think I am safe in saying that the "Pilgrim Fathers" never endured such hardships, or braved such perils, as did the early settlers of the far west.

I have mentioned the fact that I engaged to some extent in farming, after the Eastern fashion, while I lived at the mouth of Huerfano River. I constructed irrigating ditches and raised corn, wheat and other kinds of grain, and all kinds of vegetables. I think I am to-day the pioneer farmer of Colorado. What I mean by that is, that I was the first American to do any farming in the territory now embraced within the state lines. Possibly some of those who came to the country at an early day, may have engaged in farming before 1854, but I did not know of any farming being done at that time.

When I got to raising corn and wheat, I had to have some way of grinding what I wanted to use for bread, and as I was a sort of "jack of all trades," I went to work and put up a pretty good mill for those times. The mill stones we cut out of the rocks which we found along the banks of the Arkansas, and the water wheel didn't look much like the modern turbine wheel, but it answered the purpose for which it was designed. We poured a few bushels of grain into the hopper at night, and the next morning we went around and scraped up the flour. A mill of that kind would be a little slow for these times, but we managed to get along with it very well.

I came as near losing my life once or twice while I lived at that place as I ever did anywhere, and it wasn't at the hands of Indians either.

I had had in my employ more or less of the time for several years, a Frenchman by the name of Murray, who was married to a Mexican woman, and lived in a cabin only a little distance from my own.

He was an idle, drunken, worthless fellow, and had made me a great deal of trouble, but his wife was an industrious woman, who put in her time making grain sacks for me, and doing house work for my family. The woman's wages were always paid to her, and when she got a few dollars ahead, she would frequently leave the money at my house, to prevent her vagabond husband from getting hold of and squandering it. This made him very angry and he threatened to kill me because I would not give him the money which his wife worked hard to earn.

I paid no attention to his threats, because I didn't think they amounted to anything, but one day, when I was doing some odd job about the house, the click of a rifle attracted my attention, and looking up, I saw Murray standing about ten feet away from me, with his gun cocked and raised, ready to shoot. He said he intended to kill me if I didn't give him the money he wanted, and as he had the "drop" on me, it wouldn't have been good policy for me to refuse. I commenced parleying with him however, and while talking kept edging closer to him. When I got within five or six feet of him, I made a spring, and grabbed his gun, wrenching it out of his hands.

Then I turned his own weapon on him, and made him get down on his knees and beg me to spare his life. He promised to behave better in the future, and after taking his amunition away from him, I fired off his gun, and handing it back to him told him to go about his business.

I got along with him pretty well for a time after that, but one day he was with his wife when she received some money, which was left at my house for safe keeping. He came around alone in a little while and demanded the money. When I refused to give it to him, he ran out of the house in a great rage, and my former experience with him, led me to believe he meant mischief. Anyhow I proposed to keep a close watch on him, as I didn't want to take chances on again talking him out of shooting me.

I picked up my gun, which was always loaded, and walked out in front of my house, so that I could see the door of his cabin, only a hundred yards distant.

A second or two later, I saw the muzzle of a gun poked out of the door, and Murray followed it.

He caught sight of me, and was in the act of raising his gun, when he let it fall very suddenly and abruptly, about the time my gun cracked.

My first impulse was to kill the miserable fellow, who seemed determined to take my life, without any sort of provocation for it, but as I brought my gun up to my shoulder, it occurred to me that I could get along without killing him, and might feel better over it afterward. I thought shooting an arm off would answer every purpose, and aimed at his right elbow. That was the reason he dropped his gun, just as he was bringing it to bear on me. What little shooting he did after that, he did left handed, and never bothered me.

As I started out to tell you awhile ago, after two or three years of farming, I got tired of it, because it kept me too much in one place, and just at that time a proposition came to me from my former neighbor, Doyle, to go into partnership with him in the freighting business. We kept up a correspondence about the matter for some time, and finally reached an agreement, by which I was to take full charge of the business, and run all the wagon trains, while Doyle was to furnish his share of the capital that we should have to invest.

We proposed to make one trip through to Kansas City and back, starting from Fort Union, each year, and the balance of the year we expected would be taken up, freighting for the government, from Fort Union to Albuquerque. There was a military post at the latter place, and its supplies were received mainly from Fort Union.

About the time I completed my arrangements for going into the freighting business, and was preparing to move my family to Fort Barclay, my wife died, leaving me with four small children to care for.

Mrs. Wootton, was a daughter of Manuel Le Fevre, a Canadian Frenchman, who came to this country from St. Louis, at an early day, and was one of the best known traders in the mountains. He lived at Taos, and after the death of my wife, my children were cared for at his home until I married again.

After completing arrangements for the care of my children, I went down to Fort Barclay, in the winter of 1856, and commenced getting things ready for a trip to " the States " as soon as the spring opened."

THE WAGON TRAIN CORRAL.

CHAPTER XXI.

OX TEAMS AND PRAIRIE SCHOONERS.

"Now that I am going to tell you something about my experience as a freighter, I must describe more particularly than I have yet, a freighting outfit.

The old-fashioned wagon trains and the stage line were contemporaries, and both went out of existence at the same time. To-day they are reminiscenses of ten years ago, and while it seems to me that only a few years have passed, since I was "whacking" the ox teams across the plains, the country is full of people who never saw a wagon train, or went bumping over the mountains in a stage coach. Sometimes I sit here, half dreaming, after the fashion of old men, and almost expecting to hear the crack of the stage driver's whip, and the rattle of the stage wheels, when the whistle of a locomotive, as it comes tearing down the mountain, reminds me that the old days are gone, and we have a new order of things. Then, when I look around for the old fellows who handled the reins over six or eight horses, and kept a lookout for Indians at the same time, and my old partners in the freighting business, I don't find any of them, and that impresses upon

me the fact, that what I am telling about now, happened a long time ago.

The freight train with which I started from Fort
Union to Kansas City, on the first day of March,
1856, was a typical train, and a description of it will
give you a general idea of all freight trains, although
some were larger and some smaller than this one.
To begin with then, I had thirty-six wagons, and to
each of these wagons were hitched five pairs of oxen.
This made ten head of cattle to each wagon, and three
hundred and sixty in all.   In addition to these I
drove along with the train, a pretty large herd of cattle, upon which I could draw to fill out the teams, in
case any of the oxen were killed, or injured in any
way, or as frequently happened, got sore-footed. Altogether it took over four hundred cattle to keep up
the train, and when the teams were hitched, and
stood ready to start, we had a procession nearly a
mile long.

Our wagons were what we called the " prairie
schooners." They were strong, heavy wagons, with
long, high beds, and would carry loads three or four
times as big as can be carried on the ordinary farm
and road wagons in use now.

It took forty men to manage the train.   There was
one driver to each wagon, and then the wagon-mas-
ters, who had a general oversight of the train, and

the herders, who took charge of the stock, when we went into camp, brought the number up to forty.

In addition to the freight wagons, we always had an ambulance in which we carried some of our provisions, and had room for a teamster, or any one else traveling with the train, who might happen to get sick along the road. Sometimes we would carry two or three passengers in the ambulance.

The men were divided into parties of ten each, which we called a "mess," and each "mess" was furnished with a camp outfit for cooking purposes. Then each "mess" selected a cook, who was also a teamster, but got extra pay, and was relieved of guard duty, and certain kinds of work which the others had to do.

When we selected a camping place, and got ready to stop for the night, the wagons were driven up into two lines, so as to form a pen, or as we called it, a corral. The tongues of the wagons were turned outside the corral, and the fore wheel of a wagon rested against the hind wheel of the one directly in front of it. Driving them up in this way, left the cattle all outside of the corral, and they were then unyoked and driven to water, after which they were watched by the herders, while they fed on the prairie grass, until they got ready to lie down for the night. That was what we called a camp corral. What we called "a fighting corral," which we formed when we were

attacked, or likely to be attacked by the Indians, was
made by turning the wagon tongues inside the circle
of wagons.   This brought the cattle all inside the
corral, and made it easy to protect them, and keep
them from stampeding.

We always started on the drive early in the morning.   The cattle were driven inside the corral, yoked
together, and hitched to the wagons in the order in
which they were to start out, those which had been
driven behind, and had taken the dust of the train
one day, going ahead the next.

As I had charge of the train, I was called the
major domo, a term we borrowed from the Mexicians
and always used.   My two assistants were wagon-
masters.   My orders had to be obeyed by all my employes as promptly and strictly as would the orders
of the captain of a military company by the men
under his command, and we moved with about the
same precision as a military organization on the
march.   I had so many men on guard all the time
at night, and one detail was relieved by another at
regular intervals.   When the wagons were driven
into line in the morning, each man took his place
alongside his wagon, and then awaited the order to
start.   When the start was made, the wagons had to
be kept up within a certain distance of each other,
like soldiers marching in single file.

By observing these precautions and preserving perfect discipline among the men, I avoided having any stragglers to look after, when we were surprised by the savages, and could always be prepared for fight in a few minutes.

We started from camp in the morning without breakfast, and drove until about ten o'clock, when we stopped to eat. Then we rested until two or sometimes three o'clock in the afternoon, while the cattle were grazing and getting water.

In this way I always got over from fifteen to twenty miles a day, sixteen miles being an average days' travel. It usually took about four months to make the trip from Fort Union to Kansas City and return.

Our wagons were not more than half loaded as a rule, when we were going east. About all there was to be hauled that way was the peltry taken in the mountains, and I generally aimed to buy up, or trade for enough of this, to enable me to make my expenses out of the profits which I could realize, by selling in Kansas City.

When we got ready to return from Kansas City, however, we always had big loads. To put six or eight thousand pounds on a wagon was not loading uncommonly heavy, and frequently we put as high as ten thousand pounds on a wagon.

We were paid then, for carrying goods through from Kansas City to Fort Union, eight dollars per hundred, so that a freight bill on a train load of goods in those times, amounted sometimes, to many thousands of dollars.

Say for instance, that an average train load of freight for my wagons, was two hundred thousand pounds. I have loaded more than that on the thirty-six wagons, but we will call two hundred thousand pounds the average. Billed at eight dollars per hundred, this brought me in sixteen thousand dollars, out of which I had to pay my expenses, provided I had not succeeded in getting enough out of the trip eastward, to meet the outlay.

I paid teamsters twenty dollars per month, and provisions cost me perhaps a thousand dollars for the trip, so that altogether I was out perhaps four or five thousand dollars. This, you see, would leave ten thousand dollars or more, as net profits of the trip, and you can understand that freighting was a pretty good business. The men who were engaged in it at that time, however, took their lives in their hands, every time they started out on a trip, and they deserved to be well paid. When I had made one trip to Kansas City, and got back to Fort Union, my wagons were unloaded, and I commenced hauling military supplies from there to Albuquerque, and my contracts with the government yielded quite as handsome returns as teaming across the plains.

This business usually lasted until the snows fell, in the early winter. Then I drove my cattle into the prairie country, where they shifted for themselves, until I got ready to start out again the following spring.

While I was handling government freight, I made the acquaintance of many of the regular army officers, who were stationed out here at one time and another, some of whom afterward became known all over the country, on account of their prominence in the war of the rebellion.

Among them were General Albert Sidney Johnston, who was killed at Shiloh, General E. R. S. Canby, who was killed by Captain Jack's band of Modoc Indians, in the Lava Beds, in 1873, and General Henry H. Sibley, who invaded New Mexico, won a victory over General Canby at Valverde, captured Santa Fe, and was defeated at Glorietta, in 1862. After the war Sibley went to Egypt, and became a General in the Khedive's army.

The wagon trains had been crossing the plains several years before regular trips were made by the stages. If my memory is not at fault, the stages first commenced running in 1847, between Independence, Missouri, and Santa Fe. Then they made one trip each month; that is, a stage coach started each month from Independence, and at the same time one left Santa Fe, going east. After awhile the

19

company started stages from each of these points, once every week, and at a later date, three times a week.

Six mules, or horses, were attached to each stage, and when they got to making what they called fast time, they changed horses about every twenty miles, while going through the mountain region. It took about two weeks to make the trip, if there were no mishaps along the road, but a break-down or two, or a fight with the Indians, would sometimes stretch the time out several days.

Each stage coach could carry eleven passengers, nine of them going inside and two outside. The fare from Independence to Santa Fe was two hundred and fifty dollars, and the passenger was allowed to carry forty pounds of baggage. If he carried more than this, the extra charge was usually about fifty cents per pound.

The stage company boarded the passengers, but I don't suppose I am giving away any secret, when I say that they didn't live very sumptuously. " Hard tack" and pork, were the principal items on the bill of fare, aside from the buffalo and other game picked up along the way. What sleep the passengers got, they took sitting up in the stage as they rode along, because they traveled day and night from the time they started, until their destination was reached.

When the country began to settle up to some extent along the Santa Fe trail, stage stations were established, at which hotel accommodations were provided, so that, if nothing happened, passengers could get square meals at regular intervals, although if they expected to have served up to them all the delicacies of the season, at these frontier taverns, they were usually very much disappointed. There was one thing they always got, however, and that was plenty of buffalo meat and other kinds of splendidly cooked wild game.

There was but one way to break the monotony of a stage trip, and that was to get out and walk when one got tired of riding. Sometimes walking a considerable distance was compulsory, because breakdowns were frequent, and horses and mules gave out every now and then between stations. It cost just the same to walk that it did to ride, and except in case of accident, the passenger was allowed to choose his own mode of traveling, provided he kept along with the procession. This he always made a point of doing, because the hostile Indians made it very uncomfortable for stragglers.

After the plains Indians went on the war path, it became necessary to have the stages accompanied over a considerable portion of the trail, by escorts of soldiers; but prior to that time, or when an escort could not be obtained, the safety of those who crossed the plains by stage, depended mainly upon their own courage and fighting qualities, the kind of arms they had, and the amount of ammunition they carried, although the judgment, discretion and nerve of the stage driver or conductor, also counted for a good deal. The stage driver who understood his business, generally aimed to travel over that part of the road where there was most danger of Indian attacks at night, because, as a rule, the savages would not fight after dark. At daybreak in the morning, however, campers and travelers had to be on their guard, as that was the Indians' favorite time to commence hostilities.

The old Santa Fe trail, which I think should be marked on the maps, so that the line of this famous national highway, could always be traced across the plains and over the Rocky Mountains, commenced at Independence, Mo., and ended at Santa Fe. It passed through Westport, now a part of Kansas City, as I have had occasion to say already, and crossing the state line at that point, traversed the plains of Kansas, in a direction a little south of west, until it reached the great bend of the Arkansas River. Then it ran close to the river until the present western boundary line of Kansas was crossed. It cut off a corner of Colorado, and a corner of the Pan Handle of Texas, and then passed into New Mexico, and on to Santa Fe, Fort Union being left seven miles to one side. That was the line of the original Santa

Fe trail, when the Arkansas River was crossed at
Fort Dodge.   It was changed later, so that it passed
through Trinidad, and crossed the Raton mountains
on the line now traversed by the Santa Fe Railroad.
The Arkansas River was crossed at Fort Bent, near
where La Junta is now, after this change was made.

The trail was eight hundred and twenty-five miles
in length, and three hundred miles of it was certainly a rough and rugged road.   Crossing the
streams, and keeping clear of mud holes was the
most difficult feature of the first five hundred miles
travel.   The mud holes we could fill with hay, cut
on the surrounding plains, and the roads were not
hard to make.

It was different, though, in going through the
mountains.   There the trail had to be hewn out of
the steep hillsides, the ax had to be used to clear the
trees and logs out of the cañons, and when the road
makers had done their best, travel was difficult and
dangerous.

In the winter the snows would frequently drift
into the cañons, and keep piling up, until it obliter-
ated every trace of the trail, and breaking a road
through these deep snows was no easy matter.

It took a man of a good deal of nerve to drive six
bronchos over the mountains, when they had to break
through these immense snow-drifts, and stage passengers needed to have about as much nerve as the

driver.   More dangerous drives than these even, were
those which had to be made down the steep mountain
sides, when they were covered with ice, and stopping
between the crest and the base of the mountain, was
out of the question.   Then, if the driver did not thoroughly understand his business, if he did not have
a steady head and a quick eye, if he did not keep his
reins well in hand, and make every turn at the proper
time, there was certain to be trouble.   Overturning
a coach under such circumstances was a frequent occurrence, and sometimes these accidents were very
serious ones.

Being caught in one of our mountain snow-storms,
when traveling became an impossibility, and all that
could be done was to sit shivering and freezing in the
stage when it came to a stop, waiting for the storm
to abate, was another trying experience for those who
were so unfortunate as to have to travel in the winter time, but being caught out in a summer hail and
thunder storm, was even worse.

I doubt if there is another place on the American
continent, where a big electrical disturbance can be
gotten up on as short notice, as here in the Rocky
Mountains, nor do I believe there is any other place
where the hail-stones grow as large, or hit as hard
when they fall, as they do here.

When a coach load of passengers were caught in
a storm of this kind, they might expect to see the

flashing lightning, almost continuous thunder, and pelting hail stones, frighten their horses until they became unmanageable. Then to escape being crippled or killed in a " runaway," they would have to tumble out of the stage, to be pounded by the falling ice balls, as long as the storm lasted, if they were not fortunate enough to find a friendly rock or tree to shelter them. Under such circumstances as these, staging in the Rocky Mountains made life a good deal of a burden to those who had to travel that way, while under the most favorable circumstances, a trip from Independence to Santa Fe, could hardly be looked upon as a pleasure trip.

There were but two ways, however, of getting into the mountain country. One was by stage and the other by wagon train. The gold hunters who went to California could choose between the perils of an ocean voyage and those of a trip overland, but those fortune hunters who came to Colorado and New Mexico had but one route to travel over.   Whether they came by stage or wagon train depended largely on their tastes and the amount of money they happened to have in their pockets when they started out. As a rule those who came west to grow up with the country had not a surplus of ready cash, and many of the men who are now prominent in business, in professional and public life, paid their passage from Independence to Santa Fe, by driving an ox

team across the plains.   Many of the young men
who found their way into the country in this way
were men of far more than average ability, and all of
them had a vast amount of pluck and energy. When
they got into the country they turned their hand to
whatever was to be done, but most of these plucky
fellows soon rose above their surroundings, and to-day
they are the bankers, cattle kings, merchant princes,
judges and dignitaries of the country. If you were
to ask any one of the most distinguished lawyers of
Santa Fe, for instance, how long he had been in the
country and how he got there, he would most likely
tell you that he "came west in the sixties," and on
the way out, filled the responsible position of engi-
neer of a prairie schooner. I am inclined to think
that the young men who traveled into the country by
wagon train, have made rather a better showing than
those who had money enough to travel by stage.

This talk about staging, has been suggested by the
mention of my going into the freighting business,
because staging and freighting were twin occupations.
Now I must go ahead and tell you something about
my experience as a freighter."

EMIGRANTS ATTACKED BY INDIANS.

CHAPTER XXII.

"I have spoken of the systematic movement of wagon trains, and the necessity which existed for perfect discipline among the men employed in the work.

This was a matter of about as much importance in moving a wagon train across the plains and over the mountains, as it would have been aboard a ship, on the high seas. The owner of a wagon train assumed almost as great responsibilities when he started out with a train load of goods, as the vessel owner assumes when starting out on a voyage.

When we received goods for shipment, we gave to the owner a bill of lading, in which it was stipulated that we should be responsible for the goods if lost in transit, or for any damage to them, other than such as might result from "visitations of Providence," such as fire, flood, and wind storms. We were not responsible either for losses resulting from Indian attacks, although we bound ourselves to do all in our power to protect our freight, and prevent it from being captured or destroyed.

The value of a train load of merchandise was frequently one or two hundred thousand dollars, and with the responsibility of protecting this immense amount of property resting upon us, it was as absolutely necessary that a crew of teamsters should obey promptly and implicitly, the orders of one man, as it is that a crew of sailors shall obey the commands of their captain.

We were governed by practically the same laws that govern men at sea, and dealt with a mutinous or unruly band of teamsters, in pretty much the same way that a mutinous crew of sailors is generally dealt with.

The temptation to mutiny, for the purpose of robbery, was quite as strong among teamsters as among sailors. A well equipped wagon train was as rich a prize as an average vessel, and while the plunder could be more easily turned into money, and divided among the mutineers, the chances of escape were quite as good as they would be at sea under similar circumstances. I have known of a good many cases of mutiny of this sort, and in at least one that I recall now, a train was taken possession of by the teamsters near Fort Kearney, the *Major domo* was killed, the cattle and wagons were driven into Oregon and disposed of, the plunder was divided, and the conspirators escaped arrest and punishment at the time, although they may have been caught afterward.

The very first trip I made to Kansas City, I had a mutiny of no small dimensions to deal with. My wagon men, or teamsters, were nearly all Mexicans, as it was very difficult at that time to equip a train with anything else.

The bitterness growing out of the Mexican war, had in great measure subsided, but it had not entirely died out. The Mexicans still had a feeling of enmity towards the Americans, and the smouldering embers of hate were easily fanned into a flame.

I had with me on this trip about thirty Mexicans, and perhaps as many Americans. Nearly all the latter, however, were discharged soldiers and others who were going back to the states as passengers.

Going through by wagon train, was a cheap way of getting out of the country. We charged a passenger thirty dollars fare, that amount being about sufficient to pay for what he ate on the road. They were not expected to do any work, other than guard and camp duty, and were allowed to ride on the unloaded or only partially loaded wagons. We thought it an advantage, sometimes, to have a considerable number of passengers, because it strengthened our force in case we had any Indian fighting to do, and in any event, gave us a more formidable appearance, and diminished the chances of attack.

While I recognized the fact that some of the Mexicans entertained for me no very friendly feeling, on

account of war happenings, and that there was an
element of danger, about undertaking to enforce discipline, and exact from them obedience of orders,
when they were as well armed as I was myself, I
knew that every man had to be armed to the teeth,
to insure our getting safely through the Indian
country, and there was nothing but Indian country to
go through at that time.

I supplied all of them with the best arms that
could be procured, and issued to each man as many
rounds of ammunition as I thought him likely to
have immediate use for, from time to time.

We got along very well for some time, but the
strict discipline which I enforced was very obnoxious
to the wagon men, and I began to hear half-sup-
pressed mutterings against the *major domo*. That
meant me, and what I overheard now and then, and
what was told me by the Americans traveling with
us, convinced me that trouble was brewing.

I did everything I could to prevent an outbreak,
but at the same time I continued to enforce the same
discipline that I had enforced in the start, and aimed
to be constantly prepared to suppress any insubordi-
nation.

It is the unexpected that generally happens, however, and when trouble did come, I was taken entirely
by surprise.

We were just breaking camp one morning, at Ash Creek, near Pawnee Rock, when one of the Mexicans came to me to ask for something from the commissary wagon. I told him I would attend to it by and by, and a few minutes later, walked out to where he and his companions were, not dreaming of any trouble.

I left all my arms behind me with the exception of a Colt's navy revolver, and this had but four shots in it.

When I came within a few feet of the group of wagon men, I told the one who had been to see me that I was ready to wait on him. Without giving me any answer, he wheeled around, and drawing a butcher knife from his belt, advanced toward me, swearing in mixed Spanish and English, that he intended to kill me. In an instant I had leveled my pistol at his head, and ordered him to throw down his knife. This did not even have the effect of checking his advance, and hoping I shouldn't have to shoot, I backed away from him, and kept out of his reach, until I ran against one of the wagons, and could retreat no further. Then it had to be his life or mine, and in a second it was his.

As soon as my pistol cracked, the other Mexicans, seeing their mutinous comrade fall, grabbed their guns, and before I could place myself in any more advantageous position, or seek any kind of shelter, they commenced shooting at me.

I dare not empty my pistol, because I should then have been entirely at their mercy, and should have had no chance of escape. I could do little more than stand there to be shot at, hoping at the same time that my good luck and a kind providence, would let me through with a whole skin.

I don't know how many shots were fired at mė, but while I stood there, thirteen bullets pierced my clothing, but only one of them grazed the skin. I managed, after little, to get behind a tree about six or seven inches in diameter, and from that shelter I fired one more shot, wounding one of my assailants in the hip. About twenty shots were fired at me after that, but the friendly tree warded off the bullets and I escaped without even a slight wound.

I think the mutineers must have reached the conclusion that I was bullet-proof, for they ceased firing, and gave me time to seek a better shelter, and have my rifle, my other pistol and knife, along with a supply of amunition, brought to me by a brother of mine, who was along with the train.

Thus equipped, I felt pretty safe, and mounting my horse, gave directions for moving the train, and then went ahead as usual, leaving the wagons to follow.

This encounter had convinced me that my life was in constant peril. The Americans whom I had with me, had stood as though paralyzed, while I was playing target for the Mexicans, and I was satisfied that I could not look to them for any assistance in suppressing future disturbances.

The mutinous teamsters dare not leave the train, because they feared the Indians, and I could not discharge them, because that would have been leaving them without means of subsistence, with starvation or slaughter by the savages reasonably certain to be their fate. It was necessary, therefore, that we should travel along together until we reached the end of our journey, but I had determined that it should be under somewhat different circumstances.

That day I rode ahead of the train to what was known as " Bill " Allison's Fort, twenty-eight miles from my battle ground. Allison was a brave, daring fellow, who had established a trading post in the heart of the Indian country.

In addition to trading with the Indians, he did a thriving business taking wolf skins. The gray wolf was an animal which followed the buffalo, and as you already know, there were thousands of them on the plains. Their skins were valuable, and Allison was taking them by the hundred by what he called the strychnine method.

He would go out and shoot a buffalo, and leave the carcass lying on the plains, thoroughly poisoned with strychnine. Before he was out of sight, perhaps, a pack of wolves would be eating the dead buffalo, and he had a big catch by the next morning.

Allison had but one arm, but he handled a gun as well as anybody, and wasn't afraid of anything. I rode to the fort that night, told him what had happened, and asked him to assist me in disarming all the men I had with me.

He agreed to help me out, and when the train came up next morning, we rode out to meet it, with four six-shooters each, stuck in our belts, and our rifles in our hands. As the teamsters came up, we compelled them to step to one side, and lay their guns, pistols and knives in a pile. The Americans were also required to give up their arms, as I did not propose to furnish an equipment, without being able to command its use, in my own defense.

All these arms were stored away in Allison's fort, and we went on our way without any arms, except such as were in the hands of myself and a few trusted employes. This was running a great risk, but I thought I should rather fight Indians, without any assistance, than run the risk of being assassinated by an armed band of insubordinate employes.

When we reached Council Grove, we found the Kaw Indians about to go on the war-path. Seth

Hayes, who was there as a government sutler, had gotten into some trouble with one of the Indians, and killed him. The Indians swore vengeance, and things looked very warlike.

I stopped there two days, waiting for matters to quiet down, and helped Hayes patch up a truce. I was better acquainted with the Indians than he was, and knew better how to settle a quarrel of that kind. He asked me what should be done, and I told him that the way to make peace with the Indians, was to pay them for the one that had been killed. I knew that this was what they expected, and that they would not be satisfied until the affair was fixed up that way. He requested me to go ahead with the negotiations, and I invited the chief to hold a conference with me. We sat down together, and after we had had a long talk, it was agreed that if the sutler would give the Indians a pony and a hundred dollars worth of goods out of his store, they would be entirely satisfied, and peace would be established.

My friend the sutler was satisfied with this arrangement, the Indians got the pony and their goods, and I left them smoking the pipe of peace with Hayes, when I went on my way, congratulating myself on my success as a peace commissioner.

I got into Kansas City without having any more trouble of any kind, and the first thing I did was to pay off and discharge my unruly wagon men.

We were not long loading our wagons for the return trip, and I started out with a new crew of teamsters. I had no trouble with them, and got along
very smoothly on the whole trip.

We had to build bridges here and there, and had
considerable difficulty crossing the Arkansas, but
these difficulties were not unexpected, although they
would not be looked upon nowadays as slight obsta-
cles to overcome. In crossing the Arkansas, for instance, it took eighteen ox teams to drag one of our
loaded wagons through the quicksands, and I spent
the greater part of a day, standing waist-deep in the
water, superintending the work of getting wagons
and teams across safely.

Some distance this side of where we crossed the
Arkansas, I got a good scare, but as it turned out
there was no occasion for it. I was riding along, as
I usually did, some distance ahead of the train, looking up a place to camp for the night. I had not been
keeping so sharp a lookout as usual, because I was
thinking about the business in hand, and looked up
all at once to find myself surrounded by Indians;
that is to say, the Arkansas River was on one side of
me, and the Indians on all the other sides.

The band was a large one, numbering perhaps four
or five hundred, and it looked to me as though I had
no chance of escape; at any rate, there was but a
single chance, and that was to cross the river, run

down on the opposite bank, recross the stream, and join the wagon train.

I had concluded to take this one chance, and was about to make a dash for the river, when the Indians hailed me, and I discovered that they were Arapahoes. I knew then that I was among friends, and my fears subsided. They came up to where I was, and seemed to enjoy having given me a scare, as much as a practical joker enjoys one of his own jokes. They said they knew me as soon as they caught sight of me, and surrounded me, just to see what "the Cut Hand" would do.

"Cut Hand" was the name I was always known by among the Arapahoes, and what gave me the name, was the fact that I was short two fingers on my left hand, having lost them by an accident in my childhood.

The Arapahoes were returning from a campaign against the Pawnees, and they had been victorious. They were going home laden with the scalps of their enemies, and driving a large number of ponies, which they had captured. They were in a joyous mood, and proposed that night to have the scalp dance, with which they always celebrated a victory.

I gave them a barrel of hard tack, a sack of flour and a sack of sugar, and they went into camp with us, or rather alongside of us.

The chief, who was in command of the band, whom I had known for a long time, detailed four young Indians, to herd my stock during the night, and at exactly the time I had named to start in the morning, they were on hand with the cattle.

They kept up the scalp dance all night, which gave some of the "tenderfeet," who were coming out with me, a good opportunity to witness this very peculiar Indian dance, which, however, has been described so often, that I need say nothing about it. Some days after that we were attacked by the Comanches, but the fight did not last long, and nobody was injured, unless it was some of the Indians. They only made one dash at us, and that fortunately was from the side which brought the wagons between them and the teamsters. This sheltered the men from a shower of arrows, which were left sticking in the wagons, and gave them a chance to do their shooting from behind this breastwork.

About the time we crossed the New Mexico line, I fell in with William Bent, a brother of Governor Bent, who was coming though with a wagon train, and we agreed to travel together. We kept along at about an even pace for some time, until we got well towards Fort Union, when I discovered that Bent was racing me, and proposed to beat me into the fort.

He got ahead of me, and fastened a bit of paper on a stick, which he stuck in the ground near the trail.

On this bit of paper he had written " good bye," and informed me that I would find him at Fort Union, when I got there. I pocketed the note and said nothing, but made up my mind that I wouldn't follow Mr. Bent into the fort. My cattle were in first class condition, and I knew they would stand several days hard driving, without being injured by it.

The first thing to do, however, was to get past Bent, and get a good start of him, if possible, before he found out what I was up to. He was only a couple of miles ahead of me, and that night I rode down to his camp, and we made an evening of it in a social way. My being in his company, threw him off his guard, and consequently he was not looking for me to make any effort to get my teams past him. While we were having a few games of cards, and taking a few toddies together, however, my men were moving our wagon train, by a slightly circuitous route, around his camp, and when we broke camp in the morning, I was two miles ahead of him. Then it was my turn to say " good bye," and he gave up the race, falling so far behind, that I beat him into Fort Union by a day and a half.

We used to have races of this kind very frequently in the old freighting days, and sometimes a good deal of money would be staked on the result. The competition between us was not quite as strong as it is just now between Trans-Atlantic steamers, but it was worth something to a freighter to have the reputation of making quick trips. It added to his patronage and gave him a greater amount of business. If there had been no such inducement, however, we should still have raced each other across the plains when an opportunity presented itself, because in those days every man was more or less of a gambler and would back his judgment with his money, as the saying goes, on any proposition. The average mountain man would bet on a five hundred mile race between ox teams, as readily as on a mile dash of Kentucky thoroughbreds or native bronchos. I have seen them go into a herd of horses that they knew nothing whatever about, and lay a wager on one horse beating another, just for the fun of seeing the horses run, and the excitement of having something staked on the result.

WM. KROENIG

CHAPTER XXIII.

FREIGHTING FOR " UNCLE SAM."

" Keeping up military posts in this country, back in the " fifties," was an expensive business. There was scarcely anything in the way of subsistence, which did not have to be hauled from Kansas City by wagon, and the cost was enormous. Fort Union was the principle distributing point for military supplies of all kinds, and as soon as I returned from my trip to Kansas City, in 1856, my wagons were loaded for Albuquerque, with government freight. The distance between the two points was one hundred and sixty-two and one-half miles, by the old trail; and, by the way, it was at my instance that the road was measured.

We were paid for hauling government freight so much per mile, per hundred pounds. It had been understood for some years, that the distance between Fort Union and Albuquerque, was one hundred and sixty miles, and the government paid the freighters for hauling that distance.

My experience in driving ox teams, measuring distances and timing the cattle, had enabled me to calculate, almost as accurately as if I had measured it, the distance traveled every day; and after I had

made one or two trips over the Fort Union and Albuquerque trail, I was satisfied that one hundred and
sixty miles did not cover it.

When I had carried about eight hundred thousand
pounds of freight, and got ready to settle with the
authorities at the Fort, I thought the distance over
and above one hundred and sixty miles, was worth
looking after, and figuring in the freight bills. I
therefore proposed that the road should be measured,
and agreed to pay expenses of the survey, provided
the measurement did not show that the distance was
greater than one hundred and sixty miles.

As I have stated, this survey showed that the distance was two and one-half miles greater than it had
been previously estimated, and that made a difference of several hundred dollars in my cash receipts
for the work done.

I put in pretty much all my time on the road, and
rarely had more than a day or two between trips, during the freighting season.

When stopping over at Fort Union I was frequently very much annoyed by a gang of petty
thieves, who made their headquarters at a notorious
place, called La Plazarota, about three miles from
the fort. These scoundrels would steal anything,
from a halter to a two horse wagon, and I hardly
ever stopped over night at the fort, without losing
something.

The authorities were so much afraid of the gang that no officer would venture to go to the Plazarota, to arrest one of the thieves, and I finally concluded to inflict a little punishment on my own account. That's the way I happened to turn man stealer.

Now I don't want anybody to jump to the conclusion that I became a professional kidnapper, or engaged in man stealing as a regular business. I only made one expedition of that kind, but it was a very successful one.

It happened this way. One night, a wagon belonging to me was stolen from my corral, and the next day I found out where it was, and who stole it.

That night I got together a party of seven men, and sometime after dark, we rode into the Plazarota, where we located our man. Then I took one of my men with me, and we entered the house in which the man was sleeping, to bring him out, leaving the other members of the party, to keep watch outside. We found the doors open, and entering the house very cautiously, we secured the thief, and got out so quietly, that although there were several other persons in the house at the time, none of them knew until afterwards what had happened. The thief himself, only knew of our presence a moment before we laid hands on him, and a gun, shoved up against either side of his body, caused him to preserve as perfect silence as we could have wished.

We knew that if any outcry were raised, or an alarm given, it would not be five minutes, before twenty-five or thirty desperadoes would rally to the assistance of our prisoner, and then somebody was pretty sure to get killed.

We rejoined our companions, who had remained some distance from the house, without having attracted any attention, and proceeded to a place two or three miles away, which was well adapted to an old fashioned hanging.

There we stopped, and after dismounting and tying our horses, we organized a court, and tried the prisoner for stealing. He was found guilty and sentenced to be hanged; then we got out a rope and commenced getting ready for the execution.

About that time the wagon thief began to get thoroughly alarmed, and begged us to spare his life. He promised to return everything he had stolen, and never to steal anything more as long as he lived.

Finally we turned him loose, and left him to walk home. The next day my wagon came back all right, and I think the fellow kept his promise not to steal anything more, as long as he lived, because he didn't live long. He was killed in a row at a fandango, only a few days afterward.

There was one member of our own party that night, who looked upon the affair almost as seriously as the man who was put on trial for wagon stealing.

This was William Kroenig, afterward a prominent and wealthy citizen of New Mexico, with whom I have had many a good laugh over it since. Kroenig, as his name indicates, was a German, and at that time he had not been long in the country, and was not familiar with our frontier ways. When the trial commenced, there was an air of solemnity about the proceedings, which made him feel somewhat nervous; then when the jury brought in a verdict of guilty, and we began making preparations for the excution, he made up his mind that we really intended to lynch the Mexican. This was going a good deal further than his kind heart and sympathetic nature would allow, and no barrister ever pleaded more earnestly for the pardon of a condemned criminal, than did the young German for annulment of the death penalty in this case.

I made four trips across the plains in 1857-58, but as the Indians were on their good behavior at that time, I had no more thrilling experience than being caught once in a Kansas blizzard. I had to abandon the wagons, and drive my cattle to the sand hills for shelter, and when I got back to where I had left the wagons, I found the overland stage inside my corral, where the passengers were trying to keep warm around a fire, made of my ox yokes.

My last trip was from Atchison Kansas, to Salt Lake City. The distance between those two points

was twelve hundred and twenty-five miles by the
trail, and it took me ninety-seven days to get through,
although I reached Salt Lake in advance of any of
the other trains, which started out at the same time
I did.

On this trip I traveled over what was known as the
Salt Lake trail, passing near Omaha, and then on by
the way of Laramie, Pacific Springs, and Fort Bridger
into Utah.

That was a bad year for the freighters generally,
although fortune happened to favor me.

Heavy rains in Kansas made a portion of the road
almost impassable, while further along the Spanish
fever attacked the oxen and killed hundreds of them.

In some places along the trail over which I passed,
I saw the dead animals lying so close together, that
it was almost impossible to find water which had not
been polluted by their decaying carcasses. I also
passed scores of wagons, which had been abandoned
when the owners, having lost their cattle, could move
them no further.

That was the year after the Mormon war, and matters were in a very unsettled condition in Utah at
that time.

As I have already said, in speaking of Utah, when
the Mormons went there in 1847, after being driven
out of Missouri and Illinois, their intention was to
get out of the United States. They had hardly got-

ten settled down in their new location, however, when the territory was ceded to the government of the United States as a result of the Mexican war.

Then, in order that they might be able to control their own affairs, in their own way, and have no interference with the practice of polygamy, they organized the State of Deseret, which they tried to have admitted into the Union. They failed in this, but President Fillmore made Brigham Young Governor of Utah Territory, when it was organized, and this arrangement was fairly satisfactory to the Mormons.

Young didn't propose to have any other United States officials to assist him in governing the territory, unless they were in perfect sympathy with the Mormon church, and after a time he drove the United States District Judges out of Utah.

This led to his being removed from the office of governor, in 1854, and Colonel Steptoe was appointed in his place. When the new governor reached Salt Lake, he found the Mormons so hostile to the government, that he never made any effort to discharge the duties of his office.

In 1857, Alfred Cumming, who had an idea that he could compel the Mormons to respect his authority, was appointed governor of Utah, by President Buchanan, and called upon the government for twenty-five hundred soldiers, to preserve order, and enforce an observance of law in the territory.

This was what led to the uprising which has sometimes been called the Mormon war. Brigham Young
called upon the saints to arm themselves and fight,
for what he termed their liberties, and Governor Cumming declared the territory in " a state of rebellion."

When General Albert Sidney Johnston undertook
to get through to Salt Lake City, the Mormons attacked and burned his wagon train, and drove away
eight hundred head of his cattle, so that he was compelled to go into camp at Black Forks, near Fort
Bridger, in the winter of 1857-58, where the soldiers
suffered greatly on account of a scarcity of provisions.

The same year John D. Lee and his band of savages, killed one hundred and fifty emigrants at the
" Mountain Meadow," and altogether there was quite
a speck of war in Utah.

The government finally fixed up a sort of compro-
mise with the Mormons, under which they became
nominally submissive to the authorities, but the soldiers were not allowed to come into Salt Lake City.
They were stationed near Utah Lake, forty miles
from the capital city, and remained there until 1860,
when the war broke out, and they were needed elsewhere.

When I got into Salt Lake in 1858, I found the
feeling of the Mormons toward the Gentiles, as they
call all those who do not belong to their church, a
great deal more bitter than it was when I visited the

city in 1852, on my way to California. Whenever a train load of emigrants came in they were looked upon with suspicion, and none but Mormons were encouraged to settle in the territory.

Personally I was treated very kindly while I was there. My visit was a longer one than that which I made there in 1852, and I had an opportunity of forming the acquaintance of a number of the prominent Mormons.

Brigham Young was particularly kind to me. As soon as he learned that I was in the city, he sent me an invitation to visit him. I called on him one afternoon, and dined with him in the evening, spending the time very pleasantly. My opinion of Brigham Young then, was that he was a shrewd, in fact a very able man, who among other things, was making his religion very profitable; and when he died, and I learned that he had left a fortune of more than two millions of dollars, I flattered myself that I had judged him correctly.

I got my wagon train unloaded, and was ready to start home early in September. Doyle, my partner in the freighting business, was with me, and before we had gotten very far on the road back to New Mexico, I sold out my interest to him.

I returned to Salt Lake, and made an effort to get a seat in the east bound stage. This I found it impossible to do, and I then made up a small party, com-

posed of those who were equally unfortunate in the
matter of securing stage accommodations, and we
started across the mountains on horseback.

There were four of us in the party, besides a little
Mexican boy, that we brought through with us, and
I never had more agreeable traveling companions.
We made good time, and the only thing we had to
annoy us on the trip was getting short, at one time,
of something to eat. I was sent ahead to look after
game, and the only thing I could find was a badger.
I killed the badger, dressed it, and served it to my
companions as bear meat. As a bear roast they liked
it first-rate, but when I told them it was badger, they
couldn't swallow any more of it.

One of my companions on this trip was Doctor
Cavanaugh, who lived in Taos for many years, and
was well known throughout New Mexico, and another was Alexander Hicklin, a noted character
among the mountain men. Both Hicklin and Cavanaugh were from Missouri, and that State furnished
many of the men who were most prominent in the
mountain region, thirty or forty years ago. Some of
those who came out here in the "forties," are still living in the country, one of the best known being
Thomas Boggs, a son of Governor Boggs, of Missouri, now living at Cimaron City, in New Mexico.

" Zan " Hicklin, as we always called him, had a
" ranch " on the Greenhorn River, about twenty-five

miles out from Pueblo, and lived there up to the time of his death, some years ago. He was the best story teller, and the most famous practical joker in the mountains, and whenever you run across a man in the country to-day, who has been here thirty years, he will tell you something about " Zan " Hicklin.

I don't think he ever met his match as a practical joker but once, and he used to tell this story on himself, with as much relish as he told any other story.

He was riding from Pueblo out to his ranch one day, and had struck a very lonely part of the road, when he noticed a stranger coming toward nim from the opposite direction, on horseback.

Not knowing what might be the character of the man he was about to meet, and thinking himself unobserved, he turned his horse aside, and rode into a clump of bushes, intending to remain there until the stranger passed by, and had gotten out of sight.

Hicklin watched the man as he rode along, and the more he looked, the more he thought the fellow looked like a dangerous highwayman. He was just beginning to congratulate himself on having avoided a meeting with the suspicious looking individual, when the man suddenly wheeled his horse out of the path, and rode straight toward the clump of bushes in which Hicklin had concealed himself.

He rode up alongside of the practical joker, and with one hand he caught his horse by the bridle,

21

while in the other he held an ugly looking navy revolver at full cock.

He ordered Hicklin to dismount, at the same time
getting down off his own horse. Then he told the
joker to sit down on a log, which lay within a few
feet of them, and took a seat beside him.

By this time Hicklin said he began to feel uncertain whether he was dealing with a robber or a mad-
man. He didn't know what to expect next, but would
not have been surprised if the stranger had either
made a demand for his money, or informed him that
he had been commanded to offer up a human sacrifice, and had found the man who had been designated
by some mysterious agency as an acceptable victim.

For five minutes not a word was said, and all the
time Hicklin's hair was standing on end, while the
perspiration rolled down his forehead, and dropped
off the end of his nose.

Once it occurred to him that this might be somebody who had hunted him up to settle an old score,
but when he looked at the man, he could not remember that he had ever seen him before. It relieved
him a little to notice a sort of merry twinkle in the
stranger's eye, instead of the cold glitter which char-
acterizes the eye of a desperado or maniac, but still
he expected to be either robbed or murdered, and perhaps both.

Finally, the man said to him :

" Your name is Hicklin, I believe."

Hicklin, in telling the story afterward, said he was so badly scared that he wasn't quite sure what his name was, but he let the stranger have his own way about it.

" I've been looking for you, for a long time," the man went on to say. " I've got some important business with you, and I reckon you'd like to know what it is."

Hicklin thought the critical moment had come, and in spite of his effort to keep cool, he started involuntarily and made a motion to get up from where he was sitting.

" Sit still," said the man with the merry twinkle in his eye, and the gun in his hand. " I wont kill you if you'll keep quiet until I get through with you. I've heard of you, and I want to tell you a story."

" I've been in this country a good many years and I've made a stake. Now I'll tell you what I propose to do. I'm going back east, and shall buy me a farm. Then I'll build a nice little house and get married. When my children begin to grow up around me, I'll take one of them on each knee, and tell them about the hardships I have undergone in this country, and what struggles I have gone through, to get money enough to buy them a home, and make them comfortable. It will be a sad story of suffering and privation, as you can understand, Mr. Hicklin, and if those children don't cry when they hear it, I'll lick 'em like blazes. That's all I wanted to say to you, Mr. Hicklin, and I hope I haven't occasioned you any annoyance."

Without saying anything more, the man mounted his horse and rode away, leaving Hicklin to chuckle over a good joke at his own expense.

It turned out that the fellow who had scared the famous old joker nearly to death, was a miner, who had heard of him, and knowing him by sight, had concluded to beat him at his own game of practical joking."

DENVER'S FIRST CABIN; BUILT IN 1858.

CHAPTER XXIV.

AN INFANT CITY.

"When I reached home, at the end of my Salt Lake trip, I had been gone over seven months. I was forty-two years of age, and had spent twenty-three years in the mountains. I thought then that I was getting tired of that kind of life, and would enjoy getting back to "the States," where I would have fewer hardships and privations to undergo, and where I should find a better condition of society. The yearning to revisit the scenes of my childhood and meet again my friends and old-time associates, was stronger than it had been at any time in the twenty-five years which had elapsed, since I said good bye to the old folks at home, and started out on my adventurous career.

While I had not amassed a great fortune, I had enough to live on very comfortably, and after cogitating over the matter for some time, I determined to take what I had accumulated, and seek a home among the friends of my youth.

With this object in view, I settled up all my business at Fort Union, and got ready to start back to "the States."

On my way, I intended to make one more trade
with the Indians, and that was to wind-up my
affairs in the Rocky Mountain region.   I loaded several wagons with goods, pocketed the drafts on St.
Louis, in which the bulk of my fortune had been in-
vested, and early in October, found myself again on
the road, but with a different object in view from
what I had had, when setting out on my former trips.

The snows commenced falling early in the fall that
year, and I had a hard time getting over the mountains.   My first objective point was the upper Platte
River, where I knew I should find the Arapahoe and
Cheyenne Indians, and it was with them that I proposed to trade.

I followed what is now the line of the Santa Fe
Railroad from Fort Union to Trinidad, and from there
went due north by way of the Pueblo, to where Denver is now.   There I came to a stop, and all my plans
and I suppose the whole course of my after life was
changed.

There wasn't much of Denver at that time, and I
don't think anybody ever dreamed that any such city
as we find there to day would grow up inside of a
hundred years.

What is now Colorado was then a part of Kansas
Territory.   A few adventurers who had visited the
country and returned to the East had told wonderful
stories of the marvelous wealth of the Rocky Moun-

tain region, and all at once people began to get it into
their heads that the territory acquired from Mexico,
was a vast gold and silver mine.

When I reached Denver a few hundred treasure
hunters had located on Cherry Creek, and were living in rough log cabins, waiting for spring to come,
when they proposed to explore the surrounding
mountains.

It was what they had heard about the old Spanish
mines on the Platte River above Denver, which probably brought the gold hunters to that point originally,
and it then became headquarters for the prospectors.

The settlement was generally known as Cherry
Creek, but two town sites had been laid out on opposite sides of the little stream.

Auraria, now called West Denver, was the first
town laid out.   There must have been some classical
scholars among the founders of the town, because
I am told that the name has a latin origin, the
word "aura" meaning a gentle breeze.   I suppose
then that Auraria was intended to mean the town of
gentle breezes, and it was rather a pretty and appropriate name.

The first cabin had been built in Denver not more
than two months before I got there—about the first
of November, 1858, I think it was—by A. H. Barker,
who had caught the gold fever, and come out from
Ohio.   Barker is still living in Denver, and is a

young man yet to have witnessed the birth of so large a city as the capital of Colorado is to-day.

When Denver was laid out, the place was named after General James W. Denver, who was then Governor of Kansas Territory. He is still living in Ohio, and I should think would be proud of his namesake.

When I stopped my wagon train in this infant city, in December of 1858, there were, as I say, but a few hundred people there, perhaps not more than five hundred all told. They were nearly all men, who had been brought there by the mining excitement, and they were of all kinds and classes.

There was no such thing as a store or anything like one in the place, and when I got in there with the stock of goods I had picked out for the Indian trade, I was at once surrounded by the miners, who wanted flour and sugar, and other merchandise that I had with me.

I should have very much preferred to carry out my original plan of trading with the Indians, because in the first place I should have made a better profit on the goods traded, and in the second place I should have been able to go East with several loads of peltry, which would have sold at a handsome profit in Kansas City.

I found it impossible, however, to resist the importunities of the pioneer settlers of Denver, and I finally agreed to unload my goods and remain there, until I traded out what merchandise I had in stock.

My first trading on the site of the present " Queen City of the West " was carried on in a style about as primitive as Indian trading. There wasn't much more style about my first store-room than there was about the average Indian lodge.

I moved into a log cabin, and without waiting for any such thing as shelving or counters to be put in, I commenced business. I had several barrels with me which I rolled alongside of each other and used as a counter. What was in the barrels doesn't matter, but it was something that every well regulated store kept on hand in those days. I think there are a few highly respected old gentlemen still living in Denver, who will remember what it was, and would be willing to testify that it was a good article if it did " come high."

Well, it did not take me a great while to sell everything I had, and then I found I had done so well, that I concluded to buy a new stock of goods, and go into the merchandising business regularly.

So it happened that I again gave up going back to my old home, and settled down to live the remainder of my life on the frontier.

The enterprising gentlemen who owned the land on which the city of Denver has since been built, were exceedingly anxious to have me locate there

permanently, and they were generous enough to offer
some inducements in addition to that which the town
afforded as a trading point. They were short of
money, but had plenty of land, and they subsidized
me to the extent of one hundred and sixty acres of
land, in consideration of my opening and carrying on
a general store in the town. The land wasn't worth
much at that time, and did not bring me a very large
amount of money when I sold it four years later, but
it would be hard to estimate its value now, as it lies
in the heart of a city of over one hundred thousand
people.

After I had entered into this arrangement to locate
permanently in Denver, I put up a two story log
building in which to carry on my business, and commenced merchandising on a larger scale. This was
the first business block put up in the city, and in
fact the first building constructed of material so expensive as hewn logs.

There was not much money in the town, or the
camp, as we called it, but I got the most of what there
was, and when the miners didn't have money, they
generally had something to barter, and so we managed to keep business moving.

New men kept coming into the camp very rapidly
that winter, and it seemed that about nine-tenths of
all those who came were gamblers.

They would reach Denver " broke," and the first thing to do of course was to " make a raise." They nearly all came through with ox-teams, and they would come to me and leave a good yoke of cattle, as security for a loan of twenty-five dollars. On the day following they would bring back thirty dollars or forfeit the cattle. This was a matter of such frequent occurrence that loaning money in this way became a part of my business.

After I had completed my log store building, I built a frame house for a residence, which by the way is still standing, and was the first frame building put up in Denver.

The first newspaper published there, was started in 1859, by W. N. Byers—who still lives in the city which he has done much to build up—and was printed in the second story of my log " business block." It wasn't a very pretentious sheet, and was published under great difficulties. Sometimes the publishers were able to get hold of the right kind of printers' supplies, and sometimes they failed to get hold of anything better than fools-cap or wrapping paper, upon which to print an issue of the old " Rocky Mountain News," now a great metropolitan newspaper, keeping pace with the growth of the city and this rapidly developing western country.

The difficulty of procuring printers' supplies, was not the most serious with which the publishers of this pioneer newspaper had to contend.

I remember one time, when they had been carrying on something of a warfare against the lawless element in the town, that two desperate characters made their appearance in the neighborhood of the building one morning, and shot all the windows out of the printing office. The fire was returned from the inside, and before the shooting ceased one of the desperadoes was killed. About the first question Byers asked of an employe in those days, was whether he could handle a gun to good advantage, and a printer who was handy in this respect, stood well with the proprietors of the paper, even though he had a multitude of shortcomings as a compositor.

Thousands of people came to Denver in 1859. They scattered out to prospect in the mountains, or at least some of them did, while a great many, after looking about for a few days, would return to where they came from, declaring that there was not enough of the precious metal in the country to be worth looking after.

Among the thousands of prospectors who came to the country, of course there were many who were law-abiding men, and made good citizens, but there was a very large element which was utterly lawless. Murders were almost everyday occurrences, and stealing was the only occupation of a considerable portion of the population. This gang of thieves was a peculiar one. They seemed to steal for the love of it, and would take anything from a pet calf or a counterfeit gold dollar, up to a saw mill. It is an actual fact that the first steam saw mill set up in Denver, was stolen, not by the man who put it up, but before he got possession of it, from St. Joseph, Missouri.

It had been shipped to that point from St. Louis, and while aboard the boat on which it had been forwarded to St. Joseph, waiting for the owner to come and claim it, it was unloaded one night on to a flatboat, and pushed some distance up a small stream, running into the river. Then it was taken off the flatboat, loaded on to wagons, and brought through to Colorado. The man who bought it, to go into the milling business in Denver, a year or two after it was first brought to the country, hired a man to set it up for him, who identified the stolen property, and it had to be paid for a second time.

The scoundrels and thieves came pretty near running the country until the vigilantes organized. Then they took a back seat, as the saying goes. I remember the first man who was hanged under this regime. He was a Hungarian named Stoefel, who lived on Clear Creek, four or five miles above Denver, with his brother-in-law.

They started out together one day to come to Denver, and on the way, the Hungarian killed his companion, and robbed him of a little sack of gold dust, which he afterward sold to me.   A couple of Mexican boys discovered the body of the murdered man, while the Hungarian was still in town, and he was taken into custody.   He confessed to having committed the murder, and we proceeded at once to a trial of the case.

A court was organized, and a jury of twelve men empaneled.   The prisoner was defended by an able lawyer, but according to the custom in those days, his confession was admitted as evidence, and the verdict of the jury was, that he should be hanged, at two o'clock in the afternoon of the day of trial.   An executioner was appointed to carry out the sentence of the court, and at the appointed time, three men got into a two horse wagon, and were driven under a cottonwood tree on the bank of Cherry Creek.   These three men were the prisoner, the executioner, and a minister, who had found his way out from the east along with the great crowd of gold seekers.

A rope was placed around the murderer's neck and thrown over a limb of the tree.   Then the minister, a good Christian man, kneeled down in the wagon to offer up a prayer, and the executioner also got down on his knees.   The fellow who was to be hanged didn't follow their example, but stood up, until the executioner poked him in the ribs, and asked him if he didn't know better than to act like a heathen.

After prayer the wagon was driven out from under the tree, and the man who had murdered his friend to get possession of a few dollars worth of gold dust was left dangling from the Cottonwood limb until he was pronounced dead and cut down. It was as neat and orderly an execution as ever took place anywhere, and was the first of a series which revolutionized Denver society.

Within the next few months a number of notorious characters were gotten rid of in this expeditious and generally satisfactory manner, and others escaped the same treatment by heeding the warning they received and leaving the country without unnecessary delay.

So many people came into the country in the winter of 1858–59 that a strong agitation sprang up in favor of cutting loose from Kansas and organizing a new territory. In the spring of 1859 the friends of this project got together, and took steps to bring about the organization of a new territory, to be called Jefferson Territory, and B. D. Williams was sent to Washington to lay the matter before congress.

At the same time Captain Richard Sopris represented us in the Kansas legislature, and secured the passage of an act establishing Arapahoe county.

The effort to secure the organization of Jefferson
Territory was not successful, and it was not until
1861, when Kansas was admitted into the union as a
state, that we got a territorial form of government,
the new territory formed, taking the name of Colorado.
Colorado is a Spanish word, meaning " red," and it
was thought to be an appropriate name for our territory, because the country was noted for its red rocks
and a soil which gives some of its hills a reddish cast.
" Jefferson " was the name we had chosen for the territory, and we were somewhat disappointed when it
was not given that name, but we soon got used to the
new one and have always been satisfied with it.

While we were endeavoring to secure recognition
as a new territory, we organized a provisional government with R. W. Steele as governor.   One of the first
things which we undertook to do under the provisional government, was to organize a territorial militia,
for protection against the Indians.

I had the honor of being appointed a brigadier general of militia under this arrangement, but as the resources of our government were very limited, I never
had any militia to command, and consequently had
no opportunity to distinguish myself as a " general."

The Indians used to give us a good scare every
now and then in Denver.   Although they never attacked the town, they were killing miners, settlers

and emigrants, within a few miles of the place almost every day.

I suppose I came near precipitating hostilities one time when there were five or six hundred Comanches in and about the settlement, although I had no intention of doing so.

A drunken old chief, who had been terrorizing women and children and timid people generally, came into my house and became very abusive. I hadn't been used to that sort of thing in the mountains and I picked up my gun and pressed the muzzle against his body to shoot, just as he started to mount his horse, which was standing at the door. The gun missed fire, and it was a good thing it did, because if I had killed the copper-colored old vagabond, it would most likely have brought the whole band of Comanches down on the town, and we might have had serious trouble.

A great many of the adventurers who came to Denver while I was there, had a hard time of it. Some came without money and others had so little money when they reached there that it was soon exhausted. There was little or nothing for them to do, and as they could not obtain employment, many a deserving man had to go hungry in those days, while others borrowed the wherewithal to secure an occasional meal, from sympathetic friends who were more fortunately situated. There were hundreds of bitterly

22

disappointed men, who seemed to have come to Colorado thinking they could pick up gold nuggets almost
anywhere, who found it difficult to pick up a square
meal once a week.   I fed a great many of them, and
did that much, at least, towards building up the city.
One of the first, if not the first hotel started in the
town, was one in which I was interested.   That hotel
enterprise failed financially, for the reason that
neither the manager nor myself could understand
that only men who had money had a right to eat.

Whenever a man came to me and said he was hungry, and had no money, I used to send him around
to the hotel for a meal, and the manager made it
a point never to turn away a man who made the same
sort of appeal.   Our house was well patronized, but
in view of the fact that the most of our patrons were
free boarders, I suppose it is not surprising that we
did not make a success of the hotel business."

DENVER IN 1859.

CHAPTER XXV.

THE HAUNTED FORT.

"I left Denver in 1862. Looking at it from a business standpoint, I can see now that this was a mistake. If I had remained there and grown up with the capital city, I might have become a rich man, and had a big hotel or an opera house, or some-thing of that sort named after me.

I reckon I shouldn't have felt right though, after the buildings got too thick. There would have been a lack of room and breathing space, and I might have been expected to wear fine clothes. Anyhow, I should have been jostled about on the streets, instead of having the road all to myself, as I do now when I go out for a walk, and should have had the noise and dust of the city, instead of the singing of birds, and the pure air of the mountains, that I have here.

I guess I'm better off as it is, but to tell the truth, it wasn't the fear that Denver would become a city, that drove me away from there.

While I left the place at the end of a four years' stay, with about twenty times the population it had when I went there, the chances seemed to me to be, that it would get smaller rather than larger. The population had fluctuated continually during the four years I remained there, first going up and then down, until I made up my mind that it was a good place to get away from. There's where I lacked what you call foresight, but such things all go in a life time, and as I have already said, I suppose I'm just as well off where I am.

The breaking out of the war in 1861, kept back immigration, and that and the following year, were comparatively dull years in the mountains generally, and particularly dull in Denver. I sold out my business there, and concluding to try ranch life again, I started in on the Fountaine River, nine miles above Pueblo. That was where my farm was located, but I built a house first on the site of Pueblo, near the old fort which gave the place its name.

Here again I became a " squatter " on the site of a future city, without ever dreaming of any such thing. The town site had been laid out, but very few buildings had been erected, and there were not many people in the settlement. The massacre which had occurred in 1854, had operated to keep people away from there, not only because they feared another outbreak, but because they had a sort of superstitious dread of being near the old fort.

The walls of the old adobe building had been stained and bespattered with the blood of victims of the slaughter, and there were stories about its being haunted, which made some of the mountain men even, timid about stopping over night in it, when they passed that way.

I remember an amusing thing which happened there, when I was returning from my last trip to Salt Lake, which illustrates how one man at least, was affected by the stories of the haunted fort.

We had with us an old fellow named Betts. Barney Betts, I think it was, but anyhow the last name is right. He had heard of the ghosts that made their appearance from time to time about the fort, and protested mildly against camping near it, but the other members of the party laughed at his fears, and our camp fire was kindled under some cottonwood trees, not very far distant from the haunted ruins of the trapper's old headquarters.

We sat around the fire until nine or ten o'clock, telling stories, and the character of the stories we told, was not such as to allay nervousness on the part of a man who believed in ghosts, and was afraid of them, because we wanted to have a bit of fun at the expense of our timid traveling companion.

At a reasonable hour we retired for the night. That is to say, we wrapped ourselves in our blankets, and stretched ourselves out on the ground, near enough to the fire to be warmed without being burned by it.

Betts lay down close to me, and I noticed that he was not in a comfortable frame of mind for a good nights rest, but as I was not disturbed by the same, or similar fears, in ten minutes after I lay down, I was sound asleep.

I had slept perhaps an hour or two, when I felt something plucking at my blanket, and in an instant I was wide awake.

I raised up a little, so that I could look around, and discovered Betts sitting up beside me. It was a moonlight night, and I could see that his face was as pale as bleached cotton, while his teeth were chattering as I had seen men's teeth chatter when they had the old-fashioned ague down in Mississippi.

" What on earth's the matter, man! " I said to him in a whisper.

" Hear em? " said he.

" Hear what? "

" I've seen em," he whispered, crawling up so close to me that I could hear his heart beat as though it was trying to knock out some of his ribs.

" You've seen what? you old idiot," I exclaimed, thinking of Indians and beginning to get slightly alarmed myself.

" The Ghosts."

" Where? " I inquired, beginning to understand what the trouble was.

" At the fort," said he ; " don't you hear em? "

I listened, and heard what had not attracted my attention before, the plaintive notes of two whippoorwills, which were evidently perched on the adobe wall, or somewhere about the old fort.

Then I burst out laughing, and this awakened my companions. We thought the joke had gone far enough, and explained to him that what he heard was not the wailing of a perturbed spirit, but the night song of a very harmless little bird.

Poor old Barney was not entirely satisfied with our explanation. The noise might be accounted for, but he still insisted that he had seen *reboso* wrapped, but headless Mexican women wandering about the fort, and I think he really believed he had seen the ghosts of some of the *senoras* who had perished in the massacre.

While I am talking about ghosts I might as well tell you another ghost story, although I must tell you about some other things which lead up to it first.

I have already told you that when the war broke out there were some differences of opinion among the men who found themselves in Colorado and New Mexico, as to whether the northern or the southern states were in the right. The population of the mountain towns, settlements and mining camps, had been gathered from every State in the union, and I think it's a mean man who has no feeling of loyalty for his native State, and no love for his birthplace.

Colorado was made a territory in 1861, and with Texas in rebellion, Colorado and New Mexico were

border territories, and for a time there was really
some uncertainty as to whether they would fall in
line with the Federals or Confederates.

When Colonel Sibley made his raid into New Mexico with his " Texas Rangers," in 1862, he expected
to receive considerable reinforcements, in the way of
volunteer additions to his little army, along the way,
and he had been promised a thousand men when he
reached Colorado.

THE PLAZA, SANTA FE.

Whether the enthusiastic southerners, who made
this promise, would have been able to furnish that or
any other considerable addition to Sibley's force
must always remain a question, because he never
reached Colorado, and they were not put to the test.

After defeating General Canby at Valverde, he came on to Santa Fe and captured that city, but the New Mexicans did not flock to his standard as he had expected.

They treated him with a good deal of consideration, and made his stay in Santa Fe a very pleasant one, but they didn't come up with guns in their hands, ready to enroll themselves in the Confederate army.

The hospitality which they extended to him was about as detrimental to the cause which he represented as their armed opposition would have been.

Colonel Sibley had spent many years in the territory as a regular army officer, and knew almost everybody in the country of any consequence. When he got among these old time friends, he couldn't resist the temptation to enjoy himself and have a good time, even in war times.

He seemed to forget that he wasn't doing garrison duty, and had no time for dancing attendance at fan dangos, and holding convivial reunions with old friends.

He wasted time in Santa Fe, and in the meantime the "Colorado First," a regiment which had been raised by Governor Gilpin for services in the Union army, was making a forced march across the mountains to head him off before he reached Fort Union. while Canby was following him up from lower New Mexico.

The result was that he was cornered and defeated in the battle on Glorietta mountain, when he should have been at Fort Union. Had he pushed on to Fort Union from Santa Fe, he could have captured it without difficulty, as the small garrison stationed there did not expect to offer any effective resistance, and would have evacuated the fort before Sibley reached it. There he could have entrenched himself so strongly that no force which could have been brought against him for a considerable time could have driven him out, and he could have remained in the country long enough to have had some influence on public sentiment, and possibly he might have received material assistance from Colorado and New Mexico.

As it was he was whipped back into Texas, and the war ended so far as Colorado and new Mexico were concerned. Had Sibley gained a firm foothold, these territories might have been considerable of a battle ground, but when the confederate colonel was driven across the line, some of the Colorado troops were sent into Missouri, while those who remained at home had nothing to do but watch hostile Indians, and discipline those who manifested, what was thought to be too great sympathy with the Southerners, in the struggle to get out of the union, and build up a government of their own.

I was one of those looked upon by the territorial government as an erring brother, and subjected to some little discipline as a consequence. Having been born in Virginia, and raised in Southern Kentucky, I was essentially a Southern man, and naturally enough, I think, was very strongly in sympathy with the Southern states. Those who know me well, know I have never hesitated to express my opinions, and so I came to be looked upon as rather a pronounced " rebel."

At one time in 1863, when the war feeling was very bitter, I had occasion to go up to Denver from Pueblo, on some business. Before I had been long in the city, I was warned by friends, that I was looked upon by the authorities there as an enemy of the government, and was likely to be taken into custody and held as a prisoner. I wasn't at all pleased with the idea of being locked up in jail. In-door life never did agree with me, and besides I had a family to look after down at Pueblo.

I got through with my business as quickly as possible, and started for home on horseback, just as the news was brought to me that a posse had been started out to hunt me up, and put me under arrest.

I started early in the morning and rode all day, reaching the head of Kiowa Creek at night-fall. This was one of the places which the mountain men, or at

least a good many of them avoided, and here's where
my ghost story comes in.

A soldier named Fagan, belonging to Captain
Marcy's company, had dropped dead while standing
guard one night when the company was in camp
here, several years before, and the place had come to
be known as " Fagan's Camp."

The lonely grave, which was miles away from any
human habitation, had probably moved some superstitious hunter or trapper, to start the story that the
spirit of the unfortunate soldier, materialized every
night, and dressed in full uniform, with musket in
hand, tramped all night in a circle about the grave,
to guard the resting place of the body which it had
once inhabited.

I had heard the story, but did not know the exact
location of " Fagan's Camp," although it would have
made no difference if I had, as superstition has never
been one of my weaknesses.

When I got down off my horse, and went into camp
for the night,—if I may call it going into camp, for
one man to build a fire and sit down by it alone—it
chanced that I dismounted, without knowing it, inside the circle around which it had been alleged the
ghostly sentry paced every night, and when I kindled my fire, it was at the head, or the foot, I don't
know which, of Fagan's grave.

When I lay down to rest, I stretched myself alongside of this same little mound of earth, which served to protect me to some extent from the cold, raw, night wind. Tired as I was, after my long hard ride, I dropped asleep, and had slept something like two or three hours, when I was awakened,—as I always was by the slightest noise—by the tramping of horses, some distance from me.

I had left my own horse secreted in a cañon not far away, and leaving my camp-fire, I hastened to the horse, thinking it possible that the Denver posse had followed my trail, and that there might be necessity for immediate and hasty flight.

My fire, which had not been a big one to begin with, had burned down, so that when I left it, the few dying embers remaining, sent up only a sort of "will o' the wisp" blaze, which would scarcely have been noticed twenty yards away.

I stood by my horse, ready to mount and gallop away, if occasion required it, but having a fancy to see who my visitors were before starting, or becoming seriously alarmed. By and by, they came close enough to me, to enable me to hear their conversation, and although I could not make out who they were, I knew there were several men in the party.

Presently I heard one of the men say: "Look sharp now for ghosts. This is 'Fagan's camp;' and they say the dead soldier's ghost stands guard over his grave every night."

"I'd a heap rather see 'Dick' Wootton," said another member of the party, whose voice I recognized as that of a friend. "We've kept on his trail, and he must be some place in these mountains."

"We'll find him if he's here," said the first speaker, "though I tell you I don't much like prowling round a dead man's camp. If Fagan's ghost is running these parts, as I've heard lots of 'em say it is, I want to camp some place else. What the devil is that!"

They had caught sight of my little camp fire, which would blaze up now and then, just enough to throw a pale glare over its surroundings, and make the outlines of the grave distinctly visible, when it would apparently die out again so completely, that hardly a spark could be seen.

It was really a ghostly-looking kind of manifestation, and as the party stood looking at it for a minute or two, without saying anything, I thought the men were half inclined to stampede and run away from the place, without making any further investigation.

Finally, one of them said: "Might as well see what it is."

Then they all got down off of their horses, and approached the place as cautiously as though they thought themselves in danger of being, at any moment, impaled on the bayonet of the ghost sentinel.

Not one of them uttered a word above a whisper, until they reached the grave, and discovered that the light they had seen, and regarded with so much superstitious dread, came from a real fire. Then one of them blurted out:

" It's ' Dick ' Wootton's camp fire, and I'm a natural born liar if he haint been asleep on Fagan's grave."

" You're right, partner, as sure as I've got a front and a hind name," said another one of my midnight visitors. " That fellow would camp in a sepulchre without having any bad dreams, or risk going to sleep in a powder magazine with his pipe lit. He aint far away from here now either. Let's call him."

The discovery that I had slept in " Fagan's camp," seemed to dispel all their fears, and their voices rang out on the night air, calling me by name.

I had learned by this time that I had nothing to fear from that party, and when I joined them I found five friends, who were getting away from Denver as hurriedly as I was myself, and for the same reason.

We didn't look for another camping place, but raked together the remains of my fire and piled on more fuel. Nobody cared much about sleeping, but we sat around the fire and talked over war matters and nursed our grievances until morning. Then we went on to Pueblo, and never heard anything more about the proposed arrests. When it got noised around that I had not only stayed all night in "Fagan's camp," but had actually kindled a fire on the grave, and slept alongside of it until I was awakened by the party looking for me, it spoiled a very pretty ghost story, and "Fagan's camp" was no longer avoided by the mountain men or other travelers, who had occasion to go that way.

The story of my adventure was vouched for by so many witnesses, that it could not be disputed, and the haunted camp sensation was exploded."

GEN. JAMES W. DENVER.

CHAPTER XXVI.

" PLAINS " INDIANS ON THE WAR PATH.

I put up two cabins in Pueblo, among the first built there. I lived in one of them, and ran a grocery in the other, while superintending the building of some cabins on my farm.

My farming on the Fountaine River was quite extensive, and I demonstrated that grain of all kinds could be raised in Colorado. I had done that before, when farming on the Arkansas River, but I did still better on my new farm. Corn and wheat were the principal crops which I raised, and my hundred acre corn field, attracted more attention than anything else in that section of the country.

I can tell a good story in connection with that big cornfield, which will illustrate fairly well, the hardships of another phase of frontier life, and give you an idea of what gentlemen of the learned professions had to contend with sometimes, in the discharge of their duties, or pursuit of their callings.

I was sitting in my cabin one night, some time after dark, when the dogs outside of the house, commenced making a great fuss, and I knew that some stranger, or strangers perhaps, were around. I stepped to the door with my gun in my hand, and lis-

23

tened.   Pretty soon I heard some one calling, who
had gotten within hailing distance, but was afraid to
come nearer.   I couldn't make out what the man
was saying, but I quieted the dogs, and then answered his call, asking him who he was and what he
wanted.   He came up closer, and informed me that
he was Judge Allen Bradford ; that he had gotten
lost in my cornfield, and that what he wanted was to
get out of it, and find something to eat and a place
to sleep.

I went out and brought him up to the house, because I knew of Judge Bradford, although at that
time I had never seen him.

When he got up to where the light shown on him,
I think he looked less like a judge, than anybody I
ever saw, unless it was a Yuma Indian.   The cornfield was very muddy, and the mule which he was riding, a consumptive looking animal any way, had
mired down several times, and both man and mule
looked like they had been made of *adobe*, and
hadn't got dry yet.   The judge was on his way to
Conejos, where he was to hold court, and had gotten
lost, the result being that he landed in my big cornfield, and came pretty near not getting out of it.   When
he got indoors that night I traded him a trappers'
suit for his mud-stained judicial garments, and he
felt better after the change, if the clothes didn't fit
him.   He got a good night's rest, and in the morn-

ing, when I sent him on his way, riding a good horse, in place of that sickly looking mule, he looked more like a judge.

Judge Bradford afterwards became one of the most distinguished men in the state, and used to laugh over losing his way in my corn patch, every time I saw him.

It was not a great while afterward that I happened to be called on to make my appearance in the Judge's court. That was while the war was going on, and as I have already said, it stirred up a good deal of controversy between the representatives of the different sections, who were living at the time in Colorado. The question at issue, as the lawyers say, when my presence in Judge Bradford's court was required, was a political one, and I didn't agree with the court politically.

In the course of the proceedings, which from my standpoint seemed to be a little irregular, I suppose I must have gotten somewhat excited.

Anyhow I did some swearing, which wasn't of the character that men are called upon to do in court. The Judge called me to order very mildly, but he didn't fine me for contempt of court, as everybody present expected he would, and I always thought the reason he didn't fine me, was because he had not forgotten that cornfield scrape.

For three years I plowed and planted, and harvested my grain, leading almost as quiet a life as the average Eastern farmer.

The markets were good for everything in the way of farm produce, because the troops which the government kept stationed in Colorado and New Mexico, required supplies, and everything that could be raised on the small amount of land under cultivation was taken at handsome prices.

We soon made up our minds that the war of the rebellion wasn't to be fought out in Colorado, and that there was no occasion for us to get greatly excited over it out here. After we had gotten into this frame of mind, Northern and Southern men got along very comfortably together, notwithstanding their differences of opinion.

It was about this time that the most serious Indian troubles ever experienced in Colorado commenced. The influx of whites, into the territory, led the Indians to believe that their country would soon be overrun, and they looked upon every immigrant as a trespasser. The Cheyennes, a band which the mountain men had generally been on good terms with, became for some reason or other, particularly incensed against the settlers.

The Comanches, the old-time enemies of the Cheyennes, had been hostile to the whites, whether settlers, traders, or trappers, from the time they first

commenced coming into the country.   As soon as
the Comanches learned that the Cheyennes were inclined to become alarmed over the invasion of their
territory by white settlers, they made peace with
them, and did all they could to stir them up against
their common enemy, the "pale face."

The Kiowas, after being almost exterminated by
the Arapahoes and Cheyennes, had joined the
Comanches, as had also a fragment of the Apache
tribe, which became known as the "Prairie Apache"
band.

After the alliance between the Comanches and
Cheyennes, these two bands, together with the Kiowas and Prairie Apaches, scattered over a broad area
of country, constituted what I think was the largest
number of Indians that we ever had on the war path
at one time in the far west.

The Arapahoes joined them later, one of their principal grievances being the cutting down of a grove of
timber, near Fort Wallace, Kansas.

This grove, which they called "The Big Timber,"
was a favorite wintering place of the Indians.   Buffalo were numerous in the surrounding country,
and it was at this grove that the Indians gathered
after the chase to tan the buffalo skins, and prepare
them for the traders.

The contractors who built Fort Wallace, cut down
the fine old trees, and entirely destroyed the grove,

so that when the Arapahoes visited their old camping place again, they found scarcely a tree standing.
Then the Indians put on their war paint and declared
that for every tree the white men had cut down, they
would kill a white man, and I reckon they did it before they were finally subdued and forced to quit the
country.

The Comanche and Cheyenne warfare was very
shrewdly carried on. They were never all on the
war path at once, and while some of them were killing immigrants, and making forays against weak settlements, the others were claiming to be good Indians, and in that way managed to keep on good
terms with the traders. They did all the trading for
the hostiles as well as themselves, and by that means
secured large supplies of guns and amunition, which
were at once turned over to the Indians who were on
the war path. It was some time before we found out
how it was, that the Indians who were actually doing the fighting, kept themselves supplied all the
time with arms, of as good patern as those used by
the soldiers, and also with plenty of amunition.

When we made this discovery, we very naturally
came to the conclusion that all the Indians who had
entered into the understanding according to which
part of them furnished the amunition for killing
white men, women and children, while the others
did the killing, were equally guilty.

It was the necessity for punishing all the Indians who belonged to the hostile combination, whether they were actually caught scalping their victims, or only sharpening the knives for those who did the scalping, which led Colonel Chivington to march against the Cheyennes with the "Colorado First," and fight the first band he came across. Chivington was severely censured by the tender-hearted Eastern people, whose scalp locks were never in danger, for this action, and a great deal has been said by them about the "Chivington massacre." The most absurd and unreasonable stories were started about the affair in the East, and I shouldn't wonder if the Indian lovers didn't succeed in persuading people back there, that the Comanches, Cheyennes, Apaches and Kiowas, were kind hearted, industrious and peace-loving creatures, while the white people of Colorado were merciless savages.

One of the stories published, was to the effect that when the "Colorado First" got back to Denver, the citizens had a sort of combined jubilee and scalp dance, at which the scalps of the slaughtered Indians were placed on exhibition.

Now the facts were, that the people of Central and Eastern Colorado, and Western Kansas, were very glad to learn that the savages, who had for months menaced life and property, who had in cold blood killed scores of settlers and immigrants, had been severely punished by Colonel Chivington and his troops, at Sand Creek.   At a public meeting which was held in Denver, soon after the occurrence, called for the purpose of congratulating the officers and soldiers of the " First Regiment," upon the success of the campaign from which they had just returned, there were scalps on exhibition, but *they were not the scalps of Indians.*   They were the scalps of white victims of the savages, which had been found in the possession of the alleged good and peaceable Indians.   They were the scalps of immigrants who had been slain, while attempting to cross the plains in search of homes in the far West.   They were the scalps of settlers who had never wronged either Indian or white man.   They were the scalps of gray haired men and prattling children, of fair haired and dark haired women, who had suffered a thousand deaths at the hands of the red devils.

Those were the scalps which were exhibited on that occasion, and they were exhibited for the purpose of showing, that the savages who had been so severely punished, deserved the punishment.   I was never on very friendly terms with Colonel Chivington, and have censured some of his acts as a military officer, as severely as anybody, but my opinion of this particular campaign and his action in connection with it is, that if it is any part of the business of soldiers stationed in the Indian country, to protect the lives and property of settlers, he and his men did their duty and did it well.

Nothing ever had a more salutary effect upon the Indians than the result of this campaign. While no peace was made with them at that time, nor in fact for some years after that, and they kept on murdering weak parties of immigrants and isolated settlers, they kept their distance from the larger settlements and particularly from Denver. Before that it was hardly safe to ride out a dozen miles in any direction without an escort of soldiers to accompany you.

I remember that just before that time, I had occasion to escort the family of an old friend of mine, who had died, from Pueblo to Denver; and when I had gotten through safely, I felt that I had completed the most perilous trip of my life. People were killed along a portion of the road, the day before, and others the day after I passed over it, and how I had the good fortune to escape, with the lady and her children in my charge, was always something of a mystery to me.

The lady and children by the way, were very much shocked by a discovery which we made, as we drove along the road between where the town of Colorado Springs is now, and Denver. We noticed the ravens hovering about a spot not far from the road, in a small grove, and driving to one side, we found there the skeletons of four men, bound with ropes to as many trees. The flesh had been picked clean from the bones, but a bullet hole in each skull showed how the men had met their death.   Each skeleton stood in a pair of boots, which was all that was left about them in the way of clothing, and altogether this was as ghastly a find, along a lonely road, as one could imagine.   We learned afterwards that the skeletons were those of the notorious " Jim " Runnels and three of his band of robbers, who had been captured and summarily executed only a short time before.

In the summer of 1864 I again " soured " on farming, and I think my experience that summer would have soured a philosopher.   First I had to wrestle with a water spout, which rolled over my wheat and corn, and then when it made a feeble effort to stand up again, a hail storm completed the work of destruction.

I shall never forget that terrible flood of 1864.   It had been raining hard, and about the last of May, the Fountaine River and other streams were considerably swollen, but we did not think them dangerously high. I was living then on my farm on the Fountaine, and had just gotten up one morning, when I saw, what I can only describe as a great bank of water, coming down the valley.   It looked to me then as though it might be a hundred feet high and a mile or two wide. Actual measurements of the water marks taken later, demonstrated that it was eighteen and a half feet high, or deep perhaps I should say, in the main

current, and it spread out until it made a stream between one and two miles wide.

My house stood on high ground, and I felt safe so
far as my family was concerned, but I had a neighbor, some distance down the river, whose house I
knew must be swept away by the torrent. My little
fourteen year-old boy mounted a horse, and riding as
fast as possible to this neighbor's place, warned him
of the danger, just in time to enable him to escape
with his family to the hills.

We afterwards succeeded in getting some of the
furniture out of the house, but the house itself went
down the stream, and along with it went eleven hundred dollars in gold, that Dodson — that was the
neighbor's name — had left behind him, when he
made his hurried race for the hills.

The great torrent, as it came down, following the
course of the Fountaine River, uprooted cottonwood
trees, which were four or five feet in diameter, and
carried them along until they lodged against some
hill side, or were piled up with other debris.

The flood subsided almost as suddenly as it came
on. In an hour or two the river was but little higher
than at the ordinary high water stage, but in that
two hours, about everything that the settlers in the
valley had, in the way of property, had been swept
away, and nine lives had been lost. When the water
receded, so that I could look over the ground where

my growing crops had stood, I found in the place of wheat and corn, scores of uprooted trees, wrecks of log cabins, farm wagons, plows and other wreckage which had been brought down from above. The wheat and corn, while it had been leveled to the ground, had not been entirely destroyed. I cleaned off the debris as best I could, and in a few days the grain began to recover to some extent from the effects of the flood. I was beginning to congratulate myself on the prospect of having something of a crop after all, when the hail storm came which finished it.

The big hail stones knocked the heads off my wheat, and pounded my corn into the ground, so that when it was over, I had no more show of reaping a crop of either kind of grain, than I would have had if the seed had never been put into the ground.

I need not say that my farming operations did not pay that year. I need not say either, that I began to have doubts about my being able to make a fortune out of the business. With Indians on the war path, and liable at any time to sweep through the valley and drive away my stock, and hail storms and floods to destroy my crops, it didn't look to me as though the time had come to make a success of farming in Colorado, and I left the ranch the next spring."

CHIEF CONNIACH.

CHAPTER XXVII.

PATHFINDER AND BUILDER.

I had long had in mind the building of a stage road through the " Raton Pass," and when I made up my mind to quit farming on the Fountaine, I thought it a good time to put through my road project.

I had been over the mountains so often, had in fact lived in them so many years, that I knew almost every available pass in Colorado and New Mexico, and understood just about how the travel ran, in various directions. I knew that the Raton Pass was a natural highway, connecting settlements already in existence, and destined to be a thoroughfare for other settlements, which would spring up in south-eastern Colorado and north-eastern Mexico.

Barlow and Sanderson, the proprietors of the Santa Fe stage line, were anxious to change their route, so as to pass through Trinidad, which had by this time become a point of some importance, and the freighters generally wanted to come through that way. How to get through the pass, was the problem, however, with all of them.

A trail led through the cañon it is true, but that
was almost impassable for anything but saddle horses
and pack animals at any time, and entirely impassa-
able for wagon trains or stages in the winter time.

Nobody knew this better than I did, because I had
come through the pass on my way to Denver in 1858,
and spent nearly a month traveling a distance of fifty
miles with a comparatively light wagon train.

What I proposed to do was to go into this winding,
rock-ribbed mountain pass, and hew out a road, which
barring grades, should be as good as the average
turnpike.   I expected to keep this road in good repair, and charge toll for travelling over it, and
thought I could see a good business ahead of me.

The first thing to be done was to secure a charter,
or rather two charters, because the road which I intended to construct, would be an inter-territorial
highway, partly in Colorado and partly in New
Mexico.   I applied to the Colorado legislature, when
it met in the winter of 1865, for a charter, authorizing
me to construct a toll road from Trinidad to the New
Mexico line, and to the New Mexico legislature for a
charter, covering the distance from the New Mexico
line to Red River, which was to be the southern terminus of my road.

I got both charters without difficulty, although the
Colorado charter bill was not passed until just before

the adjournment of the legislature, which at that time met at Golden.

The following spring I moved down here, picked out the spot which I have since made my home, and commenced work on my mountain road.

I had undertaken no light task, I can assure you. There were hillsides to cut down, rocks to blast and remove, and bridges to build by the score.   I built the road, however, and made it a good one too. That was what brought the Santa Fe trail through this way, and as the same trail extended to Chihuahua, in Mexico, my twenty-seven miles of turnpike, constituted a portion of an international thoroughfare.

After I got my road completed, the next thing was to make it a paying investment. Such a thing as a toll road was unknown in this country at that time. I do not think there was one in either Colorado or New Mexico, until after I built mine.

People who had come out here from the Eastern states understood of course, that the object of building a turnpike, was to enable the owner to collect toll from those who traveled over it, but I had to deal with a great many people who seemed to think that they should be as free to travel over my well graded and bridged roadway, as they were to follow an ordinary cow path.

I may say that I had five classes of patrons to do business with. There was the stage company and its employes, the freighters, the military authorities who marched troops and transported supplies over the road, the Mexicans, and the Indians.

With the stage company, the military authorities and the American freighters I had no trouble. With the Indians, when a band came through now and then, I didn't care to have any controversies, about so small a matter as a few dollars toll. Whenever they came along, the toll gate went up, and any other little thing I could do to hurry them along, was done promptly and cheerfully. While the Indians didn't understand anything about the system of collecting tolls, they seemed to recognize the fact that I had a right to control the road, and they would generally ride up to the gate and ask permission to go through. Once in a while the chief of a band would think compensation for the privilege of going through in order, and would make me a present of a buckskin or something of that sort.

My Mexican patrons were the hardest to get along with. Paying for the privilege of traveling over any road was something they were totally unused to, and they did not take to it kindly. They were pleased with my road and liked to travel over it until they reached the toll gate. This they seemed to look upon as an obstruction that no man had a right to place in the way of a free born native of the mountain region. They seemed to look upon the toll-gate as a new scheme for " holding up " travelers, for the purpose of robbery, and many of them evidently thought me a kind of freebooter, who ought to be suppressed by law.

Holding these views, when I asked them for a certain amount of money, before raising the toll-gate, they naturally differed with me very frequently about the propriety of complying with the request.

In other words, there would be, at such times, probably an honest difference of opinion between the man who kept the toll-gate, and the man who wanted to get through it. Anyhow, there was a difference, and such differences had to be adjusted. Sometimes I adjusted these matters through diplomacy, and sometimes I did it with a club. They were always settled one way, however, and that was in accordance with the toll schedule, so that I could never have been charged with " unjust discrimination " in rates.

Only the Indians were exempted from paying the fixed rates, but collecting turnpike tolls in the far west, twenty years ago, was a lively business.

I did make one other exception to the rule, too, now that I come to think about it, and that was in favor of officers and parties who were in pursuit of horse and cattle thieves.

Stealing cattle and horses in Colorado, and running them into New Mexico, got to be a business about that time, and the same band of thieves that drove

24

stolen Colorado stock into New Mexico, would recross
the line with stock stolen from the Mexicans.

There was one gang of robbers in the country at
that time, headed by " Jim " Gray, a notorious
scoundrel, which was carrying on a very extensive
cattle and horse stealing business in this region.
Gray was the most daring horse thief I have ever
known. He came to my place once, in broad day
light, when a large party of soldiers were stopping
here, stole the best mule they had, rode it away and
escaped. "Jack" Ross was at the head of another
notorious gang of thieves, and members of both gangs
used to pass through here frequently.

One morning I remember, just as I was starting
out to work, I met a young fellow riding a fine looking horse, without either saddle or bridle. I suspected
it was stolen, but was not sure of it until half an hour
later, when a pursuing party came along and gave
me the information. Learning that the man they
were looking for was not far ahead, they galloped
along, and in the afternoon of the same day, they
came back, bringing with them the stolen horse.

I asked them if they had captured the thief, and
they said : " yes, we captured him, and if anybody
inquires for him, you can tell them that they can
find his remains over in New Mexico, where his
career as a horse thief ended."

Members of these bands would sometimes come along and hire to me, for the purpose of getting an opportunity to steal, and I had to be continually on the lookout for them.

On one occasion a government wagon train, with an escort of soldiers stopped here over night, and in the middle of the night they came to my room, woke me up, and informed me that all their horses and mules had been stolen. I got up, and after looking about for some time, we found all the stock, with the exception of a fine black horse.

I had in my employ, a fellow of whom I had been somewhat suspicious for some time, and when I went to the cabin in which the men were sleeping, I found him gone.

He was on hand, however, the next morning, and I set him at work in the garden. I was satisfied that he was the horse-thief, and by and by I walked down to where he was at work, leveled a pistol at his head, and ordered him to throw up his hands. He had a pistol sticking in his belt, but he made no attempt to use it, and promptly obeyed my order. I then told him that I knew he had stolen the missing horse, and that I wanted to know where it could be found.

The fellow weakened, confessed that he was the thief, and agreed to return the stolen animal, which he did later in the day.

Just about the close of the war, and in fact in
1866–67, the Indians were so bad that all wagon
trains passing over the Santa Fe trail had to be accompanied by escorts of soldiers.   These escorts
joined west-bound trains at Fort Larned, which was
located at the eastern edge of the Comanche country.

In 1865, a company composed partly of Californi-
ans and partly of Mexicans, and commanded by Captain Haley, passed through here, escorting a train of
perhaps a hundred and fifty wagons.   While they
were stopping here, one of the non commissioned
officers of the company was brutally murdered by
three soldiers, and I came near being a witness of the
murder.

The officer was a Mexican corporal, and the soldiers
were also Mexicans.   There was a feud between the
corporal and the privates, which originated at Las
Vegas, where the men had been bound and gagged,
by order of the corporal, for engaging in a disturbance at a fandango.

The soldiers were camped near the summit of the
mountain at the time they stopped here, but some of
them would come down to my place every little
while.

The corporal, whose name was Juan Torres, came
down one evening with the three men who, although
he did not suspect it, had plotted to kill him.

They left at an early hour, going in an opposite direction from their camp, and I closed my doors soon after, for the night. They had not been gone more than half an hour when I heard them talking, not far from my house, and a few seconds later I heard the half suppressed cry of a man who had, I was satisfied, received his death blow.

I had gone to bed, and lay for a minute or two thinking whether I should get up and go to the rescue of the man whose cry I had heard, or insure my own safety by remaining where I was.

A little reflection convinced me that the murderers were undoubtedly watching my house, to prevent any interference with the carrying out of their plot, and that if I ventured out I should only endanger my own life, while there was scarcely a possibility of my being able to save the life of the man who had been assailed.

In the morning, when I got up, I found the dead body of the corporal, stretched across Raton Creek, not more than a hundred yards from my house.

As I surmised, he had been struck with a heavy club or stone, and it was at that time that I heard him cry out. After that his brains had been beaten out, and the body left where I found it.

I at once notified Captain Haley of the occurrence, and identified the men who had been in company with the corporal, and who were undoubtedly his murderers.

They were taken into custody, and made a full confession, in which they stated that one of their number had stood at my door, on the night of the murder, to shoot me if I had ventured out to assist the corporal.

Two of the scoundrels were hanged afterwards at Las Vegas, and the third was sent to prison for life. The corporal was buried near where the soldiers were encamped, at the time of the tragedy, and it is his lonely grave, which frequently attracts the attention of passengers on the Santa Fe trains, just before they reach Raton Tunnel, as they travel southward.

Notwithstanding the fact that there were frequent quarrels, and now and then a bloody fight between the teamsters and others who passed over the road, that was the only murder ever committed in this neighborhood, so far as I know, since I have lived here.

My toll road was a success financially, from the time I completed it, up to the time it was paralleled by the Santa Fe Railroad. Then I got out of the way of the locomotive, and turned my business over to the railroad company.

I have but one objection to railroads, by the way, and that is, they drive the game out of the country. Cutting down the timber which must necessarily be used in the construction of a railroad, frightens away the deer and other game in the first place, and then when the road gets into operation, the whistling of the locomotives, and the noise of the trains, drives the timid animals still further away.

Before the railroad was built, I used to sit on the front porch of my house, and shoot deer, but since that time I have had to get out and skirmish around a good deal, to find even a jack rabbit.

Speaking of the disappearance of the game, reminds me that I have heard recently of a novel complaint being made by the white settlers of Western Colorado. The Ute Indians have a reservation over there, and the settlers complain that they are exterminating the game, hundreds of deer being killed for their skins alone.

This is a charge which the Indians have preferred against the whites a great many times, but I don't think I ever knew before, of the white men complaining of the Indians driving the game out of the country. They have generally been willing to see the game disappear, hoping that the Indians would disappear at the same time.

When I first located where I am living now, the Utes were about the only neighbors I had. They were always scattered around in the mountains, and I had some of them about me pretty much all the time for several years.

When they got to using guns, they would come in here very frequently, and challenge me to shoot with them. I had to humor them, and the shooting always had to be for some kind of "stake," as an Indian never missed an opportunity to gamble. I could always beat them shooting, because I have seen but very few Indians who handled a gun well; but they would try over and over again, to get the best of me, in a match.

Old Conniach, a famous Ute chief, who used to come to see me very often, was more chagrined than any of the Indians, over his failure to beat me in a shooting match.

He came in one day and insisted on wagering five buckskins, against five Mexican silver dollars, that he could beat me shooting at a mark, each of us to take a single shot.

I won, and then up went another pack of buckskins against another five dollars. I won the second pack as easily as I had the first, and then I wanted to make Conniach a present of the buckskins. I came pretty near offending the old fellow by making this proposition and he very curtly informed me that "Ute Indian always paid his debts."

He wasn't satisfied with that trial of our skill as marksmen, but tried it again a few days later. The result was the same that it had been before, and when I brought up one of my boys, " Little Dick," the Indians called him, and he too had beaten the old chief, it took all the conceit out of him.

He had boasted that no white man could beat him shooting, and he honestly believed what he said. As a matter of fact, there were few white men in the country, who knew anything about handling a gun, who could not have done better shooting than old Conniach, under any circumstances, although he was one of the best shots among the Indians.

The mountain men always had a great advantage in fighting the Indians. While they were using the bow and arrow we had the advantage of being able to shoot a much greater distance than they could, and after they got to using guns, we could shoot more accurately and handle our guns a great deal quicker. To shoot with any accuracy whatever, the Indian had to have " a rest " for his gun, and he was always slow about " taking sight," while the mountain men all shot " off hand," and lost no time in "drawing a bead " on an enemy.

At hunting game with the rifle the Indians were no match for the white hunters. They were experts at finding the game, it is true, but anybody could do that in this country twenty years ago.

When the game was discovered, however, such as deer or bear for instance, the hunter had not, as a rule, much time to hunt up a tree or rock to rest his gun on before shooting. The game usually saw the

hunter about as soon as the hunter saw the game,
and was up and away if he was not quick in his
movements. It was the habit of the Indian hunter,
when using the rifle, to carry a couple of gun rods
in his hand, and when he got ready to shoot at anything, down would go the rods on the ground in the
form of the letter X. With one hand, the hunter
held the rods together, while with the other he managed his gun, resting it between the two rods. Sometimes he would make a single rod answer the purpose,
holding it with his hand in the same manner, but
he never had sufficient confidence in himself as a
marksman to risk a shot at game without some
sort of a rest. That was when the Indians first commenced using rifles. Of late years, they have learned
to use them to better advantage."

A DUEL AT DINNER.

CHAPTER XXVIII.

STAGE COACH STORIES.

When the stage company commenced running its coaches through by way of Trinidad, and over my toll road, my place was made a stage station. Of course I had to keep a hotel then, in connection with my other business, and I entertained guests of all grades and stations, from the Vice-President of the United States, down to plain stage robbers and horse thieves.

Tavern keepers in those days couldn't choose their guests, and we entertained them just as they came along. The "knights of the road" would come by now and then, order a meal, eat it hurriedly, pay for it, and move on to where they had arranged to "hold up" a stage that night. Sometimes they didn't wait for it to get dark, but halted the stage, went through the passenger's pockets and the treasure box, in broad daylight, and then ordered the stage driver to move on in one direction, while they went off in another.

One of the most daring and successful daylight stage robberies that I remember of, was perpetrated by two men, when the east-bound stage was coming up on the south side of the Raton mountains, one day about ten o'clock in the forenoon.

On the morning of the same day, a little after sun rise, two rather genteel looking fellows, mounted on fine horses, rode up to my house and ordered breakfast. Being informed that breakfast would be ready in a few minutes, they dismounted, hitched their horses near the door, and came into the house.

I knew then, just as well as I know now, that they were robbers, but I had no warrant for their arrest, and I should have hesitated about serving it if I had, because they looked like very unpleasant men to transact that kind of business with.

Each of them had four pistols sticking in his belt, and a repeating rifle strapped onto his saddle. When they dismounted they left the rifles with the horses, but walked into the house and sat down at the table, without laying aside the arsenal which they carried in their belts.

They had little to say while eating, but were courteous in their behavior, and very polite to the waiters. When they had finished breakfast, they paid their bills, and rode leisurely up the mountain.

It did not occur to me that they would take chances on stopping the stage in daylight, or I should have sent some one to meet the incoming coach, which I knew would be along shortly, to warn the driver and passengers to be on the lookout for the robbers.

It turned out, however, that a daylight robbery was just what they had in mind, and they made a success of it.

About half way down the New Mexico side of the mountain, where the cañon is very narrow, and was then heavily wooded on either side, the robbers stopped and waited for the coach. It came lumbering along by and by, neither the driver nor the passengers dreaming of such a thing as a "hold up."

The first intimation they had of the presence of stage robbers, was when they saw two men step into the road, one on each side of the stage, each of them holding two cocked revolvers, one of which was brought to bear on the passengers and the other on the driver.

Both the driver and the passengers were politely but very positively told that they must throw up their hands, without any unnecessary delay, and the stage came to a stand-still.

There were four passengers in the coach, all men, but their hands went up, at the same instant that the driver dropped his reins, and struck an attitude that suited the robbers.

Then while one of the men stood guard, the other stepped up to the stage and ordered the "treasure box" thrown off. This demand was complied with, and the box was broken open and rifled of its contents, which fortunately were not of very great value.

The passengers were compelled to hand out their watches and other jewelry, as well as what money they had in their pockets, and then the driver was directed to move on up the road. In a minute after the robbery had been completed the robbers had disappeared with their booty, and that was the last seen of them by that particular coach load of passengers.

The men who planned and executed that robbery were two cool, level headed and daring scoundrels, known as " Chuckle-luck " and " Magpie." They were killed soon after this occurence, by a member of their own band, whose name was Steward. A reward of a thousand dollars had been offered for their capture, and this tempted Steward to kill them, one night when they were asleep in camp.

He then secured a wagon, into which he loaded the dead robbers, and hauled them to Cimaron City, where he turned them over to the authorities, and received his reward.

On one occasion I had a notorious horse thief and murderer and the man who was in pursuit of him, in my house at the same time.

The man who was hunted was a half-breed Cherokee Indian, who went by the name of " Chunk," and the man hunting him was Porter Stockdon, himself a great rascal and all round desperado, who was killed afterward while resisting arrest for some one of his numerous crimes.

"Chunk" rode up to my place early one morning, hitched his horse and went in to breakfast. After breakfast he rode away without manifesting any uneasiness, or indicating by his manner, that he had any fear of being pursued.

Stockdon was in the house at the time, but he had said nothing to me about his business, and if he saw "Chunk" he must have been afraid to undertake to arrest him. He went away by and by, and I saw no more of him until that night.

I was sitting by the fire, talking with guests, of whom there were perhaps ten or a dozen in the room, when I heard a knock at the door. Without getting up, I called out, "come in," and turned about in my chair, to see who the visitor was.

The door opened, and a man stepped inside, with a cocked "six-shooter" in each hand. We were all taken by surprise, and my guests didn't know whether they were to be "held up," or had a desperado to deal with, who would want them to stand on their heads for his amusement, and they looked mighty uncomfortable.

I recognized Stockdon in a moment, and asked him what he wanted. He had sense enough then to tell me then that he was looking for "Chunk," who had killed a man at a fandango, near Trinidad, the night before.

I told him the man he was looking for, had left the house, shortly before he left it himself in the morning, and that he would have had no trouble in finding him at that time.   I then told him which way the murderer had gone, and requested him to put up his pistols before he hurt somebody, reminding him that it wasn't a very genteel performance to come into a public house, flourishing a couple of " guns," and frightening people until their hair stood on end, when there was no occasion for it.

He had several men with him, who had been left outside the house, and they all went on together in the direction that the man they were after had taken. They killed an innocent young man over in New Mexico, by mistake, but came back without having seen anything of " Chunk," the murderer.

This fellow was killed afterward at the Clifton House, near Raton, by Clay Allison, whom the young people about here can remember as something of a " man killer " and desperado.

Allison and " Chunk " met at the Clifton House, and as their meeting was a peculiar encounter between what we called " bad men," I will tell you about it.

They had been together a half day or more, had quarreled more or less, and each was watching for an opportunity to get " the drop " on the other. They went into dinner together, and sat down at the same table, Allison laying his pistol on the table, alongside his plate, while " Chunk " held his weapon, at full cock, in his lap. They had hardly seated themselves at the table, when " Chunk " made a grab for Allison's pistol, with one hand, at the same time that he attempted to fire his own pistol, with the other hand. His pistol struck the table and was discharged without injuring his antagonist, and before he could shoot again, Allison blew his brains out.

I was never bothered by the bands of " road agents," who infested the country at that time, but once. That is, they made but one attempt to rob me, and they didn't get any satisfaction out of that.

That robbery was planned by " Jack " Ross and his gang, and after robbing me they were to go on and meet the stage, which was to be " held up," and altogether they expected to make a pretty good night's work of it.

To get through with me and meet the stage before it reached my house, they had to commence operations pretty early in the evening, and so it happened that although I had gone to bed, I had not yet gone to sleep, when four men rode very quietly up to a little thicket near the house, dismounted and hitched their horses.

In those days you couldn't run a stage station without a bar, and like every other keeper of a stage station, I had one. The robbers had to pass the

25

building in which the liquors were kept, on their way up to my sleeping apartments, and the temptation to break in and help themselves, was too strong to be resisted.

They did this very quietly, but I heard them, and looking out of a window near my bed, I saw them when they came out of the bar room.

I always slept with a couple of pistols under my pillow, and my rifle near enough to the bed, so that I could put my hand on it without getting up. When I saw the four men come out of the bar room, and start toward the building in which I was sleeping, I picked up my rifle, and poking the muzzle out through the open space, left by the breaking out of a pane of glass, waited until the leader of the gang was within ten feet of the window. I pushed my gun out of the window a little farther, so that the foremost robber could get a good look into the muzzle of it, and called a halt, threatening to shoot if they advanced an inch farther.

Ross himself was at the head of the party, and he undertook to explain to me that all they wanted was a nights lodging, and asked me to get up and let them in.

I told him that I wasn't opening my house to robbers, at that hour of the night; that I knew who they were, and what they wanted, and would shoot in two seconds if they didn't clear out.

They evidently didn't like the situation, because they lost no time in getting away. Just as they turned back, we heard the stage, which happened to be ahead of time, rattling down the mountain, not more than two hundred yards distant, and as they knew that I would give the alarm, they did not meet the stage, but rode down the road in the opposite direction.

When the stage came in, I found there were eight passengers aboard, and they were well armed. They examined their weapons carefully, to see that they were all in good order, borrowed a few guns from me, and started on towards Trinidad, prepared to give the road agents, of whose presence along the road I had informed them, about as warm a reception as robbers of any kind ever met with.

They had no occasion, however, to use their weapons, because the robbers, knowing that I would inform the stage driver and his passengers of the danger ahead of them, and that in consequence they would be on their guard and prepared for a fight, were not seen along the road.

When a stage load of people came along and stopped with me over night, they generally had some good stories to tell of their adventures on the road, which had sometimes been perilous and sometimes only amusing. Sometimes they would tell of having been chased by the Indians, when it was a race for

life, and at other times they had met with nothing
more serious than being "held up" by the genteel brigands, and losing their money and such valuables as
they happened to have along with them.

I remember one time, John Chisholm, the famous
ranchman, who owned the cattle on a thousand hills, or
at any rate had thousands of cattle, came along with
a good story about his having been robbed on his way
through, by stage, from some point in Arizona to
Santa Fe, where he took the overland stage for the
East.

He had a big contract for furnishing supplies for
the Indians down in Arizona, and had gone there a
short time before with a large band of cattle, which
he turned over to the agency. He stopped there until
he got paid for them, and then took the precaution
to send nearly all of his money and drafts ahead of
him to Santa Fe..

When he got into the stage to leave for home, he
had with him a thousand dollars in greenbacks, and
some small change, which he expected to use along
the road.

The first night out they were stopped by stage robbers, who had evidently been shadowing Chisholm,
and expected to capture the proceeds of his cattle
sale.

When the stage came to a stop, he knew what was
up, and had just time enough to get hold of his roll

of greenbacks, and drop it down the leg of his pants, before the robbers opened the door of the stage, and ordered him to get out and turn over to them what money he had with him.

He told them they could search him and take what they found, but he was not prepared to contribute very handsomely on that occasion. They had no trouble in finding his watch, which they appropriated without ceremony, and then they began a thorough search for the money they supposed he had concealed about him. He said he expected every minute they would find that roll of bills, hidden away in his pants leg; but they didn't, and all they got was a two dollar bill, which they found in his vest pocket.

He told them that two dollar bill was all the money he had to pay for something to eat, on the road to Santa Fe, and he thought they ought to let him keep it. One of the robbers finally pulled a silver dollar out of his pocket and handed it to him, remarking that a man who was mean enough to travel in a stage coach, with only two dollars in his pocket, ought to starve, but he would give him that dollar, just to let him know that he was dealing with a gentleman.

Chisholm told this story, everytime he made a stop at a stage station, and chuckled over the way he fooled the stage robbers and saved his thousand dollars.

A west-bound stage came in one night just at dark, with as much as a hundred arrow points and broken arrows sticking in the sides and running-gear of the coach, and the passengers told a story, which is but a sample of scores of stories I have heard, as I sat by the fire with my guests on an evening when we had had a lot of fresh arrivals.

There were five men, one woman and a child, in the party that arrived in the battle-scarred stage, and they were all on their way to Santa Fe.

In coming through the Comanche country, they had had a military escort, most of the way, but as they saw no Indians, the escort turned back, leaving the stage to go on its way alone. They were making good time over a perfectly level prairie, and the stage driver was beginning to congratulate himself on having made another trip over the most dangerous portion of the old trail, without having an Indian fight, when a passenger who sat beside him on the box, called his attention to what looked like a huge ant hill, not more than two hundred yards distant, near the road side.

Scanning the little mound closely, the driver at once reached the conclusion, that what he saw was an Indian, covered up in the sand, where he could see the roadway, and give the signal for an attack on the stage, at the proper time.

That a band of Indians was concealed in the long grass, and an ambush lay just ahead of him, he was certain, and how to avoid it was the question. He dare not turn back, and turning out on either side might be to plunge into the very midst of the band of savages.

He was not long in deciding what course he would pursue, because there was no time to lose. The man who sat beside him, was informed that there were Indians ahead, and he was directed to swing himself into the coach and notify the other passengers. He did so without being told a second time, and the men gathered up their guns and held them at the coach windows, ready to fire the moment they caught sight of the Indians.

Meantime the driver, who was as brave a fellow as ever cracked a whip over a stage team, had tightened his hold on the reins, shook out his long whip lash, and touching up his six bronchos, just enough to put them on their mettle, held them in check so that they would appear to the Indians to be jogging along at the regulation pace, until he got ready to make his contemplated dash through the ambuscade.

He waited until he got within forty yards of the sand-covered Indian, when he cracked his whip over the horses and uttered a series of yells which started them at once on a dead run.

At the same moment, the suspicious looking sand pile resolved itself into an Indian, who sprang to his feet, and gave a war whoop which brought a score or more of the Comanches up out of the grass, where they had been lying on either side of the road.

The drivers tactics had taken the Indians by surprise, and he was through the ambuscade before they could fairly bend their bows. The next moment, however, the arrows fell thick as hail-stones, about the stage, and a rifle ball cut a hole through the broad brim of the driver's hat.

The passengers returned the fire; but with what effect they could not tell, as they were going at terriffic speed, and the stage was rolling from side to side, like a ship in a storm.

They were soon out of reach of the arrows, for the time being, but within two hundred yards of the place where they ran into the ambuscade, they caught sight of the Indians' horses, which had been hidden in a ravine, and they knew that pursuit was certain. Realizing that there was but one chance for him to save the lives of his passengers, and his own as well, the stage driver kept his bronchos forging along at the top of their speed, hoping to reach the next stage station, four miles away, before the Comanches should overtake them.

It took the Indians some little time to get to their horses and mount them, and the stage had gotten a good start in the race, but before half the distance to the station had been covered, the arrows again commenced whistling past the driver and pelting the stage.

Fortunately the men who were inside knew how to use their guns, and although it was difficult to shoot with any degree of accuracy, on occount of the rolling motion of the stage, they managed to hit one or two of the Indians, and that caused the red-skins to fall back. They followed the stage almost to the station, however, and were in sight of it, when the panting, foaming, and almost exhausted ponies, dashed into the big stage barn, the doors of which were closed behind the coach load of thoroughly frightened passengers.

The stage station was by no means well garrisoned, and would hardly have withstood much of a seige, but the Indians knew well enough that there were a few determined men there, and they knew also that to make an assault on the station meant the killing of some of their number. For some time they hovered about, apparently waiting for the stage to resume its journey. Not until after night-fall however, and sometime after the Indians had been seen riding away in an opposite direction, did the plucky stage driver assure his passengers that it was safe to start again on their trip to Santa Fe, to which place he carried them in due time without any more thrilling adventures.

The only one of the passengers who received any injury, more serious than the terrible " shaking up " they got, was the child, a little girl about four years old, whose cheek was grazed by an arrow. The wound was little more than a scratch, however, and could only have left a slight scar, to remind her in after years, of her narrow escape from death at the hands of the savages.

The driver had his clothes torn in several places by the arrows, and there was a bullet hole through his coat, as well as his hat, but he escaped like the rest, without injury."

TRINIDAD AND RATON PEAK.

CHAPTER XXIX.

FAREWELL VISITS OF THE RED MEN

" The railroad took the place of the stage line in 1878, and since that time I have lived in a different atmosphere from that in which I formerly lived. I almost feel that I am no longer on the frontier, and that there is no frontier to go to. In my old age, I have been brought back into civilization, and I find just one unpleasant feature about it.

While I am not so foolish as to lose sight of the fact that I have grown old, and as a consequence am no longer suited to an adventurous life myself, I still fancy that I should like to live amidst such surroundings as we had in this country twenty-five years ago, so that visitors could drop in every day or two to see me, who would have something to talk about.

If the buffalo had not all been killed, if there were more deer and bear in the mountains, if the stage lines were still running, and the Indians had not been driven out of the country, the young fellows who visit me, would now and then be able to tell a story worth hearing.

As it is, I have to do pretty much all the story telling myself, except when I happen to meet somebody who tells me about the cities that have grown up on the plains where I used to hunt buffalo, and along the streams where I used to set my beaver traps. Every once in a while I meet a man too, who tells me about the gold or silver that has been dug out of the mountains that I used to tramp over when trading with the Indians, and that interests me almost as much as if I had found it myself.

Then another man comes along who happened to know one of the "old-timers," with whom I had slept in camp perhaps a hundred times, and when I inquire about my old friend, I hear something which has a sort of melancholy interest for me.

I learn that my old-time companion is dead, and that the lawyers are dividing up his estate among themselves; or in other words, that the heirs are engaged in a legal dispute over the disposition to be made of his property, which amounts to the same thing as dividing it among the lawyers.

I don't feel very old, but when I look about me for my associates of the "forties," I find that only the mountains and I are left, and before long it will be only the mountains.

The Indians disappeared from this portion of Colorado, a few years before the railroad came, and since that time I have seen as little of them as if I had been living in one of the New England States.

The Utes used to claim the land on which I am now living, and a large area of surrounding country.

They disliked to give it up, but they had to go, because as they said, " the white men wanted more room."

They were terribly whipped by a party of soldiers under command of Colonel Fountleroy and a party of volunteers under Colonel St. Vrain, only a year or two before I came here, just over the mountain on Sugarite Creek. They had killed some people, and stolen some stock, in the neighborhood of Abiquiu, and the soldiers followed them over four hundred miles, before they came up with them.

The Indians, believing they had distanced their pursuers, lay down at night to sleep, in brush covered booths, some of which were standing not many years ago, and may yet be for all I know, never dreaming that before morning, half their number would be lying dead on the banks of the little creek, beside which they were encamped.

The soldiers came on them in the middle of the night, and at once attacked the camp. The Indians were taken completely by surprise. For once they were caught napping and that very soundly. Bewildered by the sudden and unexpected attack, they could offer but little resistance, and something like a hundred of them were killed, only a remnant of the band escaping.

The last fight the whites had with the Utes in this part of Colorado, in fact the last serious trouble they

had with any of the Indians, was at Trinidad, in
1867.

It was early in the fall, when quite a large band of
the Utes came along past my house, and as usual
stopped to pay me a visit.

I knew a good many of them, and among others I
recognized a good looking chief, who was about fifty
years old, as an Indian I had seen at some time, but
I couldn't remember when or where it was.

After asking him a good many questions, I learned
that he had been with the band of Utes that gave
me so much trouble near the Uncompahgre River,
when I was on my way to California in 1852. We
talked over my encounter with old " Uncotash,"
whose life I had threatened when I didn't think my
own was worth a farthing, and whom I succeeded in
frightening into good behavior. The chief with
whom I had this talk, more than fifteen years after
the occurrence, gave me credit for being " heap
brave and " heap fool," by which he meant that I
took desperate risks.

The Indians told me that they were going to Trinidad to have " big horse race with the white men."
They said " Indian horses run fast, beat white men's
horses ; Indian win heap bets."

I thought it altogether likely that they might have
as good luck as they expected, but I knew that

those horse races generally led to trouble, and tried to persuade them not to go to Trinidad.

The chief who had charge of the band, promised me however, that they would behave well, and assured me that they would not "quarrel with the white men."

For some days after they got to Trinidad everything went along smoothly, and they were quite as fortunate in winning horse races, as they had expected to be, but just as I had anticipated, the affair wound up in a quarrel.

There were but few people at Trinidad in 1867 and when the hot tempered Utes began to make some hostile demonstrations, the settlers became alarmed and appealed to the military forces for protection.

There were no troops stationed at Trinidad, but Major Alexander got there soon after the Indians began to talk about going on the war path, with one company of soldiers.

He made an effort to patch up a truce, but it was unsuccessful, and seeing that the situation was critical, he notified the settlers scattered about in the surrounding country, to come into town, and place themselves under his protection.

I was informed that an Indian outbreak was almost certain, and that when the hostilities once commenced, I would be in very great danger, if I remained at my home in the mountains.

I thanked Major Alexander for giving me this warning, but at the same time informed him that my interests were here, and that I should stay here and protect them as far as possible.

We learned afterward, that while the parleying and threatening was going on at Trinidad, the Indians had sent couriers back into the mountains, to stir up some of the larger bands of Utes, and an effort was being made to bring about a general Ute uprising. I will tell you farther along how this uprising was prevented.

What precipitated hostilities at Trinidad, was a quarrel between Indians and Mexicans.

The Indians were encamped about two miles above the town, on the Purgatoire River, near a small Mexican settlement. They charged the Mexicans with having stolen some of their horses, and finally, as a result of the quarrel, one of the Indians was shot and killed by a Mexican.

That happened about ten o'clock in the morning, just as the Indians were getting ready to leave their camp. Of course they at once commenced a warfare on the Mexicans, and Major Alexander with his company of soldiers and a few volunteers, picked up in Trinidad, marched out to suppress the savages.

They retreated about two miles up the river, sent their women and children into the mountains, and having formed the usual ambuscade, waited for the soldiers to come up.

Their first fire killed and wounded several of Major Alexander's men, but as soon as the fire was returned, they scattered in the mountains and made their escape. The Indians always insisted that they did not lose a man in the fight, aside from the one killed by the Mexican, early in the morning, and claimed a victory for that reason.

Two of the Utes came to my house immediately after the fight, and complained bitterly of the way they had been treated at Trinidad. They were loud in their threats of vengeance, and declared that the big bands of Utes would soon be on the war path, and that much blood would be shed before their anger would be appeased.

Before the fight occurred, L. B. Maxwell, who had for years been on very friendly terms with the Utes, had learned of the trouble at Trinidad, and the contemplated general uprising of the Indians, and had sent a messenger to "Kit" Carson, who was stationed at Fort Garland, giving him full information in regard to the plans of the Indians. Maxwell advised him to go out and hold a conference with a large band of hostiles, then on their way to meet the retreating Indians, and see if he could not make peace with them.

"Kit" acted on this advice, and in doing so, probably saved Major Alexander's company from being entirely destroyed. Major Alexander was in pursuit of the band that had been driven away from Trinidad, when "Kit" met him and induced him to turn back. Had he kept up the pursuit twenty-four hours longer, he would have met a band of several hundred Ute warriors, and could hardly have escaped a disastrous defeat.

"Kit" Carson spoke the Ute language well, had been among them for years and had a great deal of influence with them. When he met the hostiles, he held a long conference with them, listened to all their complaints, and promised them that everything should be arranged to suit them, if they would turn back and abandon the idea of going on the war path. The result of this interview was that several of the Ute chiefs agreed to go to Cimaron City, the home of L. B. Maxwell, where a peace conference was to be held.

They sent for me to come over there, and I was present at the conference, and did what I could to aid Carson and Maxwell in fixing up a peace arrangement.

Maxwell made the Indians a present of a lot of ponies, and that put them again in good humor, and sent them back to their hunting grounds. He had established a peace with them on his own account, some years before this, by doing them a good turn, when they were at war with the Comanches and Kiowas.

A band of the Utes met a band of the Comanches and Kiowas near Cimaron City, and were badly defeated in the fight which followed.

The Utes lost all their horses, and Maxwell, taking advantage of the opportunity to place them under an obligation to him, called them in and gave them a fresh lot of ponies out of his own herd. They never forgot that favor, and when the old chief who had been the recipient of the gift was about to die, he called all the other chiefs in reach, around him, and exacted from them a promise that they would never harm " Maxwell the friend of the Utes."

Some time after the peace had been made at Cimaron, the Utes agreed to give up this country and they never came in here afterward.

The Arapahoes and Cheyennes used to pay me visits occasionally for several years after I came here.

Once a large band of Arapahoes came through on their way into the Ute country. " Roman Nose " was the chief of the band, and said he came out of his way to see me. He gave as an excuse for coming that he wanted to talk to me about the old hunters and trappers, and learn what had become of them.

The whole band staid with me half a day or more, and I talked over early experiences with the old chief, very much as I would have talked with an old *Compadre*.

The Arapahoes, Cheyennes, Comanches and Kiowas, and other remnants of tribes which had roamed over Kansas and Eastern Colorado, were removed to the Indian Territory early in the " seventies," some of them in fact before that time, and we saw no more of them after that.

About the time the Indians disappeared the game began to get scarce in the country, particularly the buffalo. I think it was in 1874 that I had my last buffalo hunt. I drove down into the Pan Handle of Texas, with a two-horse wagon, and loaded it with buffalo meat before I came back, but it cost me more labor than any load of meat I had ever taken before.

I found the buffalo getting scarce, and noticed that the temper of the animal had changed very materially. They had been hunted and harrassed so much, that they would fight on slight provocation, and a wounded buffalo was about as vicious and ugly as a wounded bear.

I narrowly escaped being killed by a wounded bull, that I supposed was dead, when I was getting ready to butcher him.

When I shot the bull he dropped to the ground as though he had received a death wound. I laid my gun aside, and rolling up my sleeves, walked up to the apparently dead buffalo, with my butcher knife in my hand, to begin skinning him.

When I got within about ten feet of him, the buffalo seemed to realize all at once, that he wasn't dead, and he sprang up and charged straight toward me.

You never saw a man make a quicker turn than I did, or make better time in a race of twenty yards.

As a matter of fact, there was never a time in my life when there was greater necessity for my doing my level best on a short distance foot race. The maddened animal behind me would have made short work of me if I had had the misfortune to stumble, or had met with any similar mishap. The charge was made so suddenly and unexpectedly that I was given no opportunity to call for assistance, or secure any arms other than my butcher knife, and this would have been a poor weapon to use in a fight with the kind of animal I had to contend with. My horse was so far away that I could not reach him, and there was but one direction for me to take in trying to get away.

It happened that I had to run toward a deep ravine which I knew was too wide for me to leap across, and so deep that I should be killed, or at least seriously hurt, if I fell into it. I headed for a tree which was growing up out of the ravine, with its top sticking up a few feet above the bank. The buffalo was mighty close to me when I reached the bank, and I had no time to pick out a place to light, when I made a jump for the tree, just as the bull plowed up the ground behind me, as he came to a stop at the edge of the ravine.

I caught in the branches of the tree, a good deal scratched and bruised to be sure, but not seriously injured. The buffalo stood on the bank snorting and bellowing, apparently not at all inclined to abandon the fight and move off.

I climbed down the tree after a little while, and went down the ravine some distance before I could get out. Then I beckoned to a boy who accompanied me on the trip, to bring my horse and gun, and mounted on the horse, it did not take me long to finish the wounded but not seriously injured animal.

I found it necessary to exercise a great deal more care to be successful in hunting the buffalo at that time than was necessary a few years earlier, and it took me longer to load my one wagon with meat then than it would have taken to load a dozen wagons, ten years before. I realized then for the first time how rapidly this splendid game was being exterminated, and my boys claim that the tears stood in my eyes when I came home and told them about it.

With the removal of the Indians from the country, the disappearance of the game, the abandonment of the stage lines, and the transfer of the freighting

business from wagons to railroad trains, the era of
adventure, I mean real, stirring, thrilling adventure,
ended in this portion of the mountain region.

The whole country has thrown off its wildness, so
far as the character of its inhabitants is concerned,
although eastern people still speak of it as the frontier.

Outside of its rugged mountain peaks, its thickly
wooded cañons, and its natural scenery, the " wild
west " is no longer wild.

The wildest thing we see out here, now-a-days, is
a cow-boy, and about the most thrilling experience
of a cow-boy's life, is getting pitched off a bucking
pony, before he learns to ride.

Pleasure parties roam about over the mountains,
and instead of being loaded down with fire arms and
amunition, as we used to be, when we ventured into
the same localities, they carry lunch baskets, and
amateur photographing outfits. We no longer see
"walking arsenals" on the streets of our little towns,
and cities, and like older States, we have a law on
our statute books, which prohibits persons from carrying concealed weapons.

Of all the changes, the improvements and the advance in civilization which have been made in the
vast western half of the United States, within the
past fifty years, I have been a witness. I trust I have
contributed my share toward bringing about the con-

dition of affairs which exists to-day, but at any rate I have led an active and stirring life, and have told you pretty much all about it.

What I have told you, will, I think, interest those who care to know something more than is generally known, about what was going on in this country before it was connected with the Eastern and Middle States by railroads and telegraph lines, as well as those who are always entertained by stories of adventure.

You can say to those who care to know more about me than I have already said about myself, that you left me, taking the rest to which an old man is entitled, and which I flatter myself I have richly earned."

"UNCLE DICK'S" HOME IN THE MOUNTAINS.

CHAPTER XXX.

A DIOS.

"A Dios" is what the Spanish speaking natives of the Rocky mountain region say to their friends, when bidding them farewell, and I have headed this chapter " A Dios " because in it I am to say farewell to "Uncle Dick."

It is not without sincere regret, that I take my leave of the kindly old man, the last of the early mountaineers, in whom I have become most deeply interested.

It is with regret also that I say good by to the picturesque surroundings of his mountain home.

Here for a longer time than ever before, I have held communion with the soul of nature, studied her moods, and watched her changing phases.

I have followed to its source the silvery stream which courses down the mountain side, clambered up to the top of the highest peaks, and rested in the shade of giant rocks, picked up somewhere, by titanic forces, ages since, and dropped down here and there to puzzle him who seeks to know from whence they came.

From such vantage ground as this, I have looked down upon a landscape as kaleidoscopic as any the sun shines on, more picturesque than fancy ever painted, and as pleasing to the eye, as anything to which dame nature has given birth since the world was made.

At other times, looking downward from the same aerial height, I have seen the vaporous clouds, stretched below me from mountain side to mountain side, like the fleecy covering which sometimes hides from view a casket of gems.

Standing in the little valley below, I have watched the forked and brilliant lightnings, which seemed to battle with the grizzled peaks, and have listened to the rattle of the thunder bolts, which marked the battle's progress.

Capricious nature, is in the mountains most capricious, and the sun himself seems more moody here than elsewhere. He warms and burns and smiles and frowns by turns. Sometimes he drops behind the western "Rockies," sending back an angry good night scowl, and at other times, he leaves behind, a soft and mellow light, lingering like a benediction upon the hills and rocks.

In every age and every clime, mankind has gazed with mingled wonder, awe and admiration upon the phenomena of the mountain regions.

"High Olympus" was the home of all the gods of classic ancients, and there they forged the thunder bolts, turned loose the warring elements and shaped the destinies of men.

In the lofty peaks of the Rocky Mountain range, which the Indians call *Chippewyan*, the superstitious savages of the western world, have located their " land of souls," where lives "Wacondah," "the master of life," and governor of the universe.

Whether looked upon by savage or savant, the fabled home of gods and disembodied spirits, must have for him who looks, a more than passing interest, and I turn my back upon the "secret keeping" hills, feeling like one who wanders from an enchanted land.

I leave them, however, with most pleasing recollections of their charms, their power to "drive away dull care," and the restfulness which they afford.

I leave them with pleasant memories of delightful strolls through embowered cañons, of wild flowers plucked fresh from nature's gardens, of moonlight rambles among the rustling pine trees with a prattling boy and *la petite madame* my wife to keep me company.

I leave the mountains, and the home of "Uncle Dick," with a kind regard for the genial, warm hearted old man, the story of whose adventures I have written down as it came to me from him.

It is seldom indeed that one meets so interesting a character now-a-days as "Uncle Dick."

He is interesting, not only on his own account, but because we see in him the representative of a class of men, who lived in an age that is as much a thing of the past as the revolutionary period, under circumstances which can never again exist on the American continent, unless it should happen that civilization takes a backward turn.

It was to the little band of path finders, who penetrated the wilds of the Rocky Mountains, at a thousand risks of life, and thus opened up the way for those who came after them, to turn loose their bands of cattle and horses, to till the soil and reap the harvests, to open the mines and send into the markets of the world the gold and silver which had been locked up here for ages, to build towns and cities and railroads, that " Uncle Dick " belonged, and it is of that class of adventurers that he is a most striking and perfect representative.

When therefore we study him, we study the character of the class of men to which he belonged. Through him we may study the character of the early mountaineers — the " mountain men " they called themselves—and draw conclusions as to "what manner of men they were," to whom we are indebted for opening the way for the rapid march of civilization, into the vast country which lies along the great dividing ridge of the continent.

That they were brave, hardy and self-reliant, they have proven by their acts. That they were chivalrous as well as brave, that they were generous as well as daring, that they were kind hearted as well as lion hearted, those who have read this account of the adventures and experiences of " Uncle Dick " Wootton, the typical mountaineer, will be fully and thoroughly convinced. Looking back over the fifty years which he has spent in the mountain country, he has traced his wanderings, and those of his associates, told us where they went, how they lived, and what they did. In a modest, manly way, he has related to us the story of his life.

With the simplicity and candor of a man whose every instinct is an honest one, he holds his life an open book, which he never hesitates to lay before those, who may at any time be thrown in company with him ; and as he talks of by-gone days, and tells tales of thrilling interest, his emotional nature makes the lights and shadows chase each other over a face furrowed by age, and in which the lines have been drawn deep and hard by years of toil and hardship, as lights and shadows chase each other over the face of a child, while an expression of tender sentiment, brings tears to his eyes, and the recall of a pathetic incident sends them coursing one after another down his cheeks.

In a thousand ways the kindly nature of the man becomes apparent to even a casual observer, and no one can fail to note, that beneath a rough exterior, " Uncle Dick " carries to-day, and has always carried a heart as tender as a woman's.   While he has been brave, daring, and impetuous, he has at the same time been warm-hearted, generous and kind.

If he has ever been resentful and vindictive, old age has smoothed his ruffled spirits, leaving not a trace of it to-day.   That his declining years may be as serene as the early years of his life were turbulent and eventful, is the wish of all who know the old trapper and hunter.

THE END.

Library of Congress Cataloging in Publication Data

Wootton, Richens Lacy, 1816-1893.
"Uncle Dick" Wootton, the Pioneer Frontiersman
of the Rocky Mountain Region.
(Classics of the Old West)
Reprint of the 1890 ed. published by W. E.
Dibble, Chicago.
Based on interviews between Wootton and Conard.
Includes index.
1. Wootton, Richens Lacy, 1816-1893.
2. Frontier and pioneer life—The West. 3. The
West—History. 4. Indians of North America—The
West. 5. Pioneers—The West—Biography.
I. Conard, Howard Louis. II. Title. III. Series.
[F593.W66 1980b]   978'.02'0924 [B]   80-22533
ISBN 0-8094-3952-2

Printed in the United States of America.